Congo in The Sixties

Godfrey Mwakikagile

1

Congo in The Sixties

Revised Edition

ISBN   9789987160495

New Africa Press
Dar es Salaam, Tanzania

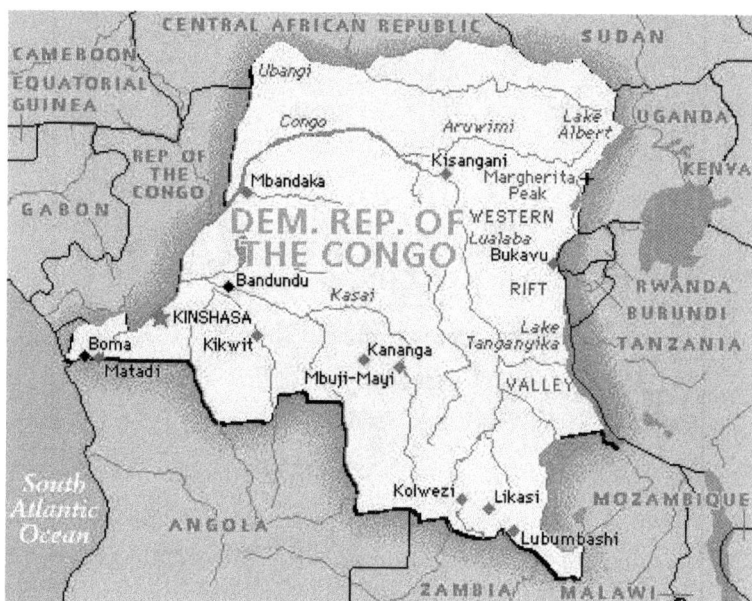

Acknowledgements

I WISH to express my profound gratitude to the sources I have used to document my work. All the sources I have cited are given full attribution. And I am very grateful to all of them without a single exception.

My work would not be what it is in terms of documentation without them except for the analysis which is entirely mine including its shortcomings.

Special thanks must go to those who conducted the interview with Frank Carlucci about his years in Congo and elsewhere in Africa and to the Foreign Affairs Oral History Collection, Association for Diplomatic Studies and Training (ADST) in Arlington, Virginia, USA, www.adst.org, the copyright holder, for permission to use their material in this book.

I am also very grateful to Jorge Castañeda whose illuminating work on Che Guevara, *Companero: The Life and Death of Che Guevara*, has been an invaluable source of information on Che's mission to Congo; a subject I have addressed extensively in this book.

Introduction

THIS WORK looks at the former Belgian Congo during the turbulent sixties when it became the bleeding heart of Africa.

It was a battleground between contending forces representing different ideological and political interests. It was also a combat theatre between ethnic and regional centres of power within the Congo itself.

The country degenerated into chaos soon after independence and also became a theatre of confrontation between the two super powers, the United States and the Soviet Union.

The violence continued to escalate with unconstrained fury, threatening to consume the heart of Africa in what came to be one of the bloodiest conflicts in the continent's post-colonial history.

The Congo also became a test case for Africa in the continent's quest for peace and stability.

The Congo imbroglio exposed, in a very painful way, the weakness of the newly independent nations as unstable political entities incapable of coping with the harsh realities of nationhood.

Probably more than anything else, the instruments or

7

institutions of authority which collectively constitute the state had to contend with the enormous task of building nations which did not exist except as a hodge-podge of different ethnic and regional groups competing for power and resources. And nowhere was this better – and tragically – demonstrated than in the Congo.

The Congo crisis also exposed the weakness of Africa in another respect.

The former Belgian Congo is potentially the richest country in Africa, richer than South Africa in terms of minerals and other resources including agricultural and hydroelectric potential. It is also one of the largest countries on the continent in terms of area, about the size of Western Europe, and had the potential to be a formidable force in the liberation of Africa.

The countries which were still under white minority rule could have expected an independent and united Congo to play a major role in their liberation. Yet it was in the Congo itself where the same forces of racial oppression, mainly from apartheid South Africa, made a mockery of African independence and exposed the continent's inability – at least militarily – to deal with white minority regimes which were oppressing black Africans.

Troops from the land of apartheid wreaked havoc across the Congo during the sixties. And they did not have the slightest fear of being punished for their wanton acts of violence against black Congolese because the country was weak and divided.

The Congolese government itself during that period after Lumumba was ousted from power and later assassinated did not care about the well-being of its people. It also did not serve African interests. It was a puppet of Western powers, especially the United States. The most powerful Congolese during that period was Joseph Mobutu who became a "darling" of the West.

During his reign, what is potentially the richest country

on the continent became one of the poorest. And it all began in the sixties.

Events in the Congo in the sixties marked a turning point in the history of Africa.

They had an impact far beyond the Congo which still reverberates across the continent today.

And the Congo itself has never recovered from the devastation wrought during those turbulent years.

The sixties were the dawn of a new era for the Congo and for Africa as a whole.

They were the best of times, as one country after another won independence from the colonial powers. But they were also the worst of times because of what happened in the Congo and in other parts of the continent in the following years.

And tragically, the Congo is still bleeding today as if it never left the sixties.

The turbulent sixties were a period which was defined by what came to known as the Congo crisis in the bleeding heart of Africa.

The sixties were also an important milestone in the history of Africa. It was the decade of independence, marked by the end of colonial rule in most parts of Africa. But while millions of people across the continent celebrated independence, as one country after another emerged from colonial rule and hoisted its own flag, some parts of the continent were also rocked by violence and other conflicts. The worst, and the most dramatic, were the Congo crisis and the Nigerian civil war.

The Congo crisis was triggered by the secession of Katanga eleven days after the former Belgian Congo won independence on 30 June 1960. Another province, Kasai, also seceded in 1960.

The region that came to be known as Congo – first as Congo Free State, then as Belgian Congo, Republic of the Congo, Democratic Republic of the Congo or Congo-Leopoldville, Congo-Kinshasa, Zaire, and now the

Democratic Republic of Congo (DRC) – has suffered so much through the centuries that it has earned the unenviable distinction as the bleeding heart of Africa. As historian Dan Snow stated in his article, "Too Rich for its Own Good: DRC: Cursed by Its Own Wealth," on BBC News Magazine, 8 October 2013:

"The Democratic Republic of Congo is potentially one of the richest countries on earth, but colonialism, slavery and corruption have turned it into one of the poorest.

The world's bloodiest conflict since World War II is still rumbling on today.

It is a war in which more than five million people have died, millions more have been driven to the brink by starvation and disease and several million women and girls have been raped.

The Great War of Africa, a conflagration that has sucked in soldiers and civilians from nine nations and countless armed rebel groups, has been fought almost entirely inside the borders of one unfortunate country – the Democratic Republic of Congo.

It is a place seemingly blessed with every type of mineral, yet consistently rated lowest on the UN Human Development Index, where even the more fortunate live in grinding poverty.

I went to the Congo this summer to find out what it was about the country's past that had delivered it into the hands of unimaginable violence and anarchy.

The journey that I went on, through the Congo's abusive history, while travelling across its war-torn present, was the most disturbing experience of my career.

I met rape victims, rebels, bloated politicians and haunted citizens of a country that has ceased to function – people who struggle to survive in a place cursed by a past that defies description, a history that will not release them from its death-like grip.

The Congo's apocalyptic present is a direct product of

decisions and actions taken over the past five centuries.

In the late 15th Century an empire known as the Kingdom of Kongo dominated the western portion of the Congo, and bits of other modern states such as Angola.

It was sophisticated, had its own aristocracy and an impressive civil service.

When Portuguese traders arrived from Europe in the 1480s, they realised they had stumbled upon a land of vast natural wealth, rich in resources – particularly human flesh.

The Congo was home to a seemingly inexhaustible supply of strong, disease-resistant slaves. The Portuguese quickly found this supply would be easier to tap if the interior of the continent was in a state of anarchy.

They did their utmost to destroy any indigenous political force capable of curtailing their slaving or trading interests.

Money and modern weapons were sent to rebels, Kongolese armies were defeated, kings were murdered, elites slaughtered and secession was encouraged.

By the 1600s, the once-mighty kingdom had disintegrated into a leaderless, anarchy of mini-states locked in endemic civil war. Slaves, victims of this fighting, flowed to the coast and were carried to the Americas.

About four million people were forcibly embarked at the mouth of the Congo River. English ships were at the heart of the trade. British cities and merchants grew rich on the back of Congolese resources they would never see.

This first engagement with Europeans set the tone for the rest of the Congo's history.

Development has been stifled, government has been weak and the rule of law non-existent. This was not through any innate fault of the Congolese, but because it has been in the interests of the powerful to destroy, suppress and prevent any strong, stable, legitimate government. That would interfere – as the Kongolese had threatened to interfere before – with the easy extraction of the nation's resources. The Congo has been utterly cursed by its natural wealth.

The Congo is a massive country, the size of Western Europe.

Limitless water, from the world's second-largest river, the Congo, a benign climate and rich soil make it fertile, beneath the soil abundant deposits of copper, gold, diamonds, cobalt, uranium, coltan and oil are just some of the minerals that should make it one of the world's richest countries.

Instead it is the world's most hopeless.

The interior of the Congo was opened up in the late 19th Century by the British-born explorer Henry Morton Stanley, his dreams of free trading associations with communities he met were shattered by the infamous King of the Belgians, Leopold, who hacked out a vast private empire.

The world's largest supply of rubber was found at a time when bicycle and automobile tyres, and electrical insulation, had made it a vital commodity in the West.

The late Victorian bicycle craze was enabled by Congolese rubber collected by slave labourers.

To tap it, Congolese men were rounded up by a brutal Belgian-officered security force, their wives were interned to ensure compliance and were brutalised during their captivity. The men were then forced to go into the jungle and harvest the rubber.

Disobedience or resistance was met by immediate punishment – flogging, severing of hands, and death. Millions perished.

Tribal leaders capable of resisting were murdered, indigenous society decimated, proper education denied.

A culture of rapacious, barbaric rule by a Belgian elite who had absolutely no interest in developing the country or population was created, and it has endured.

In a move supposed to end the brutality, Belgium

eventually annexed the Congo outright, but the problems in its former colony remained.

Mining boomed, workers suffered in appalling conditions, producing the materials that fired industrial production in Europe and America.

In World War I men on the Western Front and elsewhere did the dying, but it was Congo's minerals that did the killing.

The brass casings of allied shells fired at Passchendaele and the Somme were 75% Congolese copper.

In World War II, the uranium for the nuclear bombs dropped on Hiroshima and Nagasaki came from a mine in south-east Congo.

Western freedoms were defended with Congo's resources while black Congolese were denied the right to vote, or form unions and political associations. They were denied anything beyond the most basic of educations.

They were kept at an infantile level of development that suited the rulers and mine owners but made sure that when independence came there was no home-grown elite who could run the country.

Independence in 1960 was, therefore, predictably disastrous.

Bits of the vast country immediately attempted to break away, the army mutinied against its Belgian officers and within weeks the Belgian elite who ran the state evacuated leaving nobody with the skills to run the government or economy.

Of 5,000 government jobs pre-independence, just three were held by Congolese and there was not a single Congolese lawyer, doctor, economist or engineer.

Chaos threatened to engulf the region. The Cold War superpowers moved to prevent the other gaining the upper hand.

Sucked into these rivalries, the struggling Congolese leader, Patrice Lumumba, was horrifically beaten and executed by Western-backed rebels. A military strongman,

Joseph-Desire Mobutu, who had a few years before been a sergeant in the colonial police force, took over.

Mobutu became a tyrant. In 1972 he changed his name to Mobutu Sese Seko Nkuku Ngbendu Wa Za Banga, meaning 'the all-powerful warrior who, because of his endurance and inflexible will to win, goes from conquest to conquest, leaving fire in his wake.'

The West tolerated him as long as the minerals flowed and the Congo was kept out of the Soviet orbit.

He, his family and friends bled the country of billions of dollars, a $100m palace was built in the most remote jungle at Gbadolite, an ultra-long airstrip next to it was designed to take Concorde, which was duly chartered for shopping trips to Paris.

Dissidents were tortured or bought off, ministers stole entire budgets, government atrophied. The West allowed his regime to borrow billions, which was then stolen and today's Congo is still expected to pay the bill.

In 1997 an alliance of neighbouring African states, led by Rwanda – which was furious Mobutu's Congo was sheltering many of those responsible for the 1994 genocide – invaded, after deciding to get rid of Mobutu.

A Congolese exile, Laurent Kabila, was dredged up in East Africa to act as a figurehead. Mobutu's cash-starved army imploded, its leaders, incompetent cronies of the president, abandoning their men in a mad dash to escape.

Mobutu took off one last time from his jungle Versailles, his aircraft packed with valuables, his own unpaid soldiers firing at the plane as it lumbered into the air.

Rwanda had effectively conquered its titanic neighbour with spectacular ease. Once installed however, Kabila, Rwanda's puppet, refused to do as he was told.

Again Rwanda invaded, but this time they were just halted by her erstwhile African allies who now turned on each other and plunged Congo into a terrible war.

Foreign armies clashed deep inside the Congo as the

paper-thin state collapsed totally and anarchy spread.

Hundreds of armed groups carried out atrocities, millions died.

Ethnic and linguistic differences fanned the ferocity of the violence, while control of Congo's stunning natural wealth added a terrible urgency to the fighting.

Forcibly conscripted child soldiers corralled armies of slaves to dig for minerals such as coltan, a key component in mobile phones, the latest obsession in the developed world, while annihilating enemy communities, raping women and driving survivors into the jungle to die of starvation and disease.

A deeply flawed, partial peace was patched together a decade ago. In the far east of the Congo, there is once again a shooting war as a complex web of domestic and international rivalries see rebel groups clash with the army and the UN, while tiny community militias add to the general instability.

The country has collapsed, roads no longer link the main cities, healthcare depends on aid and charity. The new regime is as grasping as its predecessors.

I rode on one of the trainloads of copper that go straight from foreign-owned mines to the border, and on to the Far East, rumbling past shanty towns of displaced, poverty-stricken Congolese.

The Portuguese, Belgians, Mobutu and the present government have all deliberately stifled the development of a strong state, army, judiciary and education system, because it interferes with their primary focus, making money from what lies under the Earth.

The billions of pounds those minerals have generated have brought nothing but misery and death to the very people who live on top of them, while enriching a microscopic elite in the Congo and their foreign backers, and underpinning our technological revolution in the developed world.

The Congo is a land far away, yet our histories are so

closely linked. We have thrived from a lopsided relationship, yet we are utterly blind to it. The price of that myopia has been human suffering on an unimaginable scale."[1]

The sixties were some of the most turbulent years in the history of post-colonial Africa characterised by military coups and political assassinations.

What came to be known as the Congo crisis best defined that period. It not only put the bleeding heart of Africa in the international spotlight; it also, in a very tragic way, served as a microcosm of what Africa was all about: a continent in crisis, unstable, and composed of weak countries which were independent in name only.

Congo in The Sixties

THE YEAR 1960 stands out in the history of Africa in one fundamental respect. It was the year in which the largest number of African countries won independence, a feat that was not duplicated in any of the following years.

But while 1960 was hailed as Africa's Year, and Africans across the continent celebrated the dawn of a new era heralded by the achievement of independence by a large number of countries, marking the beginning of the end of colonial rule on the continent, the year was also marred by some of the bloodiest events in the history of the continent.

The initial euphoria of independence was dampened when the former Belgian Congo descended into chaos just a few days after the country won independence, turning this giant African nation into the bleeding heart of Africa. "It was the best of times, it was the worst of times," to quote Charles Dickens. And Africa has never fully recovered from the convulsions caused by the Congo crisis in the turbulent sixties. Half a century later, Congo is still bleeding.

In a very tragic way, the Congo crisis demonstrated

how vulnerable Africa was to foreign intrigue, with foreign powers turning the continent's potentially richest country into a playground and combat theatre in their contest for control of the continent.

Africans couldn't do anything about it.

While ethnic and regional rivalries fuelled and may even have helped to ignite the conflict in Congo, there is no question that the crisis was largely engineered by Western financial, economic and political interests led by the former colonial power, Belgium, and by the United States, the leader of the Western world.

Patrice Lumumba

And while Lumumba was a staunch nationalist and Pan-Africanist and wanted Congo to be genuinely independent without being dominated by either the East or West, he was not anti-Western as he was portrayed in the western media.

He even sought assistance from the West to help contain the situation and restore stability to Congo but was rebuffed by the United States and other Western powers; and for good reason, of course, since they were the ones who had engineered the whole thing.

Lumumba's predicament reminds one of what happened to Sekou Toure when he also sought assistance from the West. After the French cut off economic aid to Guinea, Sekou Toure asked for assistance from the United States but was rebuffed. President Dwight Eisenhower dismissed him as a dangerous leftist and a Soviet ally who did not deserve help from any Western country. But unlike Lumumba, he survived assassination and coup attempts through the years.

When Lumumba was assassinated, Africa entered a new era. It was a turning point in the history of the continent.

The assassination of Lumumba, and subsequent chaos that ensued following his assassination and Western intervention in Congo, was one of the biggest tragedies in the history of Africa since the advent of colonial rule. And it still haunts the continent today more than 50 years after Congo won independence from Belgium in June 1960.

Once Africa's great hope as its richest country, richer than South Africa in terms of minerals and agricultural potential right in the heart of the continent, Congo became the bleeding heart of Africa because of foreign intervention. And it is still battered and traumatised.

At the centre of this maelstrom was the United States and Belgium, the most active and most prominent players on the Congo scene in the sixties and thereafter. In fact, for decades until the fall of Mobutu in May 1997, the largest CIA station in Africa was in Congo's capital, Kinshasa. The country was then known as Zaire, renamed by Mobutu in 1971.

Lumumba's fate and that of Congo would not have turned out the way it did had Western countries not intervened, wreaking havoc on an unprecedented scale since Congo's independence in 1960 well into the 1990s and beyond at a cost of more than 6 million lives.

The civil wars which broke out in the nineties, tearing the country apart, were largely a result of that, with the West having propped up a rotten regime under Mobutu for more than 30 years, triggering an uprising against his kleptocratic and blood-soaked reign of terror during which he and his Western masters bled the country to death, leaving it an empty shell.

One of Africa's richest countries became one of the poorest. And it all started because Western countries, led by the United States, did not want Lumumba to remain in power and lead this huge, rich country in the heart of Africa.

Lumumba was a strong nationalist and Pan-Africanist leader who was determined to lead Congo as a truly independent country. And that was anathema to the West. Western countries were equally determined to secure, maintain, and perpetuate their hegemonic control over Congo and the rest of the continent in order to preserve, protect and promote their own interests to the detriment of Africans, and largely succeeded in doing so.

In many fundamental respects, Congo became a test case of what the West intended to do to African countries after they won independence. And that was to neutralise them and render their independence meaningless by turning them into client states of the West or by simply destroying them if they resisted Western intervention. Lumumba and his country became the first casualties.

The downward spiral started with the secession of Katanga Province led by Moise Tshombe.

Tshombe used the chaos that ensued soon after the country won independence as an excuse to seek assistance from Belgium to restore law and order in his province. Belgian paratroopers flew into Katanga but with a larger mission in mind: to support the secession of the mineral-rich province.

As the chaos spread across the country, Lumumba sought UN assistance and the United Nations created a peacekeeping force for the country. But just before the arrival of UN peacekeeping forces which had the mandate to make arrangements for the withdrawal of Belgian troops as requested by Lumumba, Tshombe declared independence for his province. The UN forces arrived on July 15th.

Katanga seceded on 11 July 1960, only a few days after the country won independence on June 30th under the leadership of Patrice Lumumba as the first democratically elected leader of this vast country of more than 200 ethnic groups.

Just a few days after Katanga seceded, Tshombe ordered mobilisation of his forces on July 20th to resist UN intervention and went on to recruit mercenaries to bolster his defence, making the situation worse for Lumumba as the legitimate leader of the Congolese government which wanted to keep the country united.

In the following month, Nkrumah wrote Tshombe a letter, dated 12 August 1960, in which he stated:

"You have assembled in your support the foremost advocates of imperialism and colonialism in Africa and the most determined opponents of African freedom. How can you, as an African, do this?"[2]

Lumumba assumed power as prime minister after winning a plurality of votes and was endorsed by the national parliament composed of representatives of different political parties all of which were regionally entrenched except Lumumba's Congolese National Movement – *Mouvement National Congolaise* (MNC) – which transcended ethno-regional loyalties and had support in all parts of the country. The MNC was founded on 5 October 1958. Lumumba was one of its founding members and later its president. The other founders of the party were Cyrille Adoula and Joseph Ileo.

His political base was in Stanleyville, in his home region of eastern Congo. But as a leader of a supra-tribal party, he did not see that as his only strength. He had followers across the country.

Formed less than two years before the Belgians

21

formally relinquished power, the MNC was the driving force behind the independence movement. In mid-1959, the party split into two groups.

One was more militant and was led by Lumumba, a situation similar to what happened in Ghana during the independence struggle when Kwame Nkrumah left the conservative United Gold Coast Convention (UGCC), of which he had served as secretary-general, and went on to form the more radical Convention People's Party (CPP) in 1949 which led the country to independence by campaigning on the slogan, "Independence Now."

Lumumba pursued the same goal, invoking virtually the same slogan. And his party won support across the country in a relatively short time.

The other faction of the Congolese National Movement was led by Joseph Ileo, Cyrille Adoula and Albert Kalonji. It was a moderate group and all three leaders went on to play important roles in the country soon after independence and after Lumumba was assassinated.

Ileo and Adoula each served as prime minister at different times; and Albert Kalonji – a conservative who once served as Lumumba's minister of agriculture – is remembered probably more than anything else as the leader who led another secessionist province, South Kasai, thus threatening the territorial integrity of the new republic. Among all these leaders, Lumumba emerged as the only true nationalist leader transcending tribal and regional loyalties.

And the fact that he came from a small tribe or ethnic group, the Batatele, native to Orientale, a province in eastern Congo – which includes Stanleyville, now called Kisangani – and to North Kasai where he was born, was a factor that made him more acceptable to many smaller ethnic groups across the country who feared domination by larger groups.

The large ethnic groups included the Bakongo whose most prominent son was President Joseph Kasavubu; and the Lunda, of whom Moise Tshombe was its most well-known leader who was also related to the royal family of this large ethnic group. The son of a successful business man in Katanga, Tshombe was the son-in-law of the emperor of the Lunda people.

Joseph Kasavubu

And there was the Luba, another large ethnic group dominant in Kasai Province whose most prominent member was Albert Kalonji. There were other groups which were bigger than Lumumba's, the Batatele.

President Kasavubu was the leader of *Alliance des Bakongo* (ABAKO) – the Alliance of the Bakongo – a party with an ethnic base solidly anchored among his people who constituted the largest ethnic group in the country and after whom the country itself and the Congo River were named.

But Lumumba's status as a member of a small ethnic group was also a liability since it did not provide him with a strong ethnic base from which he could derive and mobilize support the way Kasavubu did from the Bakongo; and even the way Etienne Tshisekedi did from the Luba, his people, years later when he sought the presidency in the 1990s and beyond long after Lumumba was dead.

Although Lumumba did not come from a large ethnic group, the MNC faction he led emerged victorious in the first legislative elections of May 1960 and won the largest number of votes among all the parties in the country.

His minority status as a member of the small Batatele tribe was also a powerful incentive among many members of parliament who supported him for his prime ministerial position after his party won the largest number of votes in the May 1960 elections.

But it was his appeal to nationalist sentiments transcending ethnic and regional interests more than anything else which made him the most popular leader in Congo. Many people saw him as a unifying factor and the leader of all Congolese, not just those of his small tribe or ethnic groups in the eastern part of the country where he came from.

He was the exact opposite of Moise Tshombe, his arch-enemy and the leader of secessionist Katanga Province.

The events leading to Katanga's secession occurred in rapid succession soon after the country won independence.

The army mutinied against its Belgian officers. The Belgian government deployed troops ostensibly to protect and rescue its citizens and other Europeans who were supposedly under siege and in danger of being killed by Africans. Katanga declared independence, and the country dissolved in anarchy, prompting Lumumba to seek assistance from other African countries and the United Nations to restore law and order and save the country from breaking up along ethno-regional lines. As Brian Urquhart, who was in Congo during that time, stated years later in his article "The Tragedy of Lumumba" in *The New York Review of Books*, 4 October 2001:

"Belgium's exploitation of the Congo was the darkest episode in all the murky history of European colonialism.

To feed King Leopold II's manic appetite for ivory and rubber, mutilations, mass executions, and the use of the *chicotte* - a hippopotamus hide whip that cut through skin and muscle - administered by the indigenous *Force Publique* commanded by Belgian officers had halved the population within a few years and left a legacy of oppression and cruelty that poisoned forever the relations of Congolese and Belgians.

At Congo's independence on June 30, 1960, the young King Baudoin, in a paternalistic speech, praised his ghastly ancestor's achievements. Lumumba's fiery response brought into the open the latent rage and resentment of his people (before he spoke, Lumumba was seen scribbling notes when the king was giving his speech).

Perhaps for the first time, Belgian officials realized that after independence, with Patrice Lumumba as prime minister, things would not, as they had hoped, go on much as before.

The Congo, unlike most African colonies, had no longstanding liberation movement either at home or abroad, or any internationally recognized independence leaders like Mandela, Kenyatta, Nkrumah, Nkomo, Nujoma, and others. Such liberationist activity as there was had been sanctioned only in 1957 and was led by Joseph Kasavubu, who was to become the Congo's first president.

Lumumba, a former postal clerk and beer salesman,

became the leader of the nationalist, supratribal party, the *Mouvement National Congolaise* (Congolese Nationalist Movement), in Stanleyville, his political base. He was arrested for the first time in November 1959 and then released to take part in the Brussels Roundtable that set the scene for the Congo's suddenly accelerated independence, precipitated in part by Charles De Gaulle's abrupt granting of independence to France's African colonies. Congolese independence was in every way a last-minute arrangement.

Whether because they believed that independence would be little more than a formality or because of the superiority and contempt they felt for their unfortunate African subjects, the Belgians, unlike other colonial powers, made no practical arrangements for an independent Congo.

No Congolese had ever taken part in the business of government or public administration at any important level. Only 17 (other reports say only 16) out of a population of 13.5 million had university degrees. There was not one Congolese officer in the *Force Publique*, which was to become the *Armee Nationale Congolaise* (ANC). No colony had ever faced independence so ill-prepared.

Events in the first days of independence went at a dizzying pace. The army mutinied and threw out its Belgian officers. Europeans were roughed up, and there were reports of white women being raped. The Belgian population panicked and left. Belgian paratroopers were deployed to protect the remaining Europeans.

These troops, believed by the Congolese to have been sent to reverse independence, clashed with the soldiers of the ANC – which had no officers – in the major cities. With the connivance of Belgium, the richest province, Katanga, whose president was Moise Tshombe, seceded from the new republic. Public administration, law, and order evaporated and were replaced by chaos and anarchy."[3]

Brian Urquhart was in a unique position to make those observations not only because he was in Congo during that time but also because he worked with Dr. Ralph Bunche, a black American senior diplomat who was also the UN undersecretary-general. Dr. Bunche was also in Congo during that time. As Urquhart explained:

"I should explain here my own connection with the Congo. I was Ralph Bunche's chief assistant and in that capacity was in the Congo throughout the summer and early fall of 1960.

We were in touch with Lumumba more or less on a daily basis during this time, until he broke off relations with Bunche.

In the fall of 1961, after Hammarskjold's death on a mission to the Congo, I became the UN representative in Katanga, was kidnapped and severely beaten up by Moise Tshombe's troops, and was in charge of the UN side during two weeks of fierce fighting after which Tshombe agreed to end secession and reunite Katanga with the Congo.

Bunche, who had drafted the chapters of the UN Charter on decolonization and trusteeship and was awarded the 1950 Nobel Peace Prize for negotiating the armistice agreements between Israel and its Arab neighbors, had a unique record as a promoter and expediter of decolonization and was the friend and mentor of many of the African independence leaders.

Lumumba once asked me angrily why Hammarskjold had sent 'ce negre Americain' to the Congo. I replied with some heat that Hammarskjold had only sent the best man in the world to deal with such a situation. Lumumba did not revert to this subject."[4]

Although the anarchic situation in Congo had been precipitated by a series of dramatic events soon after independence, the most tragic before Lumumba's assassination was the secession of Katanga Province.

Katanga's secession was followed by secessionist threats from other provinces. One such threat was carried out when Albert Kalonji of Kasai Province, which was the homeland of the Luba people in south-central Congo, declared himself king of South Kasai. Kasai's secession only made things worse.

Bordered by Katanga on the southeast, southern Kasai declared independence on 14 June 1960, 16 days before Congo's independence, and declared itself the Federal State of South Kasai. The northern part of Kasai province did not secede.

Moise Tshombe

On 8 August 1960, the state of South Kasai officially became a "sovereign"entity, with Bakwanga, now Mbuji-Mayi, as its capital. Albert Kalonji became president of South Kasai and Joseph Ngalula was appointed head of government or prime minister.

On 12 April 1961, an assembly of South Kasai leaders and elders declared Alber Kalonji's father an emperor, invested with the title Mulopwe which means emperor or king in the Luba language.

But the new emperor immediately abdicated his throne in favour of his son Albert Kalonji, the president of South Kasai. From then on, Albert Kalonji ruled South Kasai as Mulopwe - Emperor/King - Albert I Kalonji.

The head of the Congolese government during that chaotic period was still Patrice Lumumba. To end the secession, he sent troops to South Kasai. The soldiers, who came from the national army, were led by Joseph Mobutu. After four months of fighting, the province was retaken and brought under control. Albert Kalonji was arrested on 31 December 1961, ending the secession.

On 7 September 1962, Kalonji escaped from prison and attempted to regain the province. He set up a new government but it was dissolved less than a month later.

The secession of South Kasai was one of the major problems the country faced in the early sixties. But it was Katanga's secession which posed the greatest threat to the territorial integrity of Congo. Its leader, Moise Tshombe, was resolutely opposed to any reconciliation and the establishment of a central government as the supreme authority over the whole country.

Even before Congo won independence, Tshombe made it clear that he preferred a loose federation in which the provinces would be able to exercise considerable power over their own affairs. It was a kind of autonomy which amounted to virtual independence with a very weak central government.

Before he declared Katanga a republic soon after the province seceded from the rest of the country, Tshombe already had formidable influence in his home region because of his family ties to the royal family of the Lunda, the largest ethnic group in Katanga; also because of his dominant position as president of *Confédération des associations tribales du Katanga* (CONAKAT) – the Confederation of Associations of Katanga – the biggest and strongest political party in Katanga Province. He was co-founder of the party, together with Godefroid Munongo who became his close confidant. Munongo also played a major role in Lumumba's assassination.

The party was also supported by the Belgian colonial authorities and their government in Brussels.

Founded in the 1950s, CONAKAT was regionalist and wanted the mineral wealth of the province to benefit only the indigenous people of Katanga.

In January – February 1960, Tshombe attended the Brussels Roundtable, a conference on Congo's independence. The meeting was also attended by other Congolese leaders including Lumumba and Kasavubu under the auspices of the Belgian government.

At that meeting, Tshombe demanded that once the country won independence on June 30th it should form a loose federation of independent states based on the existing regional structure whose provinces were defined by their ethnic identities more than anything else.

He did not prevail but left no doubt in any one's mind that a unitary state for Congo was the farthest thing from his mind. He wanted no part of it; nor did his sponsors, the Belgians, who wanted to control the mineral wealth of Katanga once the province seceded.

In the general elections of 1960, CONAKAT won and secured control of the provincial legislature in Elisabethville, capital of Katanga Province, giving Tshombe considerable power not only in his home province but in the country as a whole as the leader of the richest province and of one of the most powerful and best organized political parties in Congo, even though it was regionally entrenched like the rest except Lumumba's which transcended ethno-regional loyalties.

Emboldened by this victory and support from the Belgian authorities, and his pre-eminent position on the country's political scene as the leader of the richest province, he pulled Katanga out of Congo and declared the province a republic only 11 days after the country won independence. It was a bold and dangerous move, and it had dire consequences for the entire country for decades to come. Even today, Congo has not yet recovered from what ensued in the country during those turbulent years as a result of Katanga's secession and intervention by external forces.

After Katanga's secession, Tshombe worked closely with Belgian advisers and business leaders as he had in the past and even appointed a Belgian officer as the commander of his army, in spite of the fact that the Belgians saw him as a racist who worked with whites only to secure his own interests. They denounced Lumumba the same way, although those who knew Lumumba, including his political opponents, say he was not a racist but an uncompromising nationalist and Pan-Africanist.

But there is no question that Tshombe was a tribal chauvinist and champion of the Lunda people and other Katangese but especially the Lunda, his fellow tribesmen. And he refused to cooperate with the UN and the central government under Lumumba to restore the integrity of Congo, maintaining that Katanga was an independent state and had the right to be one.

In August 1960, he was elected president of Katanga and maintained a large army of mercenaries. Many of them came from apartheid South Africa and other countries including France and Belgium. When the United Nations asked Tshombe to end Katanga's secession, he refused and opposed UN troops which had been sent to Congo to restore law and order. UN forces were later given the mandate to end Katanga's secession by force and fighting began.

As chaos continued, Congolese leaders tried to restore stability in the country. In February 1961, they formed a provisional government. Joseph Ileo was chosen to be the prime minister.

Conferences to negotiate reunification of the country

31

were held in the first half of 1961 and were attended by representatives from all of the country's six provinces.

Cyrille Adoula

In July 1961, the secession of South Kasai under Albert Kalonji formally ended, and in August, Cyrille Adoula was named Congo's prime minister.

Adoula emerged on the national scene as a moderate trade union leader before independence. Antoine Gizenga was named deputy prime minister. Earlier, Gizenga had served in the same position under Lumumba.

Lumumba served as prime minister from 24 June – 5 September 1960; Joseph Ileo from 12 September 1960 – 27 July 1961; and Adoula from 2 August 1961 – 20 June 1964.

Antoine Gizenga served as prime minister of a rival nationalist government of Lumumba's followers based in Stanleyville from 13 December 1960 – 5 August 1961.

Formation of the government of national unity in July

1961 took place after politicians from all parts of the country, including Katanga, were invited to Leopoldville in July to discuss new political arrangements under a federal constitution. They agreed to keep Kasavubu as president.

Antoine Gizenga

But to appease Lumumba's followers, Lumumba's deputy prime minister, Antoine Gizenga, was brought into the government. Before then, he was head of a rival government in Stanleyville, one of the three centres of power in the country during that period. The other two were Leopoldville, the nation's capital, and Elisabethville, the capital of the secessionist Katanga Province.

Among all three, the government in Stanleyville, Lumumba's political stronghold, claimed to be and was seen by its supporters as the only nationalist government in Congo in the tradition of Lumumba.

Although Tshombe and other politicians in Katanga were also invited to the conference, they refused to attend. It was a conference of rival groups and politicians, with different ideologies, but succeeded in reaching compromises in order to form a national government and keep the country united under a federal constitution.

While all these compromises were being made, the

situation in Katanga Province not only remained highly volatile but deteriorated. Tshombe refused to negotiate with the United Nations to end Katanga's secession and his refusal to do so was the last straw.

Pierre Mulele

UN forces began rounding up mercenaries in Katanga Province on 28 August 1960. It was the beginning of a long struggle against the secessionist province and its mercenary fighters which went on until January 1963 when Katanga's secession was finally brought to an end.

About 100,000 Congolese are estimated to have died during the Congo crisis, the bloodiest on the continent in the first years of African independence.

While Katanga's secession formally ended on 15 January 1963, and the central government took over Katanga Province with UN military assistance, another rebellion broke out in Kwilu Province in the west in January 1964 under the leadership of Pierre Mulele.

The rebellion spread to other parts of the country, followed by an uprising led by Gaston Soumialot in Kivu Province in the east. It lasted until December 1964.

In June the same year, Tshombe was recalled from exile by President Kasavubu and was appointed prime minister, replacing Cyrille Adoula, in an attempt to achieve national reconciliation. But the honeymoon between Tshombe and Kasavubu did not last long.

Disagreements between President Kasavubu and Prime Minister Tshombe led to a government paralysis. In October 1965, Kasavubu dismissed Tshombe and appointed Evariste Kimba as prime minister.

In November the same year, Mobutu overthrew the government and proclaimed himself president. Evariste Kimba served as prime minister of Congo for less than one month from 18 October to 14 November 1965. Earlier, from 1960 – 1963, he was the foreign affairs minister of the separatist Katanga Province.

Kimba and other opponents of Mobutu's regime – ex-ministers Jérôme Anany, Emmanuel Bamba and André Mahamba – were publicly hanged in the nation's capital Kinshasa in June 1966 in an attempt by Mobutu to intimidate his other opponents into submission. It was in the same year that Leopoldville was renamed Kinshasa in compliance with Mobutu's policy of Africanisation. But along with Africanisation was bloodshed because of the turmoil the country had been plunged into after Katanga's secession and because of Mobutu himself as a ruthless dictator.

All this downward spiral took place within five years after the country won independence when Lumumba became prime minister, only to be neutralised after three months in office. His biggest challenge, right away, was the secession of Katanga Province.

Joseph Mobutu

The central government under Lumumba was powerless and couldn't do anything to end the secession of Katanga Province on its own and even with the help of troops from other African countries. As Ahmed Ben-Bella, former president of Algeria who was overthrown in June 1965, said about the African countries which tried to help Lumumba and his followers and about the situation in Congo in the sixties when he was interviewed in Geneva, Switzerland on 4 November 1995: "We arrived in the Congo too late."

Ben-Bella was interviewed by Jorge Castaneda, the author of *Companero*: *The Life and Death of Che Guevara* in which he quotes the former Algerian leader.

A number of African countries – Ghana, Tanzania, Guinea, Mali, Algeria and Egypt – tried to help the nationalist forces in Congo. But, by then, Lumumba was gone. He was assassinated on 17 January 1961.

When Ben-Bella said "We arrived in the Congo too late, he was referring to the attempts made by the six African countries which intervened later in Congo to help the nationalist forces when they were fighting the Western-backed government in Leopoldville whose leaders played a major in the elimination of Lumumba.

Laurent Kabila with his wife Sifa Mahanya

But Lumumba's supporters did not give up the fight. His closest advisers and many of his followers including Laurent Kabila (who was in his twenties then) quickly left the capital Leopoldville soon after his assassination and went to the rural areas of eastern Congo, mainly Kivu, and Tanzania to mobilise forces and continue fighting.

Therefore, although Lumumba was gone, his nationalist followers who had regrouped and settled in the northeast continued to fight for his cause well into 1967.

He also had supporters in other parts of the country including Katanga, and in Kwilu Province in the west where resistance led by Lumumba's minister of education and heir apparent, Pierre Mulele, continued until Mulele's assassination by Mobutu on 9 October 1968, although the guerilla campaign by Mulele and his followers virtually ended in 1966.

Mulele, who was living in exile in Brazzaville, was tricked by Mobutu into returning to Leopoldville after Mobutu said he had given amnesty to those who had waged war against the central government and that they could return home to join their fellow countrymen in building the nation.

He didn't mean it. He sent his foreign minister Justin Bomboko to Brazzaville to lure Mulele back to Leopoldville. Bomboko had earlier also served as foreign affairs minister under Lumumba and knew Mulele well as a colleague in the first independence cabinet.

Six African leaders, more than any others on the African continent, made the most determined attempt to help the Congolese nationalist forces in their war against the puppet government in Leopoldville and its Western sponsors during the turbulent the sixties.

They were Julius Nyerere of Tanzania, Kwame Nkrumah of Ghana, Gamal Abdel Nasser of Egypt, Ben-Bella of Algeria, Sekou Toure of Guinea, and Modibo Keita of Mali.

They even had a group of their own within the Organization of African Unity (OAU) known as "the Group of Six," and secretly worked together as Ben-Bella said in the same interview with Jorge Castaneda who was then a professor at New York University. Castaneda later became Mexico's minister of foreign affairs under President Vincente Fox.

The interview with Ben-Bella is one of the most sad reminders of what unfolded in Congo in the turbulent sixties.

Tragically, Lumumba's fate was sealed from the beginning when he emerged on the political scene as the country's most influential leader. Western governments, led by the United States, saw him as a threat to their geopolitical interests in Congo and in Africa as a whole because of his strong nationalist views and beliefs as a Pan-Africanist.

On 18 August 1960, a CIA dispatch from Congo to Washington described Lumumba as "a commie playing the commie game." The American ambassador to Congo during that time was Clare Hayes Timerlake.

Americans and other Westerners saw Patrice Lumumba as another Castro and a friend of the Russians who would give the Soviets the upper hand in the heart of Africa at the expense of the West, in spite of the fact that he was not a communist or an ideological ally of the Soviets in the rivalry between the East and the West.

The Americans, including President Dwight Eisenhower and his successor John F. Kennedy and their advisors as well as congressional leaders, saw Congo as the most prized possession in Africa in pursuit of their geopolitical interests and competition with the Soviet Union because of the country's vast mineral wealth and strategic location including its proximity to the white-ruled countries in southern Africa which were ideological allies of the West against Eastern-bloc countries during the Cold War.

Therefore they did everything they could to gain control of the country and prevent the Soviets from getting it, even if it meant going to war, especially by using surrogate forces to secure Western interests. To them, Lumumba symbolized the worst they could think of. All attempts to portray Lumumba in his true colours and try to explain to the rest of the world what type of leader he really was were ignored or dismissed as lies by Western leaders, especially the Americans.

One young American reporter who was on the scene when the tragic events were unfolding in Congo during that period provided a detailed account of Western machinations against Lumumba masterminded by the United States. She produced what were probably some of the most balanced reports coming out of Congo during those tragic years.

Her name was D'Lynn Waldron. She was 23 years old in 1960 when she was in Congo. She worked for *The Cleveland Press and News* in Cleveland, Ohio, and her despatches from Congo before independence were published in that newspaper, although she complained that her editors in the United States censored and slanted her reports to portray Lumumba and the Congolese people in a negative light and added to the published reports some things she never wrote or said.

These are some of the things she said about what happened and what was going on when she was in Congo with Lumumba:

"In the spring of 1960, I was the only foreign correspondent covering Patrice Lumumba in Stanleyville just before Independence, and as such and an American, I became Lumumba's confidant and the one he entrusted to mediate between himself and the Belgian administration and to get the word to Eisenhower and the American people that he was absolutely not a Communist....

It was well known in the Congo before Independence that Belgium and the banking and mining interests were arranging for the coming Independence to disintegrate into chaos so they could take back Katanga with its gold, uranium and copper, and Kasai with its industrial diamonds, while dumping the unprofitable remainder of the Congo.

The 'White Congolese' of Belgian descent were even more aware of this and more angered by the betrayal of a trust, than almost any 'Black African,' except Patrice Lumumba.

It was these disaffected White Congolese, and especially the colonial governor of Kasai, who told me exactly what the plans of the banking and mining interests were. I even have their hand-drawn maps showing the parts of the country that would be reclaimed from the chaos. The governor of Kasai was so disgusted with the Belgian government that he took down from his wall his prized historical maps of the Congo and handed them to me (I still have them).

Before I went up the Congo River to Stanleyville,

which was Lumumba's political headquarters, I had read newspaper stories and been told by some people in the Belgian Colonial Administration that Lumumba was a madman and a Communist puppet of Russia.

What I found was a thoughtful, dignified, dedicated man who naively believed that if... Eisenhower were told the truth, Eisenhower would no longer listen to the Belgian lie that he, Lumumba, was a Communist.

My cabled newspaper stories had things added and removed by Scripps-Howard, and all references to Lumumba's admiration for America and his requests to President Eisenhower for training for his people were cut out.

Lumumba rightly believed that the Russians didn't like him any more than the Belgians did, because he was not a Communist and because he would never do the bidding of any foreign power. Lumumba only wanted what was best for the Congo and that was his death warrant. The Russians would have killed Lumumba, if the Western powers hadn't done it first.

I was with Lumumba in his living room in Stanleyville when Lumumba got the telegram which said that instead of Gizenga's staying in Accra for training with Nkrumah's people, Gizenga had been taken straight from the airport in an Aeroflot plane to Moscow. Lumumba was terrified by this and said to me, 'The Russians will use Gizenga as my Judas.'

However, Gizenga's subsequent life indicates that the Russians would have found him as dedicated to the Congo and as difficult to dictate to as Lumumba. (See the e-mail about their family's travails written to me by Dorothee Gizenga in July 30, 2003.)

The Russians had thought they would be able to wrap Gizenga in Lumumba's mantel and take control of the Congo. Gizenga did establish himself as Lumumba's heir in the Eastern Congo, but, like the rest of the Congo, the area descended into tribal war, plus Maoist inspired massacres aimed at the 'elite', which included anyone who could read, or even wore eyeglasses....

Before Independence, I know from personal knowledge, that Lumumba asked Eisenhower to provide training in government administration for Congolese, who the Belgians had deliberately kept from learning the most basic skills necessary to run a country. Eisenhower replied that would be interfering in Belgium's internal affairs, a position which was later repeated to me by the State Department.

After Independence, when the Congo needed international assistance to restore order, Prime Minister Lumumba asked Eisenhower to send American troops. However, Eisenhower continued to falsely label Lumumba a Communist and handed Lumumba's unwanted request over to Dag Hammarskjold. Hammarskjold, along with Conor Cruise-O'Brien, was part of the cabal that used the UN to destroy the Congo's Independence, in order to take back Katanga on behalf of Western mining interests.

To try to force Eisenhower to send American troops to restore order in the Congo, Lumumba threatened to bring in Russians troops. This was highly publicized by the American government, and no mention was made of the fact that this was only a threat and Lumumba was appealing to Eisenhower to send American troops. (see the book *Congo Cables* with the actual cables to and from Washington regarding the Congo and Lumumba, as assembled by Madeline Kalb).

Right up to his being turned over to Katanga to be assassinated, Lumumba pinned his hopes on America and his travelling companion and confidant was Frank Carlucci, who it has since been revealed in Congressional investigations was an American intelligence officer and presumably part of Operation Zaire Rifle, the American plot to assassinate Lumumba.

I left the Congo overland just before Independence through Ruanda and Urundi and the Mountains of the

Moon to bring Lumumba's requests for help addressed to President Eisenhower to the American Consulate in Uganda, because mail and cables were being stopped by the Belgian postal authorities. The American consulate refused to accept anything from Lumumba. They said he would have to use the Belgian Post and Telegraph in the Congo for any messages he wanted to send to President Eisenhower.

One this site, and indexed below, are newspaper stories I wrote from the Congo which were highly edited back in the States, and documents including Lumumba's own written responses to my questions on his future plans for the Congo, and in Lumumba's own handwriting with my notes using the same pen, the statement I carried to the Belgians in charge of Stanleyville at the height of the crisis."[6]

The preceding comments are on her web site which features scanned copies of some of the original pages from the *The Cleveland Press and News* containing some of her dispatches from Congo. Her web site, "Patrice Lumumba, Stanleyville, Belgian Congo D'Lynn Waldron," is:

http://www.dlynnwaldron.com/Lumumba.html

She witnessed some of the most tragic events which unfolded in Congo in the sixties.

Although she provided first-hand accounts of what was going on, and dealt with Lumumba on personal basis, she was ignored by Western leaders including her editors at her newspaper in Cleveland, Ohio, because what she wrote and said did not conform to the ideological dictates and interests of Western nations which wrongly, and deliberately, portrayed Lumumba as a communist, hence their enemy.

Frank Carlucci, whom Waldron mentioned above, provided his own account of what happened in Congo when he was there.

Frank Carlucci

Before going to Congo, he worked as a commercial officer at the American consulate in Johannesburg but was engaged in other activities as well. As he stated in an interview years later in June 1997:

"**Carlucci:** I became personally interested in the evolution of apartheid and while I was a commercial officer in essentially an economic and consulate post – Johannesburg – I undertook on my own initiative to go to a number of ANC [African National Congress] meetings....

I got a sense of what their politics were, how militant they were. Frankly, I felt they were less militant than they'd been described. I got to know some of the splinter groups. I was the first person, for example, to talk to Robert Sobukwe, who founded the Pan Africanist Congress. He later died. But I got acquainted with the movement, which, interestingly, nobody in Pretoria had been able to do.

Our embassy was constrained from the attending the meetings. The meetings were in Johannesburg. So I established a relationship, a personal relationship, with some of the political officers in Pretoria and reported to them.

I wrote a number of political – what in those days were airgrams you may recall political airgrams on these meetings on the ANC. They were well received in Washington and I think were basically responsible for my subsequent assignment to the Congo as a political officer.

Q: You went in 1960, it was to the Congo. This as a political officer. What was the situation in the Congo when you arrived there?

Carlucci: I arrived 15 days before independence. We had a Consul General who was leaving and an ambassador had been designated, Clare Timberlake. The situation was one of considerable confusion.

Nobody knew what was going to happen on the day of independence. There was a lot of focus in the consulate general on getting our independence delegation in place, making sure we were appropriately represented.

There was a feeling that we did not really know the real African leadership. What was it going to be? Who was it going to be? What did the Belgians let go of at the time of independence?

There were just a lot of unanswered questions. Some felt the Belgians had gone too fast. Everybody knew that education-wise the Congolese were not fully prepared for independence so there was anticipation of difficulty.

Q: At the beginning, were you involved in busy work or were you really starting anew?

Carlucci: The most you could get was what you could dig out of the newspaper. The bio files were inadequate to non-existent, to say the least. I set about to get to know the political figures. I did several unorthodox things which irritated the administrative officer of the embassy no end. I persuaded the DCM [deputy chief of mission], Rob McIlvaine, a marvelous man, to allow me to rent a Volkswagen so I had my own car and didn't go around in an embassy chauffeured car.

I then got myself some press credentials because the

press moved around more freely than anybody else could. Lumumba tended to hold a press conference a day and I figured it was important to get into those. Then I got myself a pass to the Parliament which was in formation. And basically spent all day outside the embassy. Just floating in from time to time.

Q: How does one get to know the new Congo and how did you set about that?

Carlucci: I'd sit in the bar in the Parliament and go up and shake hands with them and strike up a conversation. I got to know Patrice Lumumba under fairly adverse circumstances which is getting ahead of the story a little bit. But after independence when chaos broke loose-I might as well go into this story, its an interesting story. It has to do with Ralph Bunch.

Q: Yes. He was Under Secretary for Political Affairs.

Carlucci: He came out just after independence. Prior to that, we had been through the evacuation, the rapes and the pillaging. We were living in the embassy around the clock. He dictated a cable calling on the UN [United Nations] to send in a multinational force from my office. I was standing right beside him when he dictated the cable.

When the first planes came in bringing Ghanaian troops, we had a critical situation. The ambassador called me up and said, 'There is nobody at the airport, the controllers have fled, the airplanes are in the air, they're something like an hour from landing, get out there and get them down.' So I went out to the airport and spent the day acting like [an air traffic] controller, an airline attendant, and what have you.

Q: This is for a naval, an ex-naval officer?

Carlucci: That's, right. But we got the airplanes in. Meanwhile the Belgian troops had moved in to take over part of the airport.

Towards the end of the day, Rob McIlvaine, the DCM, called me and said, 'Patrice Lumumba called and wants to go to Stanleyville and would we take him.'

And he said, 'Frank, he's coming, he's on his way out.'

I guess that was early afternoon. Well, he didn't show up until about 5:00 and just drove out onto the tarmac with a big entourage. On the other side, the Belgian forces drove up and confronted him. I was standing in the middle between the two forces with machine guns pointed at each other.

Lumumba said, 'I'm here to go to Stanleyville and you're going to take me.'

The aircraft commander came up and said, 'We've just learned that the controllers in Stanleyville have been killed and all the lights are out. We're not going.'

The Belgian colonel said, 'Unless you get these people off the tarmac in five minutes, I'm opening fire.'

So I had a dilemma on my hands. I finally grabbed the aircraft commander and I said, 'I don't care if we fly up to Stanleyville. Turn around and fly back. We're getting in this airplane right now or there is going to be gunfire here.' He said, 'Okay.'

So I took Lumumba and Kasavubu, both to Stanleyville.

Q: Could you explain, at that point, who were these two?

Carlucci: Lumumba was prime minister and Kasavubu was president at that point. And there was a man named Maurice Mpolo who was accompanying them as sort of a military aide, who later became Minister of Sports. I told him that we had a problem in Stanleyville, but if they insisted on going, I would take them.

They said we insist on going. In fact Lumumba had screamed at me. He called me and he said something to the effect that 'You Europeans are all hypocrites. You promised me.'

And when we got on the airplane, I said, 'Why did you scream at me?'

He said, 'I didn't realize you were an American. I

47

thought you were European.'

The two of them stood in the cockpit. It was a Globemaster C-124. They stood in the cockpit the entire flight to Stanleyville. On the way up, I told them that there were Europeans in Stanleyville and I assumed they didn't have any objection if we took them back on the plane. Lumumba agreed. Then when we got off the plane, the Europeans came to me and said, 'We want to leave but the immigration authorities won't let us leave.'

I said, 'Well, that's your problem. You go work it out with them. I'm not your Consul.' These were basically Belgians. There were about 30 of them. They came back a couple of hours later and said, 'It's really hopeless. They won't let us leave and they are now treating us in a way that our lives are in danger.'

I said, 'Well, I'm not your Consul but I'll see what I can do.'

So I went around to the governor's house in Stanleyville where Lumumba and Kasavubu were having a cocktail party and talked to Lumumba and said, 'You had in effect said I could take them out. We have done you a favor by bringing you up here and I hoped that we could go ahead. You should let these people loose.'

And he responded with something like, 'These are bad 'Flemish' and they shouldn't be allowed to go.' But then he turned to me – he was tall and I am short – and dropped his hand on my shoulder and said, 'But I like you. Your are my friend. I give you the Belgians. It's a gift.'

I said, 'Don't give it as a gift, but I'm happy to take them.'

For several years thereafter I got cards from the Belgians thanking me for getting them out of Stanleyville. . That's how I got to know Lumumba. We became pretty good – I don't want to say friends – but every time I'd run across him, he'd have a pleasant greeting for me.

Q: Tell me, Frank, when you started this thing, when you arrived, this is obviously Cold War time and

all that, what were you getting when you arrived at the embassy about sort of American interests in the Congo and the people who seemed to be coming in – Lumumba, Kasavubu, and that?

Carlucci: Well the Congo was the focus of world attention. It was at the heart of the Cold War struggle at the time. There was a lot of feeling that Lumumba was a Communist sympathizer. We had Senator Dodd, Tom Dodd, who was an active critic of people like Lumumba and Gbenye, the latter being Lumumba's Interior Minister.

Dodd came out and I was his escort officer. I thought he had become convinced that Lumumba and Gbenye, while they may have had some sympathy for the Soviets, didn't really understand what communism was. But when he went back to the U.S., he called them communists again.

We should remember that Lumumba came to Washington and was rejected before he turned to the Soviets. How he got to Washington was an interesting story.

Q: Well, let's hear it.

Carlucci: DCM, McIlvaine called me one day and said the prime minister had just called him and he said that he wanted to go to Washington. McIlvaine had said, 'Fine, we will be glad to welcome you in Washington. Could you tell me when the visit will take place?'

The answer was 'This afternoon.' McIlvaine instructed me, 'Frank, you've got to organize this.'

I went to the consul, who was a rather strong-willed woman named Tally Palmer – Alison – who later became famous for defense of women's rights in the State Department. I said, 'Tally, I want you to prepare about 20 visas on blank sheets of paper.' She looked at me like I was crazy. I said, 'Now, just do it.' Sure enough, all of a sudden a delegation appeared on her doorstep and said, 'We want 20 visas.' She was able to issue these visas on blank sheets of paper.

49

I then went to the airport. I couldn't find an airplane. I couldn't figure out how they were going to get to the U.S. So I went to the controller's office and said, 'Do you have an aircraft coming in that is going to take the prime minister of the Congo to the United States?'

He said, 'No. The only thing we've got in is a Ghanaian Air Force plane that just landed and disembarked some troops.'

So, I went back to the radio room and at that moment, Lumumba and his entourage pulled up. I stopped them and said, 'Mr. Prime Minister, we would like to welcome you to the United States, but do you know how you are going to get there?'

He said, 'Do you see that plane over there?'

And I said, 'Yes. It's a Ghanaian Air Force plane.'

He said, 'We're going in that plane.'

I went over to the plane and said to the pilot, 'Did anybody give you any instructions to take a group of Congolese to the United States?'

He said, 'No.' And at that moment Lumumba and company approached the plane. The pilot looked at me and he said, 'What should I do?'

I said, 'You better salute and let him board and take them wherever they want to go,' which is precisely what the pilot did.

In fact, there was a humorous sequence when he got out on the tarmac ready to take off. A straggler came running out and stood in front of the airplane and wouldn't let them take off until they put him on board. They lowered the ladder and put him on board. They flew to Accra where apparently they got a plane to go to the United States.

Q: Let's go back to the time of the independence, when independence happened. What were your experiences sort of on the day and right afterward?

Carlucci: On the day of independence I had heard rumors that rioting was occurring at the Parliament

50

building so I grabbed an Lingala-speaking driver and went to the Parliament building where the troops were indeed rioting. I went up to them and through the driver asked what they were rioting about.

The answer was interesting. They were upset not so much at the Belgians as at their own leadership, Patrice Lumumba and others, who had suddenly sprouted big cars, big houses, and flashy suits. They said General Janssens, who had been made commander of the Force Publique, had written on the blackboard independence equals no change for the military. They asked, "What's in it for us Everybody else gets something and we get nothing." Subsequently, Lumumba who was an absolute spellbinder, a very charismatic man...

Q: Was he from the Leopoldville area?

Carlucci: He was from Stanleyville. He didn't have a tribal base in Leopoldville. He didn't have a strong tribal base anywhere, in fact. He'd been a postal clerk in Stanleyville. I think he'd actually been arrested for embezzlement or something similar during the colonial period. He went out to the military camp at Djelo Binza and talked to the soldiers. He managed to turn them against the Belgians. That's when anti-Belgian rioting started. I went out, I think it was either that day or the next day to the neighborhood where I was living which was past the military camp. We assembled the Americans and I led a convoy of Americans into the embassy. We were stopped a number of times by soldiers. In fact, my then two year old daughter had a bayonet poked right in her face. But we made it to the embassy. People essentially lived in the embassy until they were evacuated. We evacuated as many as we could by ferry but then the ferry...

Q: Was the ferry over to Brazzaville?

**Carlucci: Brazzaville, yes. Then the ferries were shut off. On occasion soldiers would come up and point guns at the embassy. I remember going out and confronting one.

He was pointing his gun at the embassy. I told him that he had a duty not to attack the embassy but to help me go over and rescue some Americans who were in a hotel. To my surprise he agreed and we went over and got some Americans out of the hotel. But we lived in the embassy for a couple of days. Timberlake did a marvelous job as ambassador.

Q: What was he doing at that time?

Carlucci: He was sending cables and giving instructions. It was he who told me to get out and get the planes landed. He began to feel that the Lumumba regime was increasingly erratic and very difficult to deal with. He was pushing for the UN troops to come in quickly as the only means of saving the situation. Peacekeeping has a somewhat mixed reputation these days but the Congo has to be characterized as a very successful multinational peacekeeping operation.

The troops who came in – the Ghanaians, the Moroccans, the Nigerians, Ethiopians, subsequently Indians, Pakistanis – all did a marvelous job. Basically, they restored order after a period of time. The panic with which the Belgians fled was amazing. I went around my neighborhood and remember a houseboy coming out and telling me his employer had said, 'Take everything; it's all yours.'

Another said, 'They left the phonograph playing. Should I turn it off?' People fled literally in their nightgowns. The neighborhoods were deserted for quite some time.

Q: When was the decision made to get the families out? Was this right after independence?

Carlucci: When the rioting broke out. It became very clear that it was an extremely dangerous situation. I think the rioting broke out around the early part of July, about a month after independence.

Q: Were you able to get any fix on where Lumumba and Kasavubu were or what they were trying to do at

that time?

Carlucci: Oh yes, we had some contact with them. Lumumba wasn't hard to get a fix on because he had a press conference practically every day. By talking to his aides and by attending the press conferences, we could keep track of Lumumba. It wasn't very good news.

Kasavubu kept pretty much to himself in his presidential residence, but Timberlake would call on him. He took me along as the interpreter. We called on him several times.

Lumumba, of course, at one point called on the Russians to come into the Congo which made big headlines. That's another interesting story. I attended that press conference. At the end of the press conference, I was rushing back to the embassy to file my cable and three reporters, Welles Hangen, who later was missing in Cambodia, Henry Tanner of the *New York Times* and Arnaud De Borchgrave, who was then with *Newsweek*, said, 'Frank, it's more important that the U.S. government get this message straight than it is that we file our dispatches early. So we're going to come back and help you write your cable.'

Very unusual. They came back and helped me write the cable and then went off and filed their despatches. Bob McIlvaine who was a stickler for good drafting took a look at my cable and puffed on his pipe and said, 'Well I guess it can go by cable and not by airgram. But get it down to one and a half pages, Frank.'

I said, 'But my God, he's called on the Russians to come in!'

He said, 'Go do it right.'

I learned a lesson and I went back and redrafted it.

Q: What was the analysis of why he called the Russians in?

Carlucci: I think he had become frustrated with the west. He had gone to Washington and asked us for military help. He realized, correctly it turned out we didn't agree at the time-that the Katanga secession could only be put down by force.

He wanted military assistance to do that. He went to Washington and did not get the kind of assistance that he sought. He went to Moscow and they responded by sending him some trucks-something like 100 Russian trucks came into Congo. As history can now document, in the end we had to agree to allow the UN forces to go in to Katanga and put an end to the secession. I ended up in the front wave of the troops that did that.

Q: Before we come to that, what were we saying as far as American participation or doing something when we'd helped Lumumba go to the United States? What was the embassy recommendation on his sudden coming there and how to treat him and how did it work out from your perspective?

Carlucci: Well, there wasn't much time to make any recommendation other than he's coming to the United States and wants our support. Treat him hospitably and be as responsive as you can. The embassy, as I recall, it was a long time ago, but I don't think we were arguing in favor of giving military support to Lumumba. We thought that preserving the integrity of the Congo was important and we were sympathetic on that goal. But it was the means to accomplish the goal that we could not support.

Q: What was the attitude toward the province at that time as far as American interest and the recent secession movement? How did we feel about that?

Carlucci: At that time, those were the early days, the days of Patrice Lumumba, there was very little sentiment in the United States for a separate Katanga. That changed, over the course of the next year and a half as Tshombe's very successful lobbying machine got into operation.

Q: Did we know any of the leaders in Chatting? I mean, did we have much of a fix on Chatting?

Carlucci: We did indeed. We had a consul down there named Bill Canup, who knew Tshombe as a provincial governor. I had met Tshombe during the independence ceremonies. And we knew Monongo, the Interior Minister who allegedly was present when Lumumba was killed.

Q: When you arrived in Leopoldville and started there as a political officer, what was your impression of the CIA station there and it's duty? I mean all this is brand new and I was wondering – later this became a very important thing – but what was your impression when you first arrived?

Carlucci: When I first arrived I didn't have much contact with the station. The consulate general had virtually no outside contacts. I remember being startled when the consulate general said to me, 'You need to find out what's going on here,' go down and mix with the U.S. press.

Q: Wait a minute, we're talking about Consulate General, this is before it became an embassy?

Carlucci: Before it became an embassy.

I thought to myself, that's a strange way to function to mix with the U.S. press and I proceeded to do my own thing. We weren't getting much information out of the CIA. They didn't have a lot of contacts either.

Q: What about the meeting-the press going in there – this was sort of a precursor to Vietnam. I mean this is where all the...?

Carlucci: We were swamped with press people. I think the quality was quite high. Some of them went into danger. There was one who was killed in the Kasai. He was a very bright and able young man.

Q: Did you find there was a close relationship between the embassy reporting staff and the press corps at that point?

Carlucci: Since I was the principal writer in the embassy, there wasn't a day that the press wasn't in my office. Those were the days when it wasn't a sin for the press to talk to government officials and vice versa. Those were also the days when I could say to the press, 'This is confidential,' and know that they would respect the confidentiality. They would also share information with me. So we did have a good relationship, plus the fact that I saw them all the time at Lumumba's press conferences.

Q: What about as these trucks arrived? What were we seeing by that time? Had Lumumba with his 100 trucks, Soviet trucks, I mean had this become a cause for us or...?

Carlucci: Yes. This had been blown up out of proportion to its intrinsic worth. We were all worried about the Russian technicians who had come along with the trucks and what they would do. It was a symbol that Lumumba was willing to, if necessary, play the Soviet game and that aroused a great deal of concern. Lumumba moved further and further to the left. You could argue that he was driven there by the west's lack of responsiveness. Whether it was that or whether it was his inclination, or whether he was enticed by what the Soviets had to offer, those were all fears. The fact was that he gradually became more critical in his comments toward the west and more erratic in his behavior. I came to fear that he had lost not only our confidence but he was losing the confidence of his own parliament. A lot of people thought I was nuts when I said that. One of the riskier things that I've done in my entire career was to do a nose count of the Congolese parliament in 1960. But I listed each member and where I thought he was going to vote and I concluded that Lumumba would lose. Washington couldn't believe that but we managed to persuade Washington that the UN should be allowed to hold what was called the Lovanium summit where the parliament was sequestered. It was kept insulated from political pressures and beer until they voted. Lumumba was defeated. It was out of that meeting that Adoula became Prime Minister, a much more moderate man. It's common to say that Lumumba was – there was a coup against Lumumba – but in fact he was voted out. It was then that he, as I recall the sequence, that he reacted.

He went into his residence and it was only when he left his residence to try and flee that he was captured. Had he stayed in his residence, he probably wouldn't have been captured. As it was, I was probably - I and then Senator Gale McGee - were probably the last two westerners to see him alive. We were having a drink about mid-afternoon at a sidewalk café and a truck went by. Lumumba had his hands tied behind his back and was in the rear part of the truck. The truck was on the way to the airport. As you know, he was killed either in the airplane or shortly after he got off the airplane in the Katanga.

Q: At that time, did we see the... Were the Soviets or the Soviet embassy, was it a real competition? I mean did you find yourself jostling the Soviet political officers or not?

Carlucci: No. I can't recall the Soviet embassy being that active. But I have to say I was not dealing with the diplomatic community. I was essentially the embassy's outrider and I was dealing with the Congolese. But the diplomatic relationships with the embassies were being handled at level higher than mine.

Q: You mentioned when Lumumba was using these 100 trucks, you got involved with those?

Carlucci: I didn't get involved. I was at the press conference when he called on the Soviets to come in. The trucks were sent and that caused quite a fuss, quite a stir in the western press. It was the beginning of the slippery slope that Lumumba got on.

Q: When Adoula came in, what was the feeling towards him?

Carlucci: We'd known Adoula, we liked him, there was a warm feeling, a feeling that we wanted to make his government a success. He was invited to Washington. By then I had gone back to Washington. I was his escort officer when he was in Washington. It was a whole new atmosphere.

Q: Kasavubu, where did we see him?

Carlucci: Well, we saw Kasavubu as a moderate figure, but he was very slow to action. We made efforts to persuade him that he had to move and I guess eventually, certainly when the Congress and the Parliament voted, he dismissed Lumumba. But there was no love lost between Kasavubu and Lumumba.

Q: With this group, I think wasn't there an instance where you got knifed or something like that happened to you?

Carlucci: Yes. That was during a visit of, I believe it was Loy Henderson.

Q: He was Under Secretary for Political Affairs or something like that or number two man...?

Carlucci: I think he was Deputy Secretary. Anyway, he came out. We were heading back to the airport. I was in a separate car. I wasn't part of the entourage. I was in a car that was being driven by the chief warrant officer of the Defense attaché's office. We had in the car Lieutenant Colonel Dannemiller, who was the Army attaché, and his wife. I was sitting in the front seat. The car was going too fast. I can remember telling the warrant officer that I thought he was going too fast. A bicyclist was crossing the road - one of these things where neither could guess which way the other was going and eventually we hit him and plowed into a ditch. I could see right away that he was dead. I knew what was going to happen. I told the warrant officer to run and get out of there quickly which he did. The wife of our Army attaché was in a state of shock. We couldn't get her out of the car, so I did the only thing that could be done at that point. I went over to the body to draw the crowd away from the car. I was successful. He eventually got her out of the car and they got away. But in the meantime, of course, the crowd surrounded me. Several people stopped and tried to help. Tally Palmer stopped. She had a silver convertible. I'll never forget it. I told her, 'Get out of here,' because she couldn't get close to me.

Then the crowd started beating me up. I felt what I thought was a hard blow to my back, and about that time – actually somebody else, I think Larry Detlan stopped as well – and shouted at me and said, 'Some people will take you into the village.'

I said, 'Larry, the last place I want to go is into the village.'

It was getting fairly serious when a Congolese bus driver drove his bus right through the crowd and opened his door right at my back and I just stepped into the bus. I didn't know I had been stabbed until I saw the pool of blood on the floor of the bus. He, in essence, saved my life.

Q: It was an extremely dangerous time, wasn't it there, at that point?

Carlucci: Well, yes. Subsequently there had been a lot of dangerous posts in the foreign service, but that was one of the earlier ones.

Q: What about Alison Palmer? What was your impression, because she became a figure in her own right particularly on women's affairs and this? How did she operate?

Carlucci: She was a consulate officer in the embassy. I think she showed courage, certainly by stopping and trying to help me at the time. I didn't have a lot of interaction with her. We had a cordial relationship. She didn't really comment on political affairs. She didn't spent much time outside the embassy. She just basically did visa and passport work. Certainly she might have held strong views, we didn't hear those views at the time. At least I didn't.

Q: The Kennedy administration came on in January 1961 and did you see a change in the embassy policy and all because the Kennedy administration came and Soapy Williams was the assistant secretary for African Affairs? You know there was a lot of

emphasis on Africa.

Carlucci: The major change was there had been a history of bad feelings between Chester Bowles and Clare Timberlake. I can remember Timberlake telling me when Chester Bowles was named Under Secretary of State that his days on the job were probably numbered, because he and Bowles had clashed in India. In fact, that turned out to be the case. Timberlake became increasingly critical of the UN operation, Rajeshwar Dayal in particular.

Q: Who was he?

Carlucci: He was the Indian who headed the UN operation. Not a particularly good choice, if I may say so. He was a very bright man, but he had a somewhat supercilious attitude toward the Africans – tended to look down on them. They didn't like him. In fact, it is fair to say they despised him.

Q: When you say Africans, does this also mean the troops of Guyana and from other African...?

Carlucci: No, no. The Congolese. They tended to view him as a new form of colonialism. This was post-Lumumba, but certainly Adoula had problems with Dayal. Mobutu, the military, all had problems with him. Timberlake came to feel that the UN was not being supportive enough of the central government efforts to deal with Katanga's secession as well. Timberlake was called back for consultation and never returned.

Q: This was after the Kennedy administration came in?

Carlucci: Yes, after the Kennedy administration. He was called back for consultation and never returned. At the same time, Dayal was called back for consultation and never returned. So there was an obvious swap. It looks like that's what happened. A man named Sture Linner took over, a Swede, who was much more effective. He gradually gained the confidence of the Congolese. It cost us a very able ambassador, not that we didn't have a good replacement. Mac Godley came as chargé and did a superb job.

Q: How did Mac Godley operate? Was there a difference between how he operated and maybe his outlook than Clare Timberlake?

Carlucci: Clare Timberlake was kind of a street fighter. Godley was a very courageous individual, but he had a more sophisticated approach. Timberlake was very blunt. Once when Washington told him to do something, he shot back, 'I'll go ahead and do it, but trying to do that out here is like trying to stuff a raw oyster in a slot machine.' I can remember staying up with Godley all night while we were arguing with Dean Rusk about the Lovanium Conference. At one point the State Department felt that Lumumba was going to win at Lovanium and they wanted to call the whole thing off after it had been started. We went out to a secure telephone in a trailer in a remote area and spent all night arguing with Washington. Our channel was through Sheldon Vance, the office director, but Dean Rusk was the real problem. Godley stood up to the State Department and convinced them that the Lovanium Conference ought to continue. And it had, as I mentioned earlier, it had a successful outcome. We turned out to be right, thank God.

Q: How about Mobutu? We're talking today on April 1, 1997, and Mobutu is seemingly on the ropes in Zaire now, but he's been around since that time. Did you run across Mobutu and have any dealings with him?

Carlucci: I knew him because of my habit of mixing with the Congolese down at the parliament. He'd show up at the parliament and I got to know him while he was still a Sergeant, before he became commander of the troops. I can remember one episode after he became commander of the troops. I wanted to get into the parliament and I had already missed their passes. The guard at the door wouldn't let me in and actually pushed his bayonet against my stomach. The picture was in the New York Times the

61

next day. I was very irritated. I went over and I found Mobutu having a beer at the bar. I said to him, 'Look, here are all my credentials, don't you think I should be allowed to get into the parliament?'

He said, 'Yes.'

I said, 'Well, will you please see that I'm allowed in?'

He said, 'I can't do that.'

I said, 'Why not?'

He said, 'Because I'm not in charge here.'

I said, 'Well you're commander in chief of the Army and if you're not in charge here, who is?'

And he pointed to the guy who had just jammed the bayonet in my stomach and said, 'He is.'

We developed a relationship. I don't want to say it was close, but we certainly knew each other. I think Larry Devlin and I went to see him shortly after he took over. I walked out of there saying, 'Larry, this guy can't last 10 days!' Shows you how good a political leader analyst I was.

Q: What was the reaction of the embassy on the report of knowledge of Lumumba's murder?

Carlucci: Well, we were of course distressed, but what we tried to do was report the facts as we had them. There wasn't a lot to be obtained in Leopoldville. Most of the action had taken place in the Katanga and we had to depend on our consul in Elizabethville to report in on what had transpired there. Our best assessment was that he had been killed after he arrived in the Katanga. A UN report subsequently said this, probably in the presence of Monongo.

Q: Did this cause a change? Was there at that time any concern that maybe this was part of the United Nations' effort to rid ourselves of this gentleman?

Carlucci: We had other things on our mind. When this happened, as I recall, I was in Stanleyville. This was shortly after they had arrested all the Europeans in Stanleyville and thrown them out. Timberlake asked me if

I'd go up there, back and forth and act as consul for Stanleyville. They announced on Stanleyville radio that Lumumba had been murdered and that I was the man who had done it. They claimed I was a paratroop captain or colonel, I guess. I had made it up to the rank of colonel. They were going to see that justice was done. And as I recall, Kwame Nkrumah sent a cable to Dag Hammarskjold about me killing Lumumba and a few other things like that. So we had to worry a little bit about survival. I had to find my way out of Stanleyville. I did that by hitchhiking. In fact, I hitchhiked in a UN plane to Bukavu and then to Elizabethville and then back to Leopoldville. I went back up to Stanleyville a couple of weeks later and they arrested me.

Q: What happened then?

Carlucci: Well, they put me under house arrest. They declared me persona non grata.

Q: This was the Congolese government.

Carlucci: It was a breakaway government in Stanleyville, headed by Antoine Gizenga. Kabila was a member of that government. I didn't know him well.

Q: He's now the rebel leader looking like he might take over.

Carlucci: We had Gizenga, Gbenye, Weregemere, and a number of other Lumumba supporters in Stanleyville. They had broken away when – I guess after Lovanium – I can't recall the exact sequence, certainly when Mobutu had taken over. They declared their own government. I'd been going back and forth, meeting with them, when they declared me *persona non grata.*

About then, I wanted to introduce my successor, Tom Cassilly (who later got arrested himself), so I said I'd go up one more time. I flew up and at the airport, they arrested me and they said I should get back on the airplane and go back to Leopoldville.

I said, 'I had no intention of doing that. I was staying in Stanleyville.'

By that time the airplane had left and the next airplane was four or five days away. So they said, 'Well we're going to put you under house arrest.'

So they put me in a house with a guard out in front. The guard had a machine gun. I managed to step out once or twice anyway. The day I was due to leave, the acting foreign minister, a man named Arsen Dionge, acting foreign minister of the Gizenga breakaway government, came around. He was trying to be very diplomatic. He came in and he said, 'How is everything?'

I said, 'Not very well.'

He said, 'What's your problem?'

I said, 'I certainly don't like being under house arrest and I don't like being declared *persona non grata*.'

He said, 'Oh, well, that. That, you shouldn't worry about it. It's just that it's not convenient to have you around right now. It's really not *persona non grata* or anything like that.'

I said, 'Well the next thing you are going to tell me is that I'm not under house arrest.'

He said, 'No, you're not under house arrest, no problem.'

With that, the guard, who had apparently lost his patience, came in and pointed his machine gun at the acting Foreign Minister and starting talking in a local dialect. And Dionge turned to me and said, 'Well, could you tell him who you are and who I am and that I'm the acting Foreign Minister because he doesn't seem to understand.'

Well, it was a little hard to contain my laughter. So I tried to explain to the guard that it's okay because he was the foreign minister and the foreign minister is a big man around here. Finally, the guard decided it was okay, and he put down his gun and walked back to his post. With that, the acting foreign minister turned to me and said, 'This place is terrible. Can you sell me any dollars?'

They then took me and put me on an airplane and that was my last time in Stanleyville.

Q: What were the people in our consulate general doing there?

Carlucci: Oh, they had closed that.

Q: It had been closed by that time?

Carlucci: Oh, yes. You see what happened, shortly, I guess about three or four months into Independence, they rounded up all Europeans and made them stand in the sun all day long. They chased out our consul and there was nobody up there. Timberlake called me. I'll never forget, he called me on the phone and said, 'Frank, I hate to have to ask you to do this but somebody's got to protect the American citizens in Stanleyville. Are you willing to go up there?'

I said, 'Okay.'

I must say the first airplane ride up there was pretty lonely. I was the only person on the airplane. Nobody was going near Stanleyville. I was able to, I think, restore some sense of confidence to the Americans and able to deal a little bit with the breakaway government.

Q: When you say, who were the Americans and how did they...?

Carlucci: Missionaries.

Q: Missionaries.

Carlucci: I tried to get them to leave. I can remember urging them to leave. They were very fatalistic. They didn't want to leave. And you may recall that about a year later Belgian paratroops had to go in and rescue them and some were killed.

Q: Was this...Elizabethville is now...?

Carlucci: No, this is Stanleyville.

Q: This is Stanleyville in the Katanga?

Carlucci: No Stanleyville is in Orientale.

Q: Oh, yes, Orientale Province.

Carlucci: Stanleyville was Patrice Lumumba's home.

Q: Was Michael Hoyt there at this point?

Carlucci: He was much later.

Q: Much later. And he got caught in that Dragon

Rouge operation.

Carlucci: Yes.

Q: As you are dealing with the Congolese at that time, either in Parliament or at these breakaway assemblies, what was your impression of how the government was operating?

Carlucci: The Congolese government?

Q: Yes.

Carlucci: It was chaotic. There was no government. There were ministers and soldiers who had big cars and big houses. All your conversations with them were political. Nobody was interested in restoring the country's economy or dealing with payment problems, inflation, or anything like that. Adoula's government took it a little more seriously. There was a man named Albert Adele who was governor of the central bank. He was one of the Congo's only three or four Ph.D.s, and he was very bright. He tended to take it seriously. There were others. There was an opposition politician who I gave a leader grant to, Kamitas Kamitata, who was governor of the province that included Leopoldville. He, I thought, was responsible. There were elements of leadership, but the chaos almost overwhelmed everyone.

Q: Now, I was in African INR (Bureau of Intelligence and Research) about this time, and although I had the heart of Africa, we'd look at the airgrams and all, there was a feeling that it reminded me at that time of caricatures, hostile caricatures, of what happened in the South during the early Reconstruction period when the freed slaves were taking over. This is a caricature that has gone on but the reports seem to almost define that.

Carlucci: It was pretty chaotic. I was in a hotel room one time in Stanleyville when a farce took place. A minister of the breakaway government and I were talking. He had his girlfriend in the hotel room and a man came pounding on the door shouting it was his wife. The man

66

was hauled away in a jeep. It was chaotic.

Q: Were we pretty much, except for trying to protect ourselves and all, were we trying to do the equivalent of later what would become nationbuilding?

Carlucci: Yes. When I got back to Washington, I found there were three of us working on the desk: Bill Harrop, Charlie Whitehouse, and myself. I concerned myself with internal politics, and Charlie worked on nationbuilding. Basically the first task was to get the rabble called the Congolese Army under control. Of course, 35 years later, it's still not under control. There is no discipline in it. There was no discipline then. It was a pure rabble then. It is a pure rabble now. We tried. Now, of course, we are being criticized for trying because that was characterized as military aid to Mobutu. So you're damned if you do and damned if you don't.

Q: By the way, while you were in the Congo, you were talking about being used as the point man and going out and I mean this is not a comfortable period. In fact, your exploits there became legendary within the Foreign Service. I heard about these. The aura lingers on.

Carlucci: The embassy administrative officer called me accident prone because I kept smashing up his Volkswagen. It was a rented car. It was exciting.

Q: Tell me, what about the other side of this? What about your family?

Carlucci: They were evacuated. They were sent to Ghana. They later came back. You had personal inconvenience. Our house was robbed several times. I caught a burglar cutting through the screen with a machete three feet from my baby daughter's crib. We had a lot of personal inconvenience. We were all young and lived with that.

Q: We'll finish up on the Congo side as the desk officer. With the three of you working on that, did you sense a different attitude when you got back to

Washington? Did they have a sense of the reality of the Congo?

Carlucci: No, Washington was torn. There was an acknowledgment that probably it was desirable to keep the Congo together but there was a lot of sympathy for Katanga's secession. Tom Dodd lobbied...

Q: He was the democratic senator from Connecticut.

Carlucci: ...lobbied the Kennedy administration incessantly. State Department wobbled all over. Basically the bureau of International Affairs (IO) was sympathetic to us in the African bureau. The European bureau tended to sympathize with the Katanga secessionists, and George McGee, who was Under Secretary of State, frankly would vacillate on the issue. We turned out to be very hard chargers. We had people like Bill Harrop and Charlie Whitehouse who were very able. Mac Godley became officer in charge succeeding Sheldon Vance, a very headstrong individual. A very strong team. Wayne Fredericks, who was Deputy Assistant Secretary was good. The governor, Governor Williams, bless his heart...

Q: This is Soapy Williams?

Carlucci: Soapy Williams. His heart was always in the right place, but he was no match for the bureaucrats. He'd get outmaneuvered practically all the time. We tended to ram things through. So much so that we finally ended the Katanga secession by giving the green light to the UN to move in. George Ball said no two of us should ever be allowed to serve together again.

Q: I would have thought that this whole thing would have particularly attracted somebody like Robert Kennedy and some of the activists around President Kennedy? You were young and you were hard charging. Africa was sort of the Kennedy playground...?

Carlucci: Dean Rusk did not take a deep interest. George Ball did from time to time. He generally came out right. Whenever we got into real trouble, we would use Ed Gullion, who was then the ambassador. Kennedy liked Ed Gullion. He'd met him in Vietnam or someplace and liked him personally. Gullion was a marvelous man, very bright, very articulate. So when we felt ourselves sliding down the slope, we'd call Gullion back for consultation and have him go over and see the President. And that always worked. Kennedy's instincts were quite good. He was perfectly willing to take on Tom Dodd. Some of the people in the State Department were less willing to take on Dodd.

Q: Tom Dodd was not just alone. In a way didn't he represent, you might call, the European centric but also...

Carlucci: To some extent. But he didn't have a lot of support in the Congress. The Chairman of the African subcommittee at the time was Al Gore, Al Gore, Senior. I can remember endless hearings which I used to go up and support Soapy Williams. Gore was not sympathetic to Tom Dodd's point of view. In the house, we had Barry O'Hara as chairman of the House Committee and he understood our story. Fred Dutton was the Assistant Secretary for Congressional Relations and he used to take me up there for endless briefings. We really blanketed the Congress and fairly well isolated Dodd. And as you know he was later censured by the Senate, not for the Congo activity but for some other activity.

Q: I think it's an interesting thing, and I'd like to get this, to see how able people have really essentially rather quite subordinate roles in the thing, can be quite important within a policy consideration that is not attracting the very top echelon.

Carlucci: Well, I guess the answer to that is in those days you could. I don't know if you could today. You've had people resign over Bosnia. They were subordinate people. Marshall Freeman and people like that. It's true that today there are dissent channels and people taking a different point of view is more common I suppose. We put our careers on the line, there's no question. I can remember one point when Mac Godley was ambassador I was in a meeting with Dean Rusk, who in frustration said, 'Does our ambassador over there understand what our policy is?'

Q: I thought sort of the one constant in our African policy which hangs on today is that once you start allowing these breakaway provinces and all, because of the tribal intermix, absolute chaos will be and maybe there are lousy borders, but there are borders and we better stick to those.

Carlucci: You're citing almost verbatim the standard paper that I used to write and rewrite. I'd just switch the paragraphs around saying just about that. Once you start down this slope, it's very slippery. I think there is something like 36-or I can't remember how many-52 different tribes in the Congo. They'd all be seeking their independence. Africa would fragment. The only solution is to respect the colonial boundaries. INR, I might say, at a critical point and time was very helpful. Ed Streator wrote a paper very well done on precisely that issue and said that unless we act decisively, things are going to collapse; it's all going to fall apart. That was shortly after the Kennedy administration's successful prosecution of the Cuban Missile Crisis.

Q: This had been in what October of '62?

Carlucci: Something like that. They were feeling confident about their ability to handle foreign affairs. They were flexing their muscles. They were becoming more assertive. They were becoming more cohesive. So that when we finally said, 'Hey, look, the balloon is about to go up on the Katanga. You can't vacillate any more.' They were willing to make the hard decision. The Pentagon was the first to come in and say-there was a Colonel in our meeting who said, 'I think you've got to support a military solution here. There's no other way.' Then the tide began to turn and we were able to turn a blind eye to the UN because the UN wanted to do what was quite clear was the only solution and we were holding them back. We were able to send a signal that said something to the effect don't over restrain yourselves.

Q: When I get you again, we'll go into Zanzibar. Also, I'd like to have you expand a bit more on the incident in, I think it was, Stanleyville, where you were with a Minister who was with his lady friend. If you could give me more detail on that. I think it's highly amusing and indicative of the situation.

You also mentioned off mic how your telegrams and cable and dispatches were received in Washington and the sage advice given to you about humor in the foreign service.

A final question. Did you notice any change when Kennedy was assassinated and the Johnson administration took over in the attitude toward the Congo at that point. Was there any change in emphasis or interest?

Today is the 30th of June, 1997. Frank, could you go into a little more detail about that time in Stanleyville. Do you recall the incident with the young lady?

Carlucci: Yes.

Q: You more or less eluded to it last time and I think it catches something.

Carlucci: I had struck up an acquaintance with a man who was a Minister of Mines in Lumumba's government, named Weregemere. He joined the Gizenga breakaway government. As I mentioned earlier, I went back and forth up there until they finally kicked me out. On one occasion, he asked me to come around to his hotel room. I think it was his hotel room because he wanted to talk to me. The purpose of the meeting was to warn me that the Gizenga people were out to get me. When I entered the hotel room, he had a young lady there, a rather attractive young lady. As we were discussing weighty matters-the UN presence and the Gizenga government-she apparently got tired, went over to the bed, took her clothes off and just laid

71

down on the bed. We continued talking and drinking our beer. All of a sudden, there was a pounding on the door. Weregemere went to the door - and I could hear some scuffling and a man shouting, 'I want my wife! I want my wife!' With that, the young lady went to the bathroom. I didn't know what to do, so I sort of followed her into the bathroom. The scuffling continued and eventually whoever was pounding on the door was taken by soldiers and dumped into a jeep and driven off someplace. Weregemere came back in and we resumed our conversation.

Q: I remember this vividly because there was an African INR at the time and when this came in, I think it was a despatch describing this thing. It, of course, made the rounds to everywhere. It certainly made vivid the situation there, but could you talk a bit about the fact that you were sending in these rather detailed pictures of the area?

Carlucci: Well, it was hard not to laugh. In fact, humor was the only way you kept your sanity in a place like Stanleyville unless you wanted to turn to liquor, which a lot of people did. I can remember being in the presence of the president of Stanleyville, a man named Jean Foster Manzikala, and hearing him answering the phone by saying, 'Yes, yes, Excellency.' 'Well, which Excellency are you?' They all called each other 'Excellency.'

Fist fights in the hotel were an every day event and I think sent in a dispatch about those one time. Of course, there was a humorous event, which I think I described for you, with the acting Foreign Minister Dionge.

It was kind of fun sending those things in. I don't know how they were received. It was later when I went to Zanzibar and I continued to do the same thing. Wayne Fredericks one time told me, time, he was the Deputy Assistant Secretary for African Affairs, he said, 'Frank, you're cables make the best reading in the African bureau. Keep it up and you'll never get promoted.'

There were more than a few people who thought I was a bit frivolous.

Q: You went from the Congo, were you assigned directly to Zanzibar?

Carlucci: No. I came back and I was in effect Congo desk officer during the Katanga secession. Then I had a brief tour in Personnel. When Zanzibar broke – that is to say, when they expelled our consul and closed our consulate – and a few months later, I was asked to go out there.

Q: So you went to Zanzibar. You were there from when to when?

Carlucci: I arrived 1964 and I was there just about a year. So it would have been probably – I think I would have gone out in early '64 and I think I was expelled in January 1965.

Q: What had been the situation in Zanzibar that led to the previous expulsion?

Carlucci: Zanzibar had become independent in 1964. We had a consul, Fritz Picard was his name, who has since died. The Africans rose up and slaughtered the Arabs because the Arabs had been running the place. They drove a number of them right into the sea. They took over but they had a decided communist tinge. A lot of the Africans had been trained at the Patrice Lumumba University.

Q: Which is in Moscow?

Carlucci: Moscow. Now there were a couple of Arabs involved with them. Babu and Ali Sultan Issa, who had been trained in Moscow and Beijing respectively. By the way, they have since both become capitalists. At the time, I remember shortly after I got there, the hospital was named the V.I. Lenin hospital and the stadium became the Mao Tse-tung stadium. All land was nationalized. In effect, all the Westerners were kicked out. There was a good deal of hostility toward the Americans and our consulate was shut down. Fritz Picard was marched out of the country, I think, literally at gun point. A long, intensive effort began to reopen our consulate, then turned embassy. A number of us in the State Department favored reopening the embassy as soon as possible. The upper levels of the State Department wanted us to play a secondary role to the British. The British were more cautious. They didn't want us to open and their embassy had been closed down, too. It was quite a long negotiation getting back in. Actually I went to Dar Es Salaam and worked on the issue with then Ambassador Leonhart. We struggled to try to get me over there. Eventually the Zanzibaris agreed and I went."[7]

Frank Carlucci, who years later became director of the CIA and US secretary of defence, worked at American diplomatic missions in Africa during some of the most critical periods in the continent's history. He was in South Africa from 1957 – 1959 during some of the most brutal years of apartheid and even established contacts with some of the leading figures in the African National Congress (ANC) including Robert Sobukwe who left the ANC in 1959 to form the Pan-Africanist Congress (PAC). He served in Congo from 1960 – 1962 and was there when Lumumba was assassinated on 17 January 1961. He was in Zanzibar from 1964 – 1965 and arrived there not long after the revolution took place on 12 January 1964. He was also accused of having played a role in Lumumba's assassination, a charge he strongly denied.

Patrice Lumumba, who became a martyr after his brutal assassination, was prime minister of Congo for only three months. Yet his influence went far beyond his brief term in office, and beyond Congo. He was the dominant figure on the country's political scene even after he was removed from office and even after he was arrested and put in jail towards the end of 1960.

Although there were other events which took place in different parts of Africa in 1960, there is no question that the year was dominated by the Congo crisis. Probably the most significant event which took place in that year was the secession of Katanga Province, on July 11th, only eleven days after the country won independence on June 30th. It was in the news everyday.

I remember when I was growing up in Rungwe District in the Southern Highlands in southwestern Tanzania in a region bordering what was then Nyasaland (now Malawi) and Northern Rhodesia (renamed Zambia) that the conflict in Congo was the dominant story broadcast by the Tanganyika Broadcasting Corporation (TBC) based in the capital Dar es Salaam, about 540 miles away on the east coast.

We also listened almost everyday to broadcasts from Elisabethville, the capital of Katanga Province which is also about 800 miles from my home district. We also listened to broadcasts from Leopoldville, the capital of the former Belgian Congo.

The broadcasts we listened to were in Kiswahili – a language also spoken in Congo – on shortwave radio. And they are still vivid in my memory 50 years later because of the tragic events and countless lives lost in that country in 1960 and in the following years.

Although the people of Congo celebrated independence in 1960, they also became the victims of one of the worst tragedies that befell Africa during the post-colonial era. And what happened in Congo in 1960 is indelibly etched in the minds of many people not only in that country but in other parts of Africa as well.

Probably the most significant event that occurred in Africa in 1961 was the assassination of Patrice Lumumba. And it had a profound impact on Congo and beyond for years.

The chaos that Congo endured for decades was partly attributable to the elimination of Lumumba from the country's political scene and as the most important leader and unifying force in Congo's post-colonial history.

He was assassinated on 17 January 1961. His brutal murder and the ensuing chaos in Congo dominated the news in Africa for the rest of the year and became one of the dominant subjects of discussion in the following years not only in Africa but in other parts of the world.

Right from the beginning, Lumumba's enemies within Congo, especially Moise Tshombe and Joseph Mobutu, were blamed for his assassination. And there is no question that they played a major role.

It was Mobutu who, as the head of the army and the most powerful Congolese leader, seized power on 14 September 1960. Also, it was he who supported Joseph Kasavubu as the country's president after Kasavubu dismissed Lumumba as prime minister on September 5th and replaced him with Joseph Ileo. And it was he who arrested Lumumba and later transferred him to his arch-enemy, Moise Tshombe in Katanga Province, to be killed.

Quite often, Lumumba's assassination is largely blamed on internal actors, the Congolese themselves, as a conspiracy between Mobutu, Kasavubu, Tshombe, Joseph Ileo, Albert Kalonji and Lumumba's other enemies in the country. The impression some people might get is that all these people were independent actors and made their own decisions, without external involvement, on what to do with Lumumba. And they did play a big role in his elimination.

But Lumumba's assassination involved even much bigger people and actors than Lumumba's Congolese enemies. It was a conspiracy which went far beyond the circle of his enemies within Congo. Although his fellow Congolese played an important role in his elimination, they were no more than puppets manipulated at will by outside powers, in spite of the fact that even they themselves would have killed him, on their own, if they had the opportunity to do so and even if there was no foreign intervention.

One of the biggest players on the scene and in Lumumba's assassination was Belgium, the former colonial power, which sent troops to Congo after independence ostensibly to rescue its citizens and other whites after the country descended into chaos precipitated by the secession of Katanga Province under the leadership of Moise Tshombe on 11 July 1960.

Katanga's secession was instigated and encouraged by Belgium and other western financial and political interests. And the real motive for Belgium's intervention was to provide military, economic and political support to Tshombe to ensure that the secession of Katanga was successful.

The Belgians had powerful financial interests in this mineral-rich province. They did not want it to remain an integral part of Congo under the control of the country's central authority, especially under the leadership of Lumumba whom they saw as a threat to their economic and political interests in the country because of his strong nationalist credentials as a leader who wanted to keep the country independent and united and free from external interference.

Although the Belgians were the most decisive force in Lumumba's assassination, they earned this status and unenviable distinction mainly because they were highly visible on the political scene in Congo as the former colonial rulers. Far more sinister was the involvement of the United States in Lumumba's arrest and subsequent assassination.

As the most powerful country in the West where the plot for Lumumba's elimination was conceived and hatched, it would not be an overstatement to say that it was the United States which was the dominant force in Congo. It was also the United States which could have prevented this tragic event from happening had the leaders in Washington chosen to do so. They orchestrated the whole thing, despite denials through the years and attempts to blame only the Belgians as the main architects of the conspiratorial and assassination plot against Lumumba.

As late as the 1990s, reports continued to circulate, as they had through the years since the sixties, that the Belgians were the main players on Congo's political scene and in the assassination of Lumumba. Even in the mid-seventies, a committee of the United States Senate which, under the chairmanship of Senator Frank Church of Idaho, investigated the role of the CIA in the assassination of foreign leaders concluded that there was no evidence to show that the United States was involved or played a role in Lumumba's assassination.

Yet, it was President Dwight Eisenhower who ordered Lumumba's assassination and authorized the CIA to carry out the plot. And Belgium could not have done anything without the approval of the United States as the leader of the Western world.

Laurence (Larry) Devlin in 1960 or 1961

But it is also true that CIA agents were involved right from the beginning in the plot to assassinate Lumumba, despite denials of the involvement of some of them such as Laurence Devlin who was the CIA station chief in Congo during that time. Devlin also befriended Lumumba using his diplomatic cover as just another official at the American embassy in Leopoldville to conceal his true identity as a CIA agent.

In an interview from his home in Princeton, New Jersey, in 1996, Devlin denied any personal involvement and claimed he was against Lumumba's assassination and that of other foreign leaders as a political weapon to secure and promote American interests.

He also talked to The New York Times in February 2008. According to a report by Scott Shane, "Memories of a C.I.A. Officer Resonate in a New Era," *The New York Times*, 24 February 2008:

"LOCUST GROVE, Va. — Larry Devlin is 85 now, suffering from emphysema and tethered to an oxygen tank, his Central Intelligence career long behind him. But he recalls with sunlit clarity the day in Congo nearly half a century ago when he was handed a packet of poisons, including toxic toothpaste, and ordered to carry out a political assassination.

Larry Devlin

'I was totally taken aback,' said Mr. Devlin, sitting in his den, looking out on a small lake in the Virginia

79

countryside. He uttered a mild profanity, he recalled, and asked, 'Isn't this unusual?'

It was 1960, and Mr. Devlin, the C.I.A.'s young station chief, was in the middle of a political maelstrom as Congolese factions fought for control of the newly independent nation and the United States jostled with the Soviet Union for influence and control over deposits of critical metals.

Mr. Devlin had no problems with bribery, blackmail or other varieties of skulduggery — "all part of the game" for the C.I.A. under Allen Dulles at the height of the cold war, he said. But he thought the order to kill Patrice Lumumba, the charismatic Congolese politician the Eisenhower administration feared would become an African Fidel Castro, was both wrong and stupid, a desperate plan that could easily go awry and devastate American influence in Africa.

'Worldwide it would have been disastrous,' he said.

So he stalled. And Lumumba's political rivals eventually killed him without the C.I.A.'s help.

Today, Mr. Devlin's story has new resonance amid a renewed debate about the proper limits of C.I.A. actions to counter a different global threat and their cost to the United States' standing. The C.I.A.'s destruction of videotapes of harsh interrogations is under criminal investigation. Congress has been reviewing the C.I.A.'s secret detention program and the transfer of terrorist suspects to countries that practice torture, though so far no inquiry has approached the sweep of the Church Committee in the Senate in the 1970s, whose reports quote Mr. Devlin under a pseudonym, Victor S. Hedgeman.

'I think there's an eerie and disturbing correlation between that era and this one,' said John Prados, an intelligence historian and the author of *Safe for Democracy: The Secret Wars of the C.I.A.*

He said the threat of terrorism now, like the threat of communism then, was used to justify extreme measures that 'later become controversial legally, morally and politically.'

Mr. Prados said the historical record supported Mr. Devlin's account of his actions, which he described last year in an autobiography, *Chief of Station, Congo: Fighting the Cold War in a Hot Zone*.

'I believe there's no reason to doubt that Mr. Devlin conspired to defuse the orders to kill Lumumba,' he said.

Mr. Devlin, who was station chief in Congo and in Laos during the Vietnam war and retired from the agency in 1974, said he never used force during interrogations and worried that endorsing such methods might put Americans at greater risk of mistreatment.

But he has watched the tribulations of a younger generation at the agency with sympathy. He can attest not only to the quandary of a field officer directed to take extreme measures, but also to the personal cost that can follow. Because his name got associated with the plot against Lumumba, Mr. Devlin was later told, he himself was made a target for death by both a Black Panther faction and Ilich Ramírez Sánchez, the Venezuelan terrorist known as Carlos the Jackal.

'I can put myself in the shoes of the people who did the waterboarding and who thought they'd get information to save lives,' Mr. Devlin said. 'I've often wondered: How would I react if I thought I had the man who knows about a bomb?'

The son of an Army colonel and a schoolteacher in San Diego, Mr. Devlin recalls being shaken when he read *Mein Kampf* at the age of 16 and paying 25 cents to hear lectures on foreign affairs at the local Unitarian church.

After serving in combat in North Africa and Europe during World War II, he went to Harvard to pursue a Ph.D. One Sunday afternoon, he was summoned by a professor, William Y. Elliott, a historian and longtime adviser to presidents. Waiting for him was McGeorge Bundy, who went on to be the national security adviser to Presidents

Kennedy and Johnson. Mr. Bundy urged him to join the recently formed C.I.A. to keep the cold war from turning hot.

His first job was as what C.I.A. calls a 'noc,' for nonofficial cover, traveling in the guise of a writer of travel guides. At the age of 38, he landed in the tumult of Congo, where he would be jailed, beaten and narrowly escape death on several occasions.

In September 1960, Mr. Devlin received a cable advising him that he would get an important message from 'Joe from Paris.' The envoy turned out to be Sidney Gottlieb, the agency's club-footed poisons expert, whom Mr. Devlin had met during operations to install listening devices overseas, and who would later become notorious for mind-control experiments using L.S.D.

Mr. Gottlieb said that the assassination had been approved by President Eisenhower but admitted that he had not seen the presidential orders. He explained that the poisons, including the spiked toothpaste, had been chosen to make the death appear to result from natural causes.

'Morally I thought it was the wrong thing to do,' Mr. Devlin said. 'And I thought it was a very dangerous thing to do. If I screwed up and brought in the wrong person and it got out that the United States had done this, I had visions of even Africans who didn't like Lumumba wiping out every white man they could find. It might have cost hundreds of lives.'

Mr. Devlin said he figured that if he refused his orders outright, his C.I.A. bosses would simply call him home and send a more willing replacement. So he listened sagely and hid the poisons in his office safe, scribbling a warning on the box — 'just in case someone got in and tried the toothpaste.'

After Mr. Lumumba was executed by opponents in January 1961, Mr. Devlin decided he needed to get rid of the poisons in his safe. He took the box to a rocky stretch of the Congo River where no one was likely to stumble upon it, and tossed it in.

Such episodes aside, he defends the C.I.A' s achievements in Congo, including support for the rise of Mobutu Sese Seko, who would become a symbol of corruption in his 32-year rule. 'We prevented the Soviets from taking over a very large part of Africa,' he said.

Though he retired from the C.I.A., Mr. Devlin stayed in Africa and worked in the diamond business for 12 years, until 1988. His boss was Maurice Tempelsman, a Belgian-American diamond importer best known as the companion of Jacqueline Kennedy Onassis in the last 15 years of her life.

'Diamonds are a political thing,' Mr. Devlin said. 'I knew all the ministers of mines. In short, I was in a better position to negotiate than people who knew a lot about diamonds.' When he came across interesting information, he added, he passed it to his old friends in the C.I.A.

Last year, Mr. Devlin was called back to C.I.A. headquarters to receive an award honoring his career and exchanged a few words with Jose A. Rodriguez Jr., the chief of the C.I.A.'s clandestine service. He has closely followed the news since Mr. Rodriguez came under investigation for giving the order to destroy the videotapes.

'I feel sorry for the guy,' Mr. Devlin said. 'I think I know what he's going through.'"

American involvement in Lumumba's ouster and elimination is clear. Still, some people have tried to minimize the role played by the United States in the assassination of Lumumba.

There are even those, including former UN undersecretary-general Brian Urquhart, who have tried to exonerate the United States from this crime. Yet there is plenty of evidence to refute that. The United States played a major role in the commission of this crime.

Also, America's direct involvement in the assassination

83

of Lumumba did little to help the United States win friends in Africa – besides Tshombe and Mobutu – and keep other countries out of the Congo imbroglio; it accomplished exactly the opposite.

Sidney Gottlieb

The CIA plot to assassinate Lumumba started with the Eisenhower Administration and remains, to this day, one of the saddest chapters in the history of relations between the United States and Africa. That the United States was largely responsible for his assassination is an open secret, as much as it has been for decades.

It is as much a sad story about the weakness of African countries as it is one of total disregard for the interests, rights and wellbeing of Africans – for racist reasons as well, not just economic and geopolitical – by the world's most powerful country whose white majority, according to national surveys, still refuse to accept African Americans as full human beings; hence the belief among millions of whites – if not the vast majority – that black people are genetically inferior to them and members of others races, a racist doctrine given pseudoscientific validity by *The Bell Curve* and other works.

Therefore by killing Lumumba, American leaders were just getting rid of "another nigger," although the main reasons were geopolitical, ideological, and economic:

control of Congo, the heart of Africa, by the United States and her Western allies.

Evidence against the United States is overwhelming, although some people, while conceding American complicity in Lumumba's assassination, tend to minimise her role. One of them is Jon Lee Anderson who wrote an excellent biography of Che Guevara, entitled *Che Guevara: A Revolutionary Life*, which also deals with the Congo crisis.

Yet he downplays America's role in the assassination of Lumumba. He also fails or deliberately refuses to see the United States – not necessarily as a global tyrant although it is hard to refute that after America's invasion of Iraq and threats to invade other countries – as an imperial power capable of manipulating and controlling world events to the detriment of weak countries.

The United States controls their economies; intimidates, manipulates, and even overthrows their governments, and has even ordered and sponsored the assassination of leaders the American government doesn't like.

Yet some people fail to see or are unwilling to accept that, sometimes out of blind patriotism in the case of Americans, although Anderson is not cast in that mould as a blind patriot. His book is massive and rich in detail. But that does not compensate for lack of objective analysis. As Jane Franklin stated in "Che Guevara: Guerilla Heroica," her review of Anderson's book, in *The Nation*:, 19 May 1997:

"Anderson seems not to share Guevara's view of US imperialism, and downplays the US role in global events.

Speaking at a 1961 rally to mobilize Cubans for the imminent US invasion, Guevara cited the recent murder of Patrice Lumumba as 'an example of what the empire is capable of '....In the many pages devoted to events in the Congo, Anderson contests this claim.

Though he reports a plan by Dr. Sidney Gottlieb of the CIA's 'medical division' to poison Lumumba, he states that 'before the CIA could get close to Lumumba, however, his own Congolese rivals did.'

But the CIA and the US Embassy had already connived with these Congolese rivals – Moise Tshombe and Joseph Mobutu – to murder Lumumba. Mobutu, who turned Lumumba over to Tshombe to kill, was actually on the CIA payroll.

Four years later, when Guevara left Cuba to fight against Tshombe and Mobutu on the side of Lumumba's followers, the CIA had already dispatched a band of Cuban exiles, trained for the Bay of Pigs, to fly bombing raids for Tshombe. This CIA operation, ignored by Anderson, suggests that Washington shared Guevara's view of the dimensions of the struggle."[8]

Some supporters of President Dwight Eisenhower refused – and even today probably still refuse – to accept the fact that the president could have authorised such a plot to assassinate Lumumba.

Yet he is the same leader who didn't care how many people were killed in order to "fight communism" in Latin America; nor did he have any qualms about overthrowing the populist government of Guzman Arbenz in Guatemala in 1954 or the government of Dr. Mohammad Mossadeq in Iran a year earlier in 1953 because it nationalised the oil industry which belonged to the Iranians – not to the British or the Americans.

Then there was the plot to assassinate Castro, also conceived and hatched by the Eisenhower Administration; and next, the one against Lumumba.

Just as in the case of Castro when Eisenhower felt that the CIA was not doing enough, and fast enough, to eliminate him, the president also felt that the intelligence agency was not working fast enough to get rid of Lumumba. As Christopher Andrew states in his book, *For the President's Eyes Only: Secret Intelligence and the American Presidency from Washington to Bush*:

"Just as Eisenhower had regarded the 5412 Committee's February (1960) proposals for dealing with Castro as too feeble, so he was equally critical of its initial plans for covert actions against Patrice Lumumba.

When the committee met to discuss action against Lumumba on August 25, Gordon Gray reported that the president 'had expressed extremely strong feelings on the necessity for very straightforward action in this situation, and he wondered whether the plans as outlined were sufficient to accomplish this.'

Thus admonished, the committee 'finally agreed that planning for the Congo would not necessarily rule out consideration" of any particular kind of activity that might contribute to getting rid of Lumumba."[9]

As part of the plot to eliminate Lumumba, the CIA also launched a smear campaign against the Congolese prime minister and prepared different kinds of poisons to accomplish their mission.

All that was revealed in 1975 during US Senate investigations – conducted by the Select Committee on Intelligence Activities chaired by Democratic Senator Frank Church of Idaho – into assassinations of foreign leaders by the CIA.

The hearings also covered CIA plots – some of them successful – to overthrow foreign governments including a number of them in Africa: for example, Nkrumah's in Ghana which the CIA succeeded in overthrowing in February 1966; Nyerere's in Tanzania which the CIA tried more than once in the mid-sixties to overthrow; and Lumumba's, of course, with Lumumba himself being targeted for assassination not just for removal from office. And the smear campaign against him by the CIA knew no bounds. As Christopher Andrew further states in his book:

"Allen Dulles (the CIA director, also known as the DCI – Director of Central Intelligence) told Eisenhower that Lumumba was insane; later reports alleged that he was also 'a dope fiend.'

On September 21 the DCI reported to an NSC (National Security Council) meeting, chaired by the president, that 'Lumumba was not yet disposed of.' Still fascinated by the use of poisons in covert action, Richard Bissell (head of CIA's covert operations) instructed a CIA scientist to prepare biological toxins designated to assassinate or incapacitate an unnamed 'African leader' (Patrice Lumumba)."[10]

More than a decade later, the CIA was still denying its involvement in the assassination of Lumumba in spite of overwhelming evidence implicating the American intelligence agency in the diabolical plot.

In a television interview on 27 February 1975, conducted by Daniel Schorr of CBS News, CIA Director William Colby was asked about the agency's role in assassinations: "Has the CIA ever killed anyone in this country?" Schorr asked. "Not in this country," replied Colby. The CIA chief was then asked about assassinations abroad. He refused to give any names.

Schorr suggested Dag Hammarskjold, the UN secretary-general killed in a mysterious plane crash in Ndola, Northern Rhodesia (now Zambia) in 1961. "No, of course not!" said Colby. But when Schorr mentioned Patrice Lumumba, also killed in 1961, Colby refused to comment.

The plot included infecting Lumumba's tooth paste with deadly bacteria. The CIA doctor who was responsible for these poisons, Sidney Gottlieb, flew to Congo with his poison kit. But things didn't work out well for him and the other CIA agents trying to kill Lumumba. They couldn't get the poisoned tooth paste to Lumumba.

As for Sidney Gottlieb, that was not even his real name. It was the name he used when he worked for the CIA. Born in 1918, his real name was Joseph Scheider. He joined the CIA after getting a Ph.D. in chemistry from the California Institute of Technology (CalTech).

He joined the CIA soon after he got his Ph.D. and worked as a member of the Technical Services Staff (TSS). He eventually became head of the Chemical Division at the CIA. His failure to kill Lumumba was one of his biggest disappointments. He died on 10 March 1999.

Finally, the CIA concluded that getting rid of Lumumba right away was the best solution. And that is exactly what it did, in collusion with Tshombe and Mobutu.

American involvement in Lumumba's elimination has been amply documented. There is no doubt that Washington played a critical role in his removal from power and subsequent assassination. As Dr. Stephen Weissman who was staff director of the US House of Representatives Subcommittee on Africa from 1986 to 1991 stated in his article, "Opening the Secret Files on Lumumba's Murder," in *The Washington Post*, July 21, 2002:

"In his latest film, 'Minority Report,' director Steven Spielberg portrays a policy of 'preemptive action' gone wild in the year 2054. But we don't have to peer into the future to see what harm faulty intelligence and the loss of our moral compass can do. U.S. policies during the Cold War furnish many tragic examples. One was U.S. complicity in the overthrow and murder of Congolese Prime Minister Patrice Lumumba.

Forty-one years ago, Lumumba, the only leader ever democratically elected in Congo, was delivered to his enemies, tortured and summarily executed. Since then, his country has been looted by the U.S.-supported regime of

Mobutu Sese Seko and wracked by regional and civil war.

The conventional explanation of Lumumba's death has been that he was murdered by Congolese rivals after earlier U.S. attempts to kill him, including a plot to inject toxins into his food or toothpaste, failed. In 1975, the U.S. Senate's 'Church Committee' probed CIA assassination plots and concluded there was 'no evidence of CIA involvement in bringing about the death of Lumumba.'

Not so. I have obtained classified U.S. government documents, including a chronology of covert actions approved by a National Security Council (NSC) subgroup, that reveal U.S. involvement in -- and significant responsibility for -- the death of Lumumba, who was mistakenly seen by the Eisenhower administration as an African Fidel Castro.

The documents show that the key Congolese leaders who brought about Lumumba's downfall were players in 'Project Wizard,' a CIA covert action program. Hundreds of thousands of dollars and military equipment were channeled to these officials, who informed their CIA paymasters three days in advance of their plan to send Lumumba into the clutches of his worst enemies.

Other new details: The U.S. authorized payments to then-President Joseph Kasavubu four days before he ousted Lumumba, furnished Army strongman Mobutu with money and arms to fight pro-Lumumba forces, helped select and finance an anti-Lumumba government, and barely three weeks after his death authorized new funds for the people who arranged Lumumba's murder.

Moreover, these documents show that the plans and payments were approved by the highest levels of the Eisenhower administration, either the NSC or its 'Special Group,' consisting of the national security adviser, CIA director, undersecretary of state for political affairs, and deputy defense secretary.

These facts are four decades old, but are worth unearthing for two reasons. First, Congo (known for years as Zaire) is still struggling to establish democracy and stability. By facing up to its past role in undermining Congo's fledgling democracy, the United States might yet contribute to Congo's future. Second, the U.S. performance in Congo is relevant to our struggle against terrorism. It shows what can happen when, in the quest for national security, we abandon the democratic principles and rule of law we are fighting to defend.

In February (2002), Belgium, the former colonial power in Congo, issued a thousand-page report that acknowledged 'an irrefutable portion of responsibility in the events that led to the death of Lumumba.' Unlike Belgium, the United States has admitted no such moral responsibility.

Over the years, scholars (including myself) and journalists have written that American policy played a major role in the ouster and assassination of Lumumba. But the full story remained hidden in U.S. documents, which, like those I have examined, are still classified despite the end of the Cold War, the end of the Mobutu regime and Belgium's confession.

Here's what they tell us that, until now, we didn't know, or didn't know for certain:

* In August 1960, the CIA established Project Wizard. Congo had been independent only a month, and Lumumba, a passionate nationalist, had become prime minister, with a plurality of seats in the parliament. But U.S. presidential candidate John F. Kennedy was vowing to meet 'the communist challenge' and Eisenhower's NSC was worried that Lumumba would tilt toward the Soviets.

The U.S. documents show that over the next few months, the CIA worked with and made payments to eight top Congolese -- including President Kasavubu, Mobutu (then army chief of staff), Foreign Minister Justin Bomboko, top finance aide Albert Ndele, Senate President Joseph Ileo and labor leader Cyrille Adoula -- who all played roles in Lumumba's downfall.

The CIA joined Belgium in a plan, detailed in the Belgian report, for Ileo and Adoula to engineer a no-confidence vote in Lumumba's government, which would be followed by union-led demonstrations, the resignations of cabinet ministers (organized by Ndele) and Kasavubu's dismissal of Lumumba.

* On Sept. 1, the NSC's Special Group authorized CIA payments to Kasavubu, the U.S. documents say. On Sept. 5, Kasavubu fired Lumumba in a decree of dubious legality. However, Kasavubu and his new prime minister, Ileo, proved lethargic over the following week as Lumumba rallied supporters. So Mobutu seized power on Sept. 14. He kept Kasavubu as president and established a temporary 'College of Commissioners' to replace the disbanded government.

* The CIA financed the College and influenced the selection of commissioners. The College was dominated by two Project Wizard participants: Bomboko, its president, and Ndele, its vice-president. Another CIA ally, Lumumba party dissident Victor Nendaka, was appointed chief of the security police.

* On Oct. 27, the NSC Special Group approved $250,000 for the CIA to win parliamentary support for a Mobutu government. However, when legislators balked at approving any prime minister other than Lumumba, the parliament remained closed. The CIA money went to Mobutu personally and the commissioners.

* On Nov. 20, the Special Group authorized the CIA to provide arms, ammunition, sabotage materials and training to Mobutu's military in the event it had to resist pro-Lumumba forces.

The full extent of what one U.S. document calls the 'intimate' relationship between the CIA and Congolese leaders was absent from the Church Committee report. The only covert action (apart from the assassination plots) the committee discussed was the August 1960 effort to promote labor opposition and a no-confidence vote in the Senate.

How did Lumumba die?

After being ousted Sept. 5, Lumumba rallied support in parliament and the international community. When Mobutu took over, U.N. troops protected Lumumba, but soon confined him to his residence. Lumumba escaped on Nov. 27. Days later he was captured by Mobutu's troops, beaten and arrested.

What happened next is clearer thanks to the Belgian report and the classified U.S. documents. As early as Christmas Eve 1960, College of Commissioners' president Bomboko offered to hand Lumumba over to two secessionist leaders who had vowed to kill him.

One declined and nothing happened until mid-January 1961, when the central government's political and military position deteriorated and troops guarding Lumumba (then jailed on a military base near the capital) mutinied. CIA and other Western officials feared a Lumumba comeback.

On Jan. 14, the commissioners asked Kasavubu to move Lumumba to a 'surer place.' There was 'no doubt,' the Belgian inquiry concluded, that Mobutu agreed. Kasavubu told security chief Nendaka to transfer Lumumba to one of the secessionist strongholds. On Jan. 17, Nendaka sent Lumumba to the Katanga region. That night, Lumumba and two colleagues were tortured and executed in the presence of members of the Katangan government. No official announcement was made for four weeks.

What did the U.S. government tell its Congolese clients

during the last three days of Lumumba's life? The Church Committee reported that a Congolese 'government leader' advised the CIA's Congo station chief, Larry Devlin, on Jan. 14 that Lumumba was to be sent to 'the home territory' of his 'sworn enemy.' Yet, according to the Church Committee and declassified documents, neither the CIA nor the U.S. embassy tried to save the former prime minister.

The CIA may not have exercised robotic control over its covert political action agents, but the failure of Devlin or the U.S. embassy to question the plans for Lumumba could only be seen by the Congolese as consent. After all, secret CIA programs had enabled this group to achieve political power, and the CIA had worked from August through November 1960 to assassinate or abduct Lumumba.

Here, the classified U.S. chronology provides an important postscript. On Feb. 11, 1961, with U.S. reports from Congo strongly indicating Lumumba was dead, the Special Group authorized $500,000 for political action, troop payments and military equipment, largely to the people who had arranged Lumumba's murder.

Devlin has sought to distance himself from Lumumba's death. While the CIA was in close contact with the Congolese officials involved, Devlin told the Church Committee that those officials 'were not acting under CIA instructions if and when they did this.'

In a recent phone conversation with Devlin, I posed the issue of U.S. responsibility for Lumumba's death. He acknowledged that, 'It was important to [these] cooperating leaders what the U.S. government thought.' But he said he did 'not recall' receiving advance word of Lumumba's transfer. Devlin added that even if he had objected, 'That would not have stopped them from doing it.'

By evading its share of moral responsibility for Lumumba's fate, the United States blurs African and

American history and sidesteps the need to make reparation for yesterday's misdeeds through today's policy.

In 1997, after the Mobutu regime fell, the Congolese democratic opposition pleaded in vain for American and international support.

Since then, as many as 3 million lives have been lost as a result of civil and regional war. The United States has not supported a strong U.N. peacekeeping force or fostered a democratic transition. The collapse in late April 2002 of negotiations between Congolese factions threatens to reignite the smoldering conflict or ratify the partition of the country.

Our government's actions four decades ago in Congo also have special meaning after the tragedy of Sept. 11. They warn that even as we justly defend our land and our people against terrorists, we must avoid the excessive fear and zeal that lead to destructive intervention betraying our most fundamental principles."[11]

Such intervention by the United Stated led to one of the worst crises in the history of post-colonial Africa. And the Congo crisis continued to be a dominant news item throughout the sixties.

The year 1961 was one of the worst right from the beginning. Lumumba had just been assassinated early that year, and Katanga's secession continued to threaten the territorial integrity of one of Africa's biggest countries right in the heart of the continent.

But it was Lumumba's assassination that dominated the news. Almost everything that unfolded in Congo during those tragic years was directly or indirectly related to his ouster from power and subsequent assassination.

Probably the only way Lumumba could have been saved would have been to prevent him from leaving his official residence in Leopoldville. Instead, he left the nation's capital,. determined to go to Stanleyville, his political stronghold in eastern Congo.

The situation in the Congo was out of control because of a combination of factors: Katanga's secession, internal disputes including secessionist threats from other provinces; and power rivalry between Lumumba and Kasavubu instigated and fueled by the United States and Belgium whose officials and intelligence agents backed Kasavubu and did everything they could to sow seeds of confusion and discord with Lumumba's camp.

When in July 1960 Lumumba appealed to the United Nations for help to send troops to end Katanga's secession and restore law and order, and ask Belgian troops to withdraw from Congo, NATO allies, especially the United States, Belgium and France expressed strong reservations on such involvement by the UN.

However, the UN Security Council finally authorised the provision of military assistance to the beleaguered nation until Congo's own security forces would be ready to take over. In spite of such an offer of assistance, UN forces couldn't do much. They were sent to Congo but only with limited mandate. They were not authorised to intervene in internal conflicts and could use force only in self-defence.

The first UN troops to go to Congo were from African countries: Ghana, Guinea, Ethiopia, Liberia, Morocco and Tunisia, They arrived two days after the UN Security Council authorised the mission. More than troops, initially all from African countries, were deployed throughout the country towards the end of July 1960 except in the secessionist province of Katanga whose army included mercenaries from South Africa, Belgium, France and other countries.

By the end of July, the total UN military contingent was 8,396, of whom 2,340 were Ghanaians, 2,087 Tunisians, 1,220 Moroccans, 1,160 Ethiopians, 741 Guineans, 225 Liberians and 623 Swedes. A little later, an Irish battalion was added. Eventually 28 countries contributed troops, making a total of 19,828 UN soldiers in Congo.

The UN force in Congo – known as UNOC, a French acronym for "UN Congo" – remained predominantly African. White troops, Swedish and Irish, came from countries which were considered to be neutral.

But it was clear that, because of their limited mandate, and given the size of the country roughly equal to the size of Western Europe, they were not enough for the task. Compounding the problem was the fact that Belgian troops did not want to leave Congo for obvious reasons and because of the kind of support they had including encouragement from the United States whose leaders did not like Lumumba anymore than the Belgians and the leaders of the other Western countries did. They wanted him out of power, and dead.

Finally, after the Belgian troops left Congo, Lumumba's primary concern was to find ways to end Katanga's secession. But because of their limited mandate, UN troops could not intervene and use force to try to end the secession of Katanga even though most of them came from African countries and may have wanted to reunite the country.

African leaders were sympathetic towards Lumumba and wanted to end Katanga's secession. They included Ghanaian President Kwame Nkrumah whose troops were the first to arrive in Congo. But he was also fully aware of the inability of the independent African countries alone to end the secession of Katanga even if Lumumba had invited them to do so without external help.

The problem was compounded by the unwillingness of Western powers to authorise the UN to send a much larger force to Congo to end Katanga's secession. Their refusal to do so amounted to *de facto* recognition of Katanga as a legal sovereign entity, to the consternation of Lumumba and other African leaders.

In August 1960, the first UN troops arrived in Katanga in a gradual attempt to replace Belgian troops which, in spite of denials by the Belgian authorities, provided the backbone of the secessionist province together with the mercenaries who also helped sustain Moise Tshombe in power. But UN forces did not go into Katanga on a combat mission. And Katanga continued to defy the central authority under Lumumba, insisting that it was an independent state and no longer an integral part of the former Belgian Congo.

In response to such defiance, and because of the inability of UN troops to end the secession by force, Lumumba sent troops from his national army – *Armee Nationale Congolaise* (ANC) – to the secessionist province in August 1960 to try to end the rebellion.

He also sent troops to Kasai Province where secessionists in the southern part of the province under the leadership of Albert Kalonji also declared independence.

Unfortunately, the soldiers from the Congolese national army were not well-trained and therefore not prepared to engage the secessionist forces in both provinces. With the UN equivocating, Lumumba was compelled under very difficult circumstances to seek assistance from the Soviet Union to try to defeat the secessionists. The Soviets responded by sending military advisers, trucks and ten transport planes.

But even they were not enough. The situation in the secessionist provinces was too dangerous and the Soviet advisers and their planes were forced to withdraw. Although troops from the national army was no match for the secessionist forces in Katanga, they were able to engage the secessionists in Kasai Province whose dominant ethnic group was and still is the Luba, but with tragic consequences.

More than 1,000 Lubas – or Baluba – were killed in August 1960 in the unsuccessful operation. About 250,000 ended up as refugees, further alienating and infuriating many people in the province who were already against Lumumba.

Lumumba's enemies used this tragedy in Kasai

Province as an excuse to undermine his authority; and President Joseph Kasavubu, with the encouragement of American and Belgian officials including CIA agents, dismissed Lumumba from the government on September 5th accusing him of using arbitrary powers as prime minister and plunging the country into civil war.

About 30 minutes later, Lumumba retaliated and announced on the radio that he had dismissed President Kasavubu from office and appealed to the Congolese people to rally around him. Lumumba's enemies were aware of what they were facing: With his popularity and oratorical skills, Lumumba had the ability to rally support across the country no other Congolese could match.

He was such a powerful orator that his enemies thought he had something else working in his favour. As Keith Kyle, a BBC reporter who was in Congo during the crisis and the ensuing civil war ignited by Katanga's secession, stated in his 1995 paper, "The UN in Congo: Initiative on Conflict Resolution and Ethnicity":

"Lumumba was a charismatic speaker whose power over other people was so compelling that many of his enemies felt that there was witchcraft in it. It was probably one of the reasons he had to die that, like the Roman consul Marius, when under arrest he could bewitch his jailers."[12]

His enemies had already decided what they were going to do. And Western countries sided with Kasavubu whom they had supported all along in his rivalry with Lumumba.

And in spite of his dismissal by Kasavubu, Lumumba still commanded support.

He maintained that he was the legitimate head of the Congolese government and his claim was confirmed by the vote of confidence he got in parliament.

But nine days later on the evening of September 14th after Lumumba and Kasavubu dismissed each other from office, Joseph Mobutu – ostensibly to fill the vacuum left by the two leaders who had dismissed each other – seized power, urged by American and Belgian officials to do so. He said Kasavubu, Lumumba and the parliament were suspended until the end of the year.

He went on to explain that this was only a temporary measure, for three months, during which the country would be governed by a "College of Commissioners" comprising technocrats – Congolese university graduates and others; a ridiculous proposition in a country which had only 16 university graduates when it won independence a few months earlier. He said the "College of Commissioners" would be headed by one of the Congolese university graduates.

It was an act of betrayal.

Mobutu once served as Lumumba's personal secretary and at the time of the coup was the head of the national army, appointed by Lumumba. And all that time, he was on the CIA payroll, without Lumumba's knowledge. Lumumba was also betrayed by another close political associate, Victor Nendaka, who was secretly working with the American and Belgian officials against him in Leopoldville.

But Mobutu was Lumumba's most conspicuous former ally who betrayed him. It is true that he broke with Lumumba. But it later became obvious that he had been against him all the time when he was working under him.

And when he executed the CIA-inspired coup with just as much Belgian support, he established his own power base but also in alliance with the Kasavubu camp.

He announced on the radio that he had temporarily seized power to neutralise two rival governments, Lumumba's and Kasavubu's, and the national parliament until the end of the year. Other western countries, besides Belgium and the United States, also supported Mobutu. But Kasavubu remained head of state. And under pressure from the United States, the UN General Assembly recognized the Kasavubu/Mobutu regime as the country's legitimate authority.

As the country further degenerated into chaos, Lumumba was being guarded by UN troops in his official residence in Leopoldville. His enemies wanted him arrested but the UN secretary-general, Dag Hammarskjold, refused to authorise UN troops to do so.

Throughout the crisis, the American ambassador in Leopoldville asked Kasavubu and Mobutu to arrest Lumumba.

But they did not and could not do so for a number of reasons including opposition by the UN to such a move whose repercussions no one could fully anticipate and which could have gone beyond anyone's imagination.

The recognition of the Kasavubu/Mobutu alliance by the UN General Assembly as the new legitimate authority in Congo further weakened Lumumba who was already isolated in his official residence in Leopoldville, guarded by UN troops.

The UN troops surrounded his house to prevent his enemies from entering the premises to capture or kill him. Forming the outer ring, surrounding UN troops, were Mobutu's soldiers waiting for an opportunity to grab Lumumba should he venture out and beyond the premises of his official residence.

All that was too much for Lumumba. The last straw for him was when, in a move orchestrated by the United States, the UN General Assembly recognised the government of Kasavubu allied with Mobutu, thus virtually withdrawing formal recognition from Lumumba as the legitimate leader of Congo.

In an attempt to mobilise support, Lumumba decided to leave Leopoldville and go to Stanleyville, his home and political base. He hid in the back of a car and left his official residence in an attempt to get to Stanleyville on the same day Kasavubu was celebrating his victory at the United Nations where his government had won formal recognition from the General Assembly as the legitimate authority in Congo in place of Lumumba.

Lumumba's departure from Leopoldville was undoubtedly motivated by good intentions and nationalist commitment. But it was a tragic mistake. He had been under protection for two months.

He had been repeatedly warned by UN officials that if he left his residence, it would no longer be their responsibility to protect him, and he would be doing so at his own risk. Yet, as the country's elected leader, he was powerless and became virtually a prisoner under the UN's protective custody.

The head of the UN mission in Congo gave orders to UN troops across the country not to take sides between Lumumba and his enemies.

This was in compliance with UN's policy of neutrality and non-interference in the internal affairs of Congo. UN soldiers were given orders not to stop Lumumba from going to Stanleyville or anywhere in the country. They were also ordered not to stop Lumumba's enemies from pursuing or hunting him down.

His enemies finally caught up with him at Mweka in Kasai Province. Born in the small village of Onalua in Katako Kombe district, northern Kasai Province, on 2 July 1925, it was ironic and tragic that the beginning of his end took place in the same province in which he was born.

After his arrest at Mweka, he was flown back to Leopoldville. All these events – Lumumba's secret departure from his official residence and subsequent arrest – took place in December 1960.

This was the last chance the UN troops had to protect Lumumba. They could have saved him. Had the UN intervened before he was captured at Mweka, his enemies would not have had the chance to lay their hands on him. After all, the UN had protected him at his residence for two months and could have extended the same protection to him outside his residence and anywhere else in the country, since he was entitled to such protection as Congo's elected national leader.

After his capture, photographs were taken showing him dishevelled and with his hands tied behind his back. He was then imprisoned together with his compatriots, Joseph Okito and Maurice Mpolo at Thysville, a military camp outside the capital.

One of the photographs shows Mobutu with his hands across his chest and his soldiers laughing at Lumumba and his colleagues who were also brutally manhandled. Even more than 50 years later, it remains one of the most tragic images of Congo, and Africa, from those turbulent years.

Yet, even in custody under strict guard by his enemies, Lumumba still inspired awe and fear among them. To avoid any mistakes and his escape with the help of his loyal supporters, they first decided to transfer him secretly to Kasai Province where one of his arch-enemies, Albert Kalonji, swore to get rid of him and use his skull as a flower vase.

Lumumba after being captured

But before they flew him to Kasai, they found out at the last minute that there were UN troops stationed at

Bakwanga airfield in Kasai Province. So Kasavubu and Mobutu together with Belgian and American officials and Lumumba's other enemies in leadership positions in Congo decided to send him to another place, Katanga, where another big enemy of Lumumba, Moise Tshombe, was in charge.

He was flown from Leopoldville to Elisabethville, the capital of Katanga, on 17 January 1961 and was brutally beaten by Luba guards throughout his six-hour flight to the province. When the plane landed in Elisabethville, Lumumba was pushed out and shoved down the steps together with Maurice Mpolo and Joseph Okito.

Lumumba and his colleagues were so badly beaten by the Luba soldiers on the plane that when they arrived in Elisabethville, Katengese officials and soldiers said the three captives were almost dead on arrival. And the Luba soldiers on plane felt justified in what they did to Lumumba and his compatriots because of what they said Lumumba did to their people in Kasai Province when he sent troops to fight the secessionists; a mission which ended in the tragic death of many innocent people massacred by undisciplined Congolese soldiers from the national army (ANC). And as John Reader stated in his book, *Africa: A Biography of the Continent*, about the last days of Lumumba and his compatriots:

"Lumumba's supporters regrouped in Stanleyville. At the end of November Lumumba decided to join them – a fatal move. He was arrested en route and handed over to Mobutu's army.

Lumumba was consigned to a military prison, but his supporters continued to have an unsettling effect on the country at large....Kasavubu and his (American and Belgian) advisers decided that he should be sent to Elisabethville, the Katangan capital, where the errant Tshombe was in charge.

On 17 January 1961, Lumumba and two colleagues

(Maurice Mpolo and Joseph Okito) were flown to Katanga, where a Swedish warrant officer with the United Nations forces witnessed their arrival:

'The first to leave the aeroplane was a smartly dressed African. He was followed by three other Africans, blind-folded and with their hands tied behind their backs. The first of the prisoners to alight had a small beard [Lumumba].

As they came down the stairs, some of the *gendarmes* ran to them, pushed them, kicked them and brutally struck them with rifle butts; one of the prisoners fell to the ground. After about one minute the three prisoners were placed in a jeep which drove off....'

Neither Lumumba nor his colleagues were ever seen again. It is believed they were taken to a farmhouse on the outskirts of Elisabethville, where they died at the hands of Katangese officials and Belgian mercenaries."[13]

A UN investigation years later concluded that Lumumba was shot by a Belgian officer in the presence of Moise Tshombe and other Katangese officials including the highly notorious Godefroid Munongo, a cabinet member in Tshombe's government who was interior minister and in charge of security in Katanga.

Munongo was also, together with Tshombe, a founding member of the Confederation of Associations of Katanga (CONAKAT), the largest political party in Katanga Province and one of the largest in the country.

He was of Tanzanian origin, a descendant of King Msiri. Born in 1830 near Tabora in western Tanganyika, Msiri was a trader – in slaves, copper, ivory and guns – and a member of the Nyamwezi ethnic group in western Tanzania (then Tanganyika) who settled in Congo and established a kingdom in Katanga in the 19th century.

He and some of his fellow Nyamwezi tribesmen from what is now Tanzania settled in southern Katanga around 1856. By 1868, he had taken control of much of Katanga and was crowned king of Garaganja, what came to be known as Katanga Province, after he succeeded in taking over most of the mineral-rich region from its previous rulers of the dominant Lunda ethnic group.

Godefroid Munongo, Tshombe's hatchet man, was not only Msiri's direct descendant; he was also the most prominent "immigrant" in the government of the secessionist region. So, when he served in the Katangese government dominated by Tshombe's dominant ethnic group, the Lunda, he was not a member of a large ethnic group.

Ironically, in spite of his minority status as a member of the small Bayeke ethnic group, he was notorious for having been responsible for the persecution of the members of the Luba ethnic group living in Katanga Province. While the Lunda dominated Katanga, the Luba were the dominant ethnic group in neighbouring Kasai Province, although their historic – hence ancestral – home is northern Katanga where many of them have always lived.

Yet, in carrying out this persecution, Munongo felt that he was more of an authentic Katangan than the Luba from Kasai were, despite his Tanzanian origin as a Nyamwezi.

So, he had a reputation as a tribalist like his boss, Moise Tshombe. And both were delighted to see that Lumumba had been arrested and sent to Katanga for them to preside over his fate.

Also present during Lumumba's execution were American CIA agents and Belgian officials as well as intelligence officers. And as Professor Adam Hochschild of the University of California-Berkeley stated in his book, *King Leopold's Ghost: A Story of Greed, Terror, and Heroism in Colonial Africa*:

"An inspired orator whose voice was rapidly carrying beyond his country's borders, Lumumba was a mercurial and charismatic figure. His message, Western governments feared, was contagious. Moreover, he could not be bought. Anathema to American and European capital, he became a leader whose days were numbered.

Less than two months after being named the Congo's first democratically chosen prime minister, a U.S. National Security Council subcommittee on covert operations, which included CIA chief Allen Dulles, authorized his assassination. Richard Bissell, CIA operations chief at the time, later said, 'The President [Dwight D. Eisenhower]...regarded Lumumba as I did and a lot of other people did: a mad dog...and he wanted the problem dealt with.'

Alternatives for dealing with 'the problem' were considered, among them poison – a supply of which was sent to the CIA station chief (Laurence Devlin) in Leopoldville – a high-powered rifle, free-lance hit men. But it proved hard to get close enough to Lumumba to use these, so, instead, the CIA supported anti-Lumumba elements within the factionalized Congo government, confident that before long they would do the job. They did.

After being arrested and suffering a series of beatings, the prime minister was secretly shot in Elizabethville in January 1961. A CIA agent ended up driving around the city with Lumumba's body in his car's trunk, trying to find a place to dispose of it...

The key figure in the Congolese forces that arranged Lumumba's murder was a young man named Joseph Desire Mobutu, then chief of staff of the army and a former NCO in the old colonial *Force Publique.* Early on, the Western powers had spotted Mobutu as someone who would look out for their interests. He had received cash payments from the local CIA man and Western military attaches while Lumumba's murder was being planned....

I had been writing about human rights for years, and once, in the course of half a dozen trips to Africa, I had been to the Congo.

That visit was in 1961. In a Leopoldville apartment, I heard the CIA man, who had too much to drink, describe with satisfaction exactly how and where the newly independent country's first prime minister, Patrice Lumumba, had been killed a few months earlier.

He assumed that any American, even a visiting student like me, would share his relief at the assassination of a man the United States government considered a dangerous leftist troublemaker."[14]

Lumumba and his compatriots Maurice Mpolo and Joseph Okito were physically and verbally abused, brutally tortured and humiliated in every conceivable way until the very last minute of their lives.

Even after they were pushed out of the plane and hit with rifle butts and dumped at the airport in Elisabethville by the Luba guards, they continued to suffer. They were given a thorough beating by Tshombe's henchmen at the airport. And the Luba guards who had tortured them all the way from Leopoldville participated in this orgy of violence. As Brian Urquhart who once served in Congo during the crisis and later as UN undersecretary-general stated in his article, "The Tragedy of Lumumba," in *The New York Review of Books*, October 4, 2001:

"After Lumumba and his two companions (Maurice Mpolo and Joseph Okito) were dumped, bloody and disheveled, in a remote corner of the Elisabethville airfield, they were beaten again with rifle butts, and thrown onto a jeep and driven two miles from the airport to an empty house in the bush, where a veteran Belgian officer, Captain Julien Gat, took charge.

A series of visitors – the notorious Katangese interior minister Godefroid Munongo and other ministers, Tshombe himself, and various high-ranking Belgians – came to the house to gloat over the prisoners, who were again beaten.

Some of the Belgian visitors later spoke of Lumumba's courage and dignity under this treatment, but none saw fit to stop it.

The soldiers were ordered to kill Lumumba if UN troops located the house.

During the evening, drinking heavily, Tshombe and his ministers decided that the three should be executed at once.

Around 9:30 PM the inebriated Katangese ministers returned to the house in the bush. After once again being beaten up, the prisoners were stuffed into a car with Captain Gat and police commissioner Frans Verscheure, and, in a convoy that also carried Tshombe, Munongo, and four other 'ministers,' were driven at high speed to a remote clearing fifty kilometers out in the wooded savanna.

Joseph Okito, the former vice-president of the Senate, was the first to face the firing squad; next came Maurice Mpolo, the first commander of the Congolese National Army; and finally Patrice Lumumba. Their corpses were thrown into hastily dug graves.

This was not the end of the atrocious affair. During the night, the Belgians, increasingly apprehensive, began to concoct an elaborate cover plan under which Lumumba and his companions had been well treated, but had later managed to escape and had been killed by the inhabitants of an unnamed 'patriotic' village.

The Belgians also decided that the corpses must disappear once and for all. Two Belgians and their African assistants, in a truck carrying demijohns of sulphuric acid, an empty two-hundred-liter barrel, and a hacksaw, dug up the corpses, cut them into pieces, and threw them into the barrel of sulphuric acid.

When the supply of acid ran out, they tried burning the remains. The skulls were ground up and the bones and teeth scattered during the return journey.

The task proved so disgusting and so arduous that both

Belgians had to get drunk in order to complete it, but in the end no trace was left of Patrice Lumumba and his companions. Lumumba was 36 years old."[15]

Lumumba's dignified composure was evident throughout his ordeal since his capture. It was also reflected even in his last message to his wife written before he was flown to Elisabethville and handed over to Katangan authorities for execution. The letter was also a farewell message to Congo and to Africa as a whole:

"My dear wife,

I am writing these words not knowing whether they will reach you, when they will reach you, and whether I shall still be alive when you read them.

All through my struggle for the independence of my country, I have never doubted for a single instant the final triumph of the sacred cause to which my companions and I have devoted all our lives.

But what we wished for our country, its right to an honourable life, to unstained dignity, to independence without restrictions, was never desired by the Belgian imperialists and the Western allies, who found direct and indirect support, both deliberate and unintentional, amongst certain high officials of the United Nations, that organization in which we placed all our trust when we called on its assistance.

They have corrupted some of our compatriots and bribed others. They have helped to distort the truth and bring our independence into dishonour.

How could I speak otherwise?

Dead or alive, free or in prison by order of the imperialists, it is not myself who counts.

It is the Congo, it is our poor people for whom independence has been transformed into a cage from whose confines the outside world looks on us, sometimes with kindly sympathy, but at other times with joy and pleasure.

But my faith will remain unshakeable.

I know and I feel in my heart that sooner or later my people will rid themselves of all their enemies, both internal and external, and that they will rise as one man to say No to the degradation and shame of colonialism, and regain their dignity in the clear light of the sun.

We are not alone. Africa, Asia and the free liberated people from all corners of the world will always be found at the side of the millions of Congolese who will not abandon the struggle until the day when there are no longer any colonialists and their mercenaries in our country.

As to my children whom I leave and whom I may never see again, I should like them to be told that it is for them, as it is for every Congolese, to accomplish the sacred task of reconstructing our independence and our sovereignty: for without dignity there is no liberty, without justice there is no dignity, and without independence there are no free men.

Neither brutality, nor cruelty nor torture will ever bring me to ask for mercy, for I prefer to die with my head unbowed, my faith unshakable and with profound trust in the destiny of my country, rather than live under subjection and disregarding sacred principles.

History will one day have its say, but it will not be the history that is taught in Brussels, Paris, Washington or in the United Nations, but the history which will be taught in the countries freed from imperialism and its puppets.

Africa will write its own history, and to the north and south of the Sahara, it will be a glorious and dignified history.

Do not weep for me, my dear wife. I know that my country, which is suffering so much, will know how to defend its independence and its liberty.

Long live the Congo! Long live Africa!

Patrice"[16]

His death was not announced until almost a month later on 13 February 1961.

The tragic news of Lumumba's death sent shock waves throughout Africa and many parts of the world. His death only plunged the country deeper into chaos.

The country was already in deep crisis. When Lumumba was killed, Katanga Province, which he tried to subdue although at a great risk since his national army was not strong enough to end the secession, was still defiant and refused to reunite with the rest of the country. And his death only encouraged the secessionists even further to assert their independence.

Many other parts of the country were also in a rebellious mood since there was no strong central authority to exercise control over this vast expanse of territory. Besides the secession of Katanga Province, secessionists in South Kasai, whom Lumumba tried to neutralise when he sent troops there in August 1960, continued to pose a big threat to the territorial integrity of Congo and were emboldened to pursue their goal after their nemesis had been eliminated.

Also, different groups in other provinces contemplated similar moves, only in varying degrees.

Then there were the supporters of Lumumba. Saddened and angered by his assassination, many of his supporters in different parts of the country vowed to carry on the struggle for Congo's liberation from the clutches of Western imperialists who played a major role in the ouster and elimination of their leader, the only true nationalist politician of national stature Congo had produced just before independence.

Lumumba's loyalists constituted the core of the nationalist forces which went on to launch guerilla warfare in an attempt to topple the Western-backed government in

Leopoldville. The strongest insurgencies were in the eastern part of the country, Lumumba's political stronghold, and in Kwilu Province in the west, the home of Lumumba's education minister and heir-apparent, Pierre Mulele.

But it was not until three years after Lumumba was assassinated that these insurgencies got underway, first in Kwilu Province in January 1964. However, some of the civil unrest in the country was fuelled by Lumumba's supporters who refused to recognise the regime in Leopoldville.

Even before the uprising started in Kwilu Province in the west in 1964, and which spread to east, the country was still in chaos. But there was also some good news. On 15 January 1963, the secession of Katanga Province came to an end. It was a victory not only for the people of Congo but for the rest of Africa.

Had Katanga succeeded in separating from the rest of the country, it would have set a bad precedent for other countries on the continent. There was a danger that some groups and regions in a number of countries would also try to secede and establish their own independent states.

Therefore Katanga's re-integration into Congo, after the secessionists capitulated to UN forces, was a victory for all African countries which were determined to maintain their territorial integrity. Many of them were already threatened by ethno-regional rivalries as they still are today.

And they were young, fragile nations whose survival depended on the willingness of the members of different ethnic groups to live and work together as one people constituting viable political entities also known as countries.

Fifteen years later, Katanga again posed a serious threat to the security of Congo, then known as Zaire, renamed in 1971 by President Mobutu Sese Seko who also changed his name from Joseph Mobutu in 1972 in pursuit of his policy of authenticity – restoration of African identity.

Again, the imperial ambitions of Western powers led by the United States, and Cold War politics, played a major role in the new conflict, but in a different context of post-colonial Africa in which African countries were more assertive of their independence in practical terms than they were in the turbulent sixties.

The conflict was also different. The Katangese *gendarmes* who threatened Mobutu's government were not puppets of any major power; nor were they surrogate forces of any other country as claimed by the West.

It was in that context that President Nyerere addressed the crisis on 8 June 1978 when he summoned to the State House members of the diplomatic corps accredited to Tanzania. In the audience were Western ambassadors and those of the Eastern-bloc countries as well as others including African diplomats. As he stated in his statement, "Tanzania Rejects Western Domination of Africa":

"I have been very concerned indeed about world reactions to recent events in Africa, and it seems to me to be necessary that I should make Tanzania's position clear. For the events of the past few weeks have once again demonstrated that although our legal independence is officially recognised, our need and our right to develop our countries and our continent in our own interests has not yet been conceded in practice. The habit of regarding Africa as an appendage of Western Europe has not yet been broken.

Soviet Forces in Africa

In Angola the M.P.L.A. did almost all the fighting against the Portuguese colonialists. As independence approached after the Revolution in Portugal, various Western countries – led by the United States of America –

114

decided to try to prevent the establishment of an M.P.L.A. Government in that country. They conspired with South Africa, and gave under-cover finance and arms to rival nationalist movements which had previously been almost inactive.

Faced with this conspiracy and the consequent attacks on Angola from South Africa and across the Zaire border, the M.P.L.A. Government sought help from those who had given support to the Movement during the independence struggle. Cuba and the Soviet Union responded to those requests. With their help the Angolan Government overcame the immediate military threat to its existence, pushed South African troops back across the border into Namibia, and pushed the F.N.L.A. troops back to where they had come from – Zaire.

Cuban troops are still in Angola; and the Soviet Union continues to give military assistance to Angola. The Angolan Government is forced to ask for this assistance to be continued because the threat to the integrity of Angola still exists.

Only last month South African troops entered Southern Angola again, and inflicted heavy casualties upon Namibian refugees. UNITA continues to get outside support. There have been continual attacks made across the Angolan/ Zaire border by F.N.L.A. troops, who are financed and supplied with weapons by external forces and who operate with the active or tacit support of the Zaire Government.

That all this is happening, is known to the Secret Services of South Africa, and of U.S.A., France, and some other western countries. It would not be happening without their connivance and their involvement. It would be incredible if the Governments of those countries did not know what their Agencies were doing.

The history of the ex-Katangese Gendarmes pre-dates the independence of Angola. It was not actions of the M.P.L.A. which took them to Angola; nor were they trained by M.P.L.A. They are a living reminder to Africa of the determined and shameless attempt by the West to dismember the former Congo (Leopoldville) in their own economic interests. When that attempt was defeated, some of these Gendarmes moved into Angola and remained there as refugees.

Now things have changed; the West has a different view of Zaire and is using it to de-stabilise Angola. It would therefore not be surprising if Angola, on its part, felt forced to withdraw the restraints it had been imposing on those Zairean refugees in Northern Angola.

Whether such a policy of retaliation is correct or wise is a matter of judgment; it is nevertheless understandable. But one thing is clear. There is no evidence of Cuban or Soviet involvement in this retaliation. The U.S. State Department was at one time reported to have said as much; the Cubans have persistently and convincingly repudiated such allegations.

So Cuba and the Soviet Union went into Angola and are still in Angola for understandable reasons, at the request of the Angolan Government. There is no evidence at all that they have been involved, directly or indirectly, in any fighting within Zaire.

Cuban and Soviet Forces are also in Ethiopia, at the request of the Ethiopian Government. The reasons for their presence are well known. They have helped the Ethiopians to defend their country against external aggression. They have not – and nor has the Ethiopian Government – engaged in any fighting outside Ethiopia's borders. And there is some evidence to suggest that the Cuban Government at any rate makes a distinction between the fighting in the Ogaden and the fighting in Eritrea.

Apart from those two countries, where else in Africa are there Soviet or Cuban Forces? There are a few Cuban and Soviet Nationals, and a few Chinese Nationals, helping to train the Freedom Fighters of Southern Africa in the use of weapons Africa gets from Communist countries for the liberation struggle in Rhodesia and Namibia. Apart from vague generalities, and rumours based on the jackets people wear, there is no serious suggestion that these Forces are operating or stationed anywhere else in Africa.

It is, then, on the basis of Soviet and Cuban Forces in two African countries that there is a great furore in the West about a so-called Soviet penetration of Africa. And those Forces are in those two countries at the request of the legitimate and recognised Governments of the countries concerned, and for reasons which are well known and completely understandable to all reasonable people. Yet Western countries are objecting, and are holding meetings ostensibly about how to defend the freedom of Africa against what they call Soviet Penetration.

Let me make it quite clear. Tanzania does not want anyone from outside Africa to govern Africa. We regret, even while we recognise, the occasional necessity for an African government to ask for military assistance from a non-African country when it is faced with an external threat to its national integrity. We know that a response to such a request by any of the Big powers is determined by what that Big Power sees as its own interests. We have been forced to recognise that most of the countries acknowledged as World Powers do not find it beneath their dignity to exacerbate existing and genuine African problems and conflicts when they believe they can benefit by doing so.

We in Tanzania believe that African countries, separately and through the O.A.U., need to guard against such actions. But we need to guard Africa against being used by any other nation or group of nations.

The danger to Africa does not come just from nations in the Eastern Bloc. The West still considers Africa to be within its Sphere of Influence and acts accordingly. Current developments show that the greater immediate danger to Africa's freedom comes from nations in that

Western Bloc.

A Pan-African Security Force

It might be a good thing if the O.A.U. was sufficiently united to establish an African High Command, and a Pan-African Security Force. If, having done so, the O.A.U. then decided to ask for external support for this Force, no-one could legitimately object. But the O.A.U. has made no such decision. It is highly unlikely that the O.A.U. meeting in Khartoum will be able to agree unanimously on the creation of such a military Force, or – if it did – that it would be able to agree unanimously on which countries to ask for support if that was needed.

Yet until Africa, at the O.A.U., has made such a decision, there can be no Pan-African Security Force which will uphold the freedom of Africa. It is the height of arrogance for anyone else to talk of establishing a Pan-African Force to defend Africa. It is quite obvious, moreover, that those who have put forward this idea, and those who seek to initiate such a Force, are not interested in the Freedom of Africa. They are interested in the Domination of Africa.

It was from Paris that this talk of a Pan-African Security Force has emanated. It is in Paris, and later in Brussels, that there is to be a meeting to discuss this and related matters pertaining to the 'freedom' of Africa. The O.A.U. meets in Khartoum in July; but we are told that African freedom and its defence is being discussed in Paris and Brussels in June.

There is only one reason why the idea of Europe setting up, or initiating, a Pan-African Security Force – or an African Peace Force – does not meet with immediate and world-wide amazement and consternation. It is the continuing assumption that Africa is, and must always remain, part of the West European 'Sphere of Influence'. This assumption is hardly being questioned yet. Even some African states take it for granted.

We all know the facts of power in the world. But we cannot all be expected to accept without question this new insult to Africa and to Africans. We may be weak, but we are human; we do know when we are being deliberately provoked and insulted.

The French have troops in many countries of Africa. In Chad, in Western Sahara, in Mauretania, and now also in Zaire, French Forces are engaged in combat against Africans. France continues to occupy Mayotte. But there are no meetings in Washington, or even in Moscow, to discuss the threat to Africa's freedom by the French Penetration of Africa. Nor should there be. But not even Africa, in Africa, discusses the question.

The reason is very simple. It is the continued assumption that it is natural for French troops, or Belgian troops, or British troops, to be in Africa, but it is a threat for troops from any Non-member of the Western Bloc to be in Africa. A threat to whom? To African freedom, or to the domination of Africa by ex-colonial powers and their allies, operated now through more subtle means and with the help of an African Fifth Column?

The answers to those questions are very obvious. There have been continued incursions by South Africa and Rhodesia into Angola, Botswana, Zambia, and Mozambique. The West has not shown much concern about these; nor have their new-found surrogates in Africa.

When the U.S.S.R. sent its troops into Czechoslovakia in 1968 Tanzania was one of the many countries which protested. Is it expected that we should not protest when Western Powers send their troops into an African country? These 'rescue operations' almost always seem to result in the death of a lot of innocent people and the rescue of a Government. But that is apparently not regarded in Europe as interference in African affairs. Instead, the same country which initiated the military expedition then calls a meeting to discuss, they say, the freedom of Africa!

There should be no mistake. Whatever the official Agenda, the Paris and Brussels meetings are not discussing the freedom of Africa. They are discussing the continued domination of Africa, and the continued use of Africa, by Western Powers. They are intended to be, taken together, a Second Berlin Conference.

The real Agenda, inside and outside the formal sessions of these meetings, will be concerned with two things. It will be concerned with neo-colonialism in Africa for economic purposes – the real control of Africa and African states. That will be led by the French. It will be concerned also with the use of Africa in the East-West conflict. That will be led by the Americans. These two purposes will be coordinated so that they are mutually supportive, and the apportionment of the expected benefits – and costs – will be worked out. It is at that point – the division of the spoils – that disputes are most likely to occur.

But the costs may also be higher than the participants anticipate. Tanzania is not the only nationalist country in Africa. There are nationalists everywhere. Sooner or later, and for as long as necessary, Africa will fight against neo-col0nialism as it has fought against colonialism. And eventually it will win. western Block countries which try to resist the struggle against neo-colonialism need to recognise that it will not only be African countries which will suffer in the process.

Nor will the whole of Africa acquiesce in being used in the East-West confrontation. We are weak, but weak countries have before now caused a great deal of embarrassment and some difficulty for Big Powers. If the West wants to prove, either to the Russians or to their own people, that they are not soft on Communism they should direct their attention to where the Soviet tanks are, and the Soviet front-line is. They should not invent an excuse to bring the East-West conflict into Africa. For if they succeed in doing that Africa will suffer, and African freedom will suffer; but it may also turn out to be very expensive for those who choose Africa as another site for East-West confrontation.

The African people have the same desire as every other people to be free and to use their freedom for their own benefit. They have the same determination to work and to struggle to that end. They know that no-one else is interested in their freedom. This talk in Europe about a Pan-African Security Force is an insult to Africa, and a derogation of African freedom.

It makes little difference if the European initiators of this plan find Africans to do their fighting for them. There were Africans who fought with the colonial invaders; there were Africans who assisted in the enslavement of fellow-Africans; and there were Africans who fought against the freedom movements. But we ask those African Governments which may have. agreed to participate in this plan to consider well be fore they go further.

We have the O.A.U. With all its faults and its incapacities, it is the only Pan-African organisation which exists and which is concerned with African freedom. Do not let us split it – and Africa – between those who are militarily allied with the West and those who may in consequence find themselves forced to seek assistance from elsewhere against the African-assisted neo-colonialism."[17]

Back in the sixties, not long after Katanga was reunited with the rest of the country in January 1963, Africa witnessed another major step towards unity when African leaders formed the Organisation of African Unity (OAU). It was formed in Addis Ababa, Ethiopia, on May 25 1963.

Unfortunately, the OAU failed to resolve the Congo crisis because of its weakness and because of the complex nature of the problem involving intervention in Congo by the world's major powers which turned the bleeding heart of Africa into a battleground between the two ideological camps: the East led by the Soviet Union and the West led by the United States.

Almost exactly one year after Katanga surrendered on 15 January 1963, ending the secession of this mineral-rich province, followers of Lumumba launched a rebellion in Kwilu Province in the western part of the country in an attempt to replace the western-backed government in Leopoldville.

The rebellion started on 22 January 1964 under the leadership of Pierre Mulele, Lumumba's minister of education and heir-apparent, coincidentally in the same month, and the same year, the Zanzibar revolution took place a few hundred miles east of Congo.

And like the leaders of the Zanzibar revolution, Pierre Mulele and his colleagues were socialist-oriented and had the support of socialist countries including Cuba, the Soviet Union and the People's Republic of China. Lumumba's followers in Congo also had the support of neighbouring Tanzania, their strongest supporter among all the African countries. Tanzania was also used a conduit for sending weapons and other forms of material assistance to the Congolese nationalist forces inspired by the martyred Lumumba.

The rebellion in Kwilu Province started almost exactly a year after the secession of Katanga Province ended in January 1963. Moise Tshombe went into exile in Spain and there was some hope that the country would start enjoying relative peace and stability after so much fighting had taken place since independence. But that was not the case. And that was because of what happened to Lumumba and the fiasco that followed his assassination. His followers were not ready to give up the fight.

The Kwilu rebellion quickly spread to other parts of the country, mainly eastern Congo, Lumumba's political stronghold and his home region. The leader of the rebellion in eastern Congo was Gaston Soumialot.

Before the rebellion started in the east, Soumialot was living in Congo-Brazzaville where the National Liberation

Council – *Conseil National de Liberation* (CNL) – was based. It was an umbrella organisation of nationalist groups following Lumumba's ideals and was opposed to the western-backed national government in Leopoldville, the nation's capital.

Gaston Soumialot on the left in 1965

In January 1964, Soumialot was sent by the CNL to Burundi to mobilise forces and launch a rebellion in eastern Congo which would be coordinated with the uprising in Kwilu to topple the regime in Leopoldville.

When he moved to the east, he was able to mobilise thousands of recruits in eastern Kivu, a region bordering Burundi in the eastern part of Congo. Many people joined the rebellion because they were disgusted with the leadership in Leopoldville that was riddled with corruption and paralyzed by incompetence. The uprising in eastern Congo came to be known as the Simba rebellion, with Stanleyville, Lumumba's political stronghold, as its nerve centre.

The 1964 rural insurgency in Congo received extensive coverage during that period. And many observers have offered thoughtful insights into this phenomenon in a larger national context to explain how and why it happened. According to Herman Kinder and Werner Hilgemann in *The Anchor Atlas of World History, 2:*

"From January to August 1964, rural insurgency engulfed five *provincettes* out of twenty-one and made substantial inroads into another five, raising the distinct possibility of a total collapse of the central government.

The extraordinary speed with which the rebellions spread among the rural masses attests to the enormous insurrectionary potential that had been building up in previous years.

Prolonged neglect of the rural sectors, coupled with the growing disparities of wealth and privilege between the political elites and the peasant masses, inefficient and corrupt government, and ANC (*L'Armée Nationale Congolaise*) abuses, created a situation ripe for major uprising.

Further aggravating the frustration of the rural masses, the promise of a life more abundant made at the time of independence had remained unfulfilled. It seemed to many, especially disaffected youths, that nothing short of a 'second independence' would bring them salvation.

Among the several factors that combined to precipitate rebellion, none was more consequential than the dissolution of parliament in September 1963, a move spurred by the incessant divisions and bickering among deputies. The immediate result was to deprive the opposition of the only remaining legitimate avenue for political participation.

Faced with this situation, several deputies affiliated with the MNC-Lumumba, among them Christophe Gbenye and Bocheley Davidson, decided to move to

Brazzaville, in the former French Congo, and organize a National Liberation Council (*Conseil National de Liberation*--CNL). In time the CNL became the central coordinating apparatus for the eastern rebellion.

Another major factor behind the insurrection was the anticipated withdrawal of the UN forces by June 30, 1964. The prospective elimination of the only reliable crutch available to the central government acted as a major incentive for the opposition to mobilize against Adoula.

Finally, with the arrival in the Kwilu area of Pierre Mulele in July 1963, a key revolutionary figure entered the arena. Once affiliated with Antoine Gizenga's PSA, Mulele traveled widely in Eastern Europe before reaching China, where he received sustained training in guerilla warfare.

Upon arriving in Kwilu, Mulele proceeded to recruit a solid phalanx of followers among members of his own ethnic group, the Mbunda, as well as among Gizenga's kinsmen, the Pende, both of whom had long been the target of government repression.

The Kwilu rebellion began in January 1964, when Mulelist insurgents attacked government outposts, mission stations, and company installations. On January 22 and 23, four European missionaries were killed, and on February 5 the chief of staff of the ANC was ambushed and killed. Troops were immediately sent to the area, and by April a measure of stability had been restored to the area. The Kwilu rebellion did not finally end until December 1965, however.

The central figure behind the eastern rebellion was Gaston Soumialot, who, in January 1964, was sent to Burundi by the CNL, with the mission of organizing the rebellion.

With the full support of the Burundi authorities, and thanks to his own skill in exploiting local conflicts and working out tactical alliances with Tutsi exiles from Rwanda, Soumialot was able to recruit thousands of dedicated supporters in eastern Kivu, along the border with Burundi. On May 15, the town of Uvira fell to the rebels, and, shortly thereafter, so did Fizi."[18]

The Simba rebellion spread quickly throughout the east and towards the south. In the northern part of Katanga, the mineral-rich province in southeastern Congo, the town of Baudoinville – which was renamed Virungu, and now Moba – fell on 19 July 1964. Others followed.

Kindu, in Maniema, was taken on July 24th. And in early August the Soumialot forces, now calling themselves the National Liberation Army – *Armée Nationale de Libération* (ANL) – captured the Lumumbist stronghold of Stanleyville. It was a great victory for the nationalist forces.

Units of the Congolese national army were routed and fled, leaving a lot of weapons behind which Soumialot's forces added to their arsenal as they pushed forward into other parts of the country to capture more territory and consolidate their gains. The Simba fighters pushed on north and west of Stanleyville, eventually penetrating as far west as Lisala on the Congo River in the western part of the country hundreds of miles away from the east.

Prospects seemed bleak for the central government in Leopoldville.

By 5 September 1964, with the proclamation of a revolutionary government under the leadership of the National Liberation Council in the provisional or new capital of Stanleyville, almost half of the entire country was in rebel hands. And seven local capitals out of 21 had also been captured by September 5th.

It seemed the nationalist forces were headed for victory.

But the United States intervened, with a vengeance, to stop the advance of the nationalist forces.

However, it must be conceded that the nationalist forces themselves were partly responsible for undermining their victory. As the rebel movement spread across the country, discipline became a problem among many of its fighters and atrocities were committed by some of them, unleashing terror and terrorising villagers for no apparent reason and without provocation.

The people who were seen as liberators now became enemies of the people, especially those who were :westernized,: an euphemism for "privileged," "educated" or "civilized." These were usually the middle-class "guilty of" aping the consumption proclivities of the West.

But American intervention played a much bigger role in neutralizsing the nationalist forces in spite of the fact that the Simba rebels also played a role in undermining themselves because of the excesses of many of their fighters who could not be contained or disciplined.

The United States increased its support for the central government in Leopoldville and the CIA organised an air force for aerial bombings of the Simba nationalist forces and their targets to support the weak Congolese national army fighting the rebels. Now the Simba rebellion faced its biggest and toughest opponent.

Also on the side of the government and the CIA in the Congo were the white mercenaries, many of them from apartheid South Africa, Rhodesia, Belgium and France. And the bombing missions masterminded by the CIA against the nationalist forces of the Simba uprising had Cuban pilots flying the planes.

These were some of the same Cubans who had been involved in the abortive Bay of Pigs invasion against Cuba on 17 April 1961 during the Kennedy administration when President Kennedy tried to overthrow Castro by using Cuban exiles living in the United States and trained by the CIA for the Cuban invasion. After the disastrous Cuban invasion, they went on another mission, this time in Congo, again at the behest of the CIA.

The CIA also had high-speed patrol boats on Lake Tanganyika to interdict supply lines for the Lumumbist nationalist forces. A lot of supplies which passed through Tanganyika, later renamed Tanzania, were shipped across the lake and some of them were intercepted by the CIA and the mercenaries. Some of the weapons sent to the rebels through Tanzania came from Egypt, which was then known as the United Arab Republic, a strong supporter of Lumumba's former vice premier Antoine Gizenga who was the head of the revolutionary government in Stanleyville.

Yet, in spite of American intervention and clandestine efforts by the CIA to undermine the insurgency, the Simba rebellion gained momentum and spread further, although it had its own weaknesses from internal dynamics which threatened to wreck the rebel movement.

Indiscipline among a significant number of its fighters remained a problem and threatened to alienate even more people whom the insurgents were supposed to be fighting for – the Congolese people in general – against the puppet government in Leopoldville. However, the insurgency was able to forge ahead in spite of its own weaknesses. And as Herman Kinder and Werner Hilgemann further state:

"No less astonishing than the swiftness of rebel victories was the inability of the insurgents to consolidate their gains and establish an alternative system of administration to one they had so easily destroyed.

Corruption, administrative inefficiency, and ethnic favoritism turned out to be liabilities for the rebel leaders as much as they had been for previous provincial administrators. Heavy reliance on specific ethnic communities (Tetela-Kusu in the east, Pende and Mbunda in Kwilu) for manning the military and administrative apparatuses of the rebellions was seen by many as a reversion to tribalism.

Further complicating ethnic tensions between the ANL leadership and the Simbas, serious conflicts erupted at the *provincette* level over who should get the lion's share of the property seized from the enemy. Finally, countless disputes disrupted the CNL leadership in exile, stemming from personality differences as well as disagreements over questions of tactics and organization.

The rapid decline of popular support for the eastern rebellion is in large part a reflection of the very inadequate leadership offered by the CNL and local cadres.

The military setbacks suffered by the ANL in the fall of 1964 were not just the result of poor leadership, however; even more important in turning the tide against the insurgents was the decisive contribution made by European mercenaries in helping the central government regain control over rebel-held areas."[19]

In a desperate move to unite the country, President Joseph Kasavubu invited Moise Tshombe in July 1964 to return to Congo and appointed him prime minister, replacing Cyrille Adoula. And the American government agreed to help Tshombe recruit a force of mercenaries to fight the Simba rebellion which the national army had failed to defeat. The CIA also decided to expand its air strike unit, using more firepower and aerial bombings against the rebels.

The CIA started using more advanced aircraft and more firepower in aerial bombings in August 1964. They were to prove decisive in the outcome of the conflict.

Cuban exile pilots learned how to use the aircraft as soon as the planes arrived in Congo in the same month of August. The Simba rebels had no antiaircraft guns to shoot down the planes and no aircraft of their own for aerial combat and bombing missions. Compounding the problem was the indiscipline and incompetence of the Simba rebels, making them easier targets and less effective in combat against the mercenaries directed by the CIA.

The central government under Prime Minister Tshombe relied heavily on the mercenaries who had a lot of combat experience. There were hundreds of them in Congo.

Tshombe also used his former fighters, the Kantangan *gendarmes*, who fought for the secession of Katanga Province and went to live in neighbouring Angola after they lost the war.

He called them back and, with their combat experience, they proved to be effective fighters against the Simba rebels. They were also integrated into the Congolese National Army (ANC – *L'Armée Nationale Congolaise*). The mercenaries led the national army into combat against the rebels and proved to be very effective in the conduct of military operations.

The mercenaries had several advantages. They were experienced fighters; they had technical superiority; and they were a disciplined force. And with the support of air strikes against the rebels and rebel strongholds, they made impressive advances against the Lumumbist nationalist forces.

But the fighting became more intense and brutal as the mercenaries started to recapture rebel strongholds. And both sides committed atrocities which could not be justified under any rules of military engagement. Caught in the crossfire, and often deliberately targeted, were innocent civilians, men, women and children in villages and towns across the country.

As the fighting continued, the white mercenaries proved to be more and more effective. They played a decisive role in recapturing Lisala from the Simba rebels on September 15th, Buende on October 24th, and Kindu on November 6th.

The Lumumbist nationalist forces were now on the defensive and the revolutionary government in Stanleyville decided to take some local whites hostage as a bargaining tool in negotiations with the central government in order to reach some kind of compromise acceptable to both sides. About 1,650 whites, mostly Belgians and some Americans including priests and nuns, were taken hostage.

The Americans and the Belgians deliberately distorted and misinterpreted what the Simba rebels said, and their intention of holding some whites hostage, and used it as an excuse to launch an invasion of Stanleyville which cost countless lives. The invasion was a joint American-Belgian parachute rescue operation code-named Dragon Rouge, or Red Dragon, and was launched on 24 November 1964 to coincide with the arrival of some units of the Congolese National Army and the mercenaries in an area near Stanleyville, the capital of the eastern province. It lasted until November 27th.

Stanleyville was captured by the Americans and the Belgians, with the help of the mercenaries, in one of the bloodiest battles in Congo in the sixties. It was a devastating blow to the Simba rebels, and their leaders, Christophe Gbenye who led the rural rebellion in eastern Congo, and Gaston Soumialot, went into exile in Cairo, Egypt.

The invasion of Stanleyville by the Americans and the Belgians was widely condemned in Congo and across Africa as well as in other countries. It was also discussed at the UN. Thousands of innocent lives were lost because of this American-Belgian operation.

And Moise Tshombe alienated many people in his own country and other parts of Africa and elsewhere around the world because he was the prime minister of Congo when Stanleyville was attacked by the Americans and the Belgians with his approval. The Americans, the Belgians and the mercenaries were now in full control of Stanleyville, with troops from the Congolese National Army playing only a subordinate role to these foreign invaders.

After the loss of Stanleyville, the Simba rebellion was seriously weakened. The rebels were demoralised, indiscipline continued to be a problem, some of them left, and by the end of the year, the eastern rebellion was reduced to isolated pockets of resistance without strong leadership and enough weapons to mount an effective counter-offensive, although the fighters continued to be inspired by the ideals of Lumumba.

From left: Milton Obote, Chirstophe Gbenye, Jomo Kenyatta, and Julius Nyerere at a meeting in Mbale, Uganda

The CIA brought in more combat aircraft and other weapons in January 1965 for mop-up operations and to effectively neutralise the rebels. And by the end of the year, the Simba rebellion had been suppressed in most areas.

Fighting continued here and there for more than one year after that but the war was, for all practical purposes, over by then. In late 1966 and early 1967, the CIA withdrew its most effective combat aircraft that were used against the rebels in the Congo.

The 1964 insurgency in Congo, and its failure to

achieve its goals, provided a textbook lesson for other revolutionaries in the country and elsewhere in Africa. One of the things many of them did not learn through the years, no more than many other people aspiring to national office did, was that articulation of ideas is not enough by itself.

Lofty ideals may inspire the people, but they do not represent concrete reality. They must be implemented to be meaningful. And that requires national involvement which is impossible if the people don't identify themselves as a collective national entity.

Also, ethnic affiliations compromise national objectives if the leaders themselves appeal to ethno-regional loyalties to secure power ostensibly to implement a national agenda. That has been one of the biggest tragedies in Africa for decades since independence.

Leaders like Pierre Mulele and Antoine Gizenga may have been true nationalists, as they indeed were. But their inability to expand beyond their regional strongholds and win considerable support from the people of other ethnic groups across the country was a major setback for the insurgency.

Mulele was a Mbunda, and Gizenga, a Pende. And both leaders, like their ethnic groups, were native to Kwilu Province. Attempts by both leaders to transcend their ethnic and regional identities were not very successful.

There were other problems they had to contend with. And as Leonce Ndikumana and Kisangani Emizet explain what happened during that period in their paper, "The Economics of Civil War: The Case of the Democratic Republic of Congo":

"The Kwilu rebellion:
22 January 1964 - 31 December 1965

(i) The political and ideological background

In the post-Lumumba period, the United Nations invested diplomatic efforts to press for national reconciliation and unification of the Congo. The United Nations organized a conference including parliamentarians and leaders of the provincial governments of Katanga, South Kasai, Haut Congo, and Kinshasa in a neutral venue at Lovanium University.

From the conference, a new central government was formed led by Adoula, who had unanimous approval from parliament. Adoula formed a diverse government, including such key pro-Lumumbists as Gigenza and Gbenye.

To appease regionalist demands, the Adoula government submitted to parliament an amendment to the *Loi Fondamentale* aimed at restructuring the country into 21 autonomous provinces (up from the six provinces initially created by the *Loi Fondamentale).* The amendment was promulgated on 27 April 1962.

While the Adoula government tried to find a constitutional solution to the political crisis in Congo, the opposition organized itself with the aim of a revolutionary overthrow of the regime. Pierre Mulele led the Kwilu rebellion while the *Conseil National de Libération* (National Liberation Council, CNL) organized the eastern rebellion

One of the most dedicated Lumumba supporters, Mulele, was Secretary General of the radical wing of the *Parti Solidaire Africain* (PSA) of Gizenga in 1959-1960 and served as Minister of Education in the Lumumba government. He also served as representative of the Gizenga's Stanleyville provincial government in Egypt and in socialist countries. Having sojourned in Peking, Mulele was influenced by Maoist ideology.

At the end of the Stanleyville government in August 1961, Mulele refused national reconciliation and chose exile, during which he perfected his revolutionary ideology and prepared his strategies for organizing a peasant guerilla force.

Mulele accused the central government of having sold out to the interests of the West and advocated a second 'liberating independence,' which attracted enthusiastic support from rural mass

(ii) Support for the rebellion:
Ethnic base with no mineral resource base

Mulele was from the Mbunda ethnic group while Gizenga was an ethnic Mpende, both groups were from the Kwilu province and claimed to be marginalized by the central government. The ethnic orientation of the Mulelist rebellion facilitated recruitment of combatants but also prevented the rebellion from gaining ground beyond the Mbunda-Mpende territory.

Unlike the Katangan and Kasai rebellions, the Kwilu rebellion was not motivated by the control of provincial mineral resources. Thus, the rebellion could not count on external economic interests for support. The war effort was entirely supported by the local population.

There are no specific factors that triggered the Kwilu rebellion. Upon his return from exile in July 1963, Mulele mobilized and trained his combatants who were subjected to a rigid code of discipline. The Mulelist rebels posed stiff resistance to government troops despite the rudimentary nature of their military equipment.

The rebellion was eventually defeated in December 1965, leaving only pockets of isolated resistance in the rural area.

The eastern rebellion:
15 April 1964 - 1 July 1966

(i) The political context

The Adoula government failed in its mission of

135

national unification and instead became a vehicle of recolonization of the Congo by Belgium via military occupation and control of the economy.

Antagonism between the parliament and the government - this time with the president and the prime minister on the same side - led President Kasavubu to suspend the parliament on 29 September 1963. The same day, opposition nationalist parties opened an extraordinary conference that ended on October 3 with the creation of the CNL whose objective was to overthrow the Adoula government and to achieve "total and effective decolonization of the Congo thus far dominated by a coalition of foreign powers" (Vanderlinden, et al. 1980: 124).

(ii) The ideological factor

The leaders of the CNL fled to Brazzaville and formed a cartel of Lumumbist- nationalist parties, the most important ones being MNC-Lumumba led by Gbenye and PSA led by Gizenga (Vanderlinden, et al. 1980).

The CNL had a socialist orientation with both pro-Soviet and pro-Chinese leanings. This socialist orientation proved useful in mobilizing the masses against the central government, which was accused of selling out to capitalist interests, but it also prevented the CNL from obtaining foreign assistance.

(iii) Organization of the rebellion

In January 1964, the CNL sent Gaston Soumialot and Laurent Kabila to Burundi with the mission of preparing the rebellion in the east (Kabila in north Katanga and Soumialot in Kivu).

On 15 April 1964, the rebellion started in the Ruzizi plain south of Bukavu and a month later, Uvira was under the control of the simba (which means lions), the rebel forces of the *Armée Populaire de Libération* (Popular Liberation Army, APL) of the CNL.

The rebellion drew its forces from the large population of young, uneducated, and unemployed Congolese. The APL advanced quickly with little resistance from the government forces. The Simba were believed to possess magic powers acquired from taking a traditional potion that was purported to transform enemy bullets into water (Verhaegen, 1969).

In two months, the rebels conquered northern Katanga, Maniema, Sankuru and Orientale province. On 5 September 1964, the "people's government" of Stanleyville was installed in Haut Congo, headed by President Gbenye of the MNC-Lumumba who was also president of the CNL.

By the end of September, about half of the country was under control of the APL. The rich endowment in mineral resources of the eastern provinces was a major motivation and source of financing for the rebellion. In this respect, the eastern rebellion has numerous similarities with the secessionist wars of Katanga and southern Kasai. Furthermore, like the Katangan, southern Kasai, and Kwilu rebellions, the eastern rebellion was also supported by a large ethnic base dominated by the Bakusu and Batetela.

(iv) Tshombe returns and defeats the rebellion

The Adoula government continued to experience instability and its army was unable to contain the rebellion. The government turned to Tshombe (in exile in Spain) who still had some influence in the Katanga region and had the backing of Belgian officials and private actors. More important, he had contacts with both the CNL and the Adoula government. Tshombe was believed to be the man who could achieve national reconciliation and control the rebellion (Gibbs 1991).

137

He returned on 26 June 1964 and President Kasavubu gave him the mission of forming a transitional government. To the surprise and anger of many, Tshombe's government did not include representatives from key opposition groups, most notably the CNL.

Tshombe rallied his former Katangan gendarmes with the assistance of Belgian mercenaries and advisers and with backing from the United States and Belgium.

The rebels unsuccessfully tried to use white hostages to stop the advance of Tshombe's forces. Stanleyville was captured on 24 November 1964, but as many as 200 Europeans and some 46,000 Congolese were killed.

The leaders of CNL retreated from the provincial capitals but continued to fight in rural areas. It was only in 1967 that the Orientale province and Maniema province were fully controlled by government forces.

The APL retained limited control over some rural areas in southern Kivu (Fizi and Baraka) under the command of Kabila. The rebellion was completely defeated by 1968."[20]

In spite of Tshombe's success in fighting the Simba rebels in his capacity as prime minister of Congo during that period, he did not last long in power. He became involved in a power struggle against President Joseph Kasavubu and lost.

In October 1965, he was replaced by Evariste Kimba as prime minister and returned to Spain, where he lived before, after he failed in his secessionist effort to keep Katanga out of Congo.

Kasavubu remained president but not for long. On November 25th the same year, he was overthrown by Joseph Mobutu who became the new head of state.

In spite of all those changes during that period, the year 1964 stood out as the most decisive in the history of nationalist resistance in the sixties when the Simba rebels were finally defeated by a combined force of American and Belgian paratroopers.

When they lost Stanleyville, the capital of their revolutionary government, they knew their days were numbered. And they never recovered from that loss. But they did not abandon the struggle for the liberation of Congo. One of their strongest supporters was Tanzania. As Professor Piero Gleijeses of Johns Hopkins University states in his book, *Conflicting Missions: Havana, Washington, and Africa, 1959 – 1976*:

"Of all the African leaders who proclaimed their support for the liberation struggle in Africa – Nkrumah, Nasser, Ben Bella, Sekou Toure – he (Nyerere) was the most committed. And by the second half of 1964, spurred by events in Zaire and the obvious failure of peaceful attempts to end white rule in southern Africa, this commitment, and his a disappointment with the Western powers, was increasingly evident.

By the time Che arrived (in 1965), Dar es Salaam had become the Mecca of African liberation movements....Dar es Salaam 'has become a haven for exiles from the rest of Africa,' the CIA lamented in September 1964. 'It is full of frustrated revolutionaries, plotting the overthrow of African governments, both black and white'....

In September 1964, Frelimo, the movement against Portuguese rule in Mozambique, had launched the opening salvo of its guerrilla war from bases in southern Tanzania, its only rear guard.

Following Stanleyville, Nyerere had thrown his full support to the Simbas, and Tanzania had become their main rear guard and the major conduit of Soviet and Chinese weapons for them.

It was also the seat of the Liberation Committee of the OAU. The head offices of Frelimo and a host of other movements struggling against the white regimes in South Africa, Namibia, and Rhodesia were in Dar es Salaam.

The Cuban embassy there was, the CIA reported accurately in March 1965, 'the largest Cuban diplomatic station in sub-Saharan Africa.' The ambassador, Captain Pablo Ribalta, was a close friend of Che Guevara.

In early 1964 Ribalta had been the commander of the Libertad air force base near Havana. 'One day,' he told me, 'Che arrived and said, 'Listen, Fidel wants to send you to Tanzania.' He told me I had to establish good relations with the liberation movements there. So they sent me to the Foreign Ministry to learn about Africa, and especially about Tanzania.'

Ribalta arrived in Tanzania on February 25, 1964, with four trusted aides from Libertad...."[21]

The year 1965 was an important milestone in the history of Africa as a whole.

Julius Nyerere

It marked the end of what came to be known as the Congo crisis which began with the secession of Katanga Province just eleven days after the country won independence from Belgium. The crisis came to an end after the defeat of the Lumumbist forces – by Western powers – in their heroic attempts to achieve genuine independence with the help of a few African countries.

The crisis formally ended when Mobutu seized power on 25 November 1965 and consolidated his rule with the help of Western powers, especially the Untied States. In fact, throughout his 32-year reign, the largest CIA station in Africa was in Kinshasa. And although pro-Lumumbist forces were defeated, pockets of resistance to Mobutu's rule continued to exist in different parts of the country, especially in the eastern part until 1968.

Coincidentally, it was also in the same year in which the white minority rulers of Rhodesia declared independence in defiance of the wishes of the black majority who demanded democratic rule.

The unilateral declaration of independence (UDI) on 11 November 1965 demonstrated Africa's military impotence against the white minority who were not even a formidable military force sharply contrasted with apartheid South Africa.

There is no question that the Rhodesian crisis was a setback for Africa in her struggle for independence. But it was during the Congo crisis that Africans suffered total defeat and humiliation at the hands of the imperial powers led by the United States.

It was a such a humiliating defeat that it still haunts Africa today as the Democratic Republic of Congo (DRC) desperately tries to recover from more than a generation of ruin sponsored by Western powers.

After more than five years of fighting since 1960, Western powers were still embroiled in the Congo imbroglio as much as they were when the crisis first broke out soon after independence.

It was Western powers who engineered and fuelled the Congo crisis; it was the same Western powers who were responsible for the ouster and assassination of Patrice Lumumba.

But there were other important players, although not as powerful.

Che Guevara in Congo

Che Guevara and Fidel Castro

One of the most prominent figures who appeared on the Congo scene in 1965 was the legendary Che Guevara whose involvement in the crisis was inextricably linked with the efforts of a few African countries which were trying to help the Congolese achieve Lumumba's dream of genuine independence.

One of those countries was Tanzania, Congo's neighbour and the strongest supporter of the Congolese pro-Lumumbist nationalists, under the leadership of Julius Nyerere which provided material, diplomatic and moral support and served as a conduit for the nationalist forces fighting against the puppet regime in Leopoldville and its Western allies.

Western countries, including apartheid South Africa

which was an integral part of the Western world, wreaked so much havoc across Congo and with such impunity that their actions could have meant only one thing: the lives of black people meant absolutely nothing to them.

Fellow Africans across the continent could not do anything to stop the carnage. And the rest of the world did nothing to stop it, while it increased in its ferocity and intensity.

United Nations forces sent ostensibly to restore the integrity of Congo and keep the Cold War out of Africa, left the country by July 1964 while the situation was still volatile. They did not help as much as they should and could have, including saving Lumumba and his colleagues Maurice Mpolo and Joseph Okito as well as others who were assassinated.

The United Nations did not play a neutral role in Congo.

Dominated by Western powers in the Security Council who were supported by their client states in the General Assembly including some African countries, the United Nations served Western interests in Congo, polarising the situation and exacerbating the conflict.

The assassination of Lumumba and his colleagues Maurice Mpolo and Joseph Okito in January 1961 only fuelled the conflict during the following years, with the massacre of the Congolese and destruction of the country by the mercenaries continuing unabated.

The intervening powers showed total disregard for the well-being of black people, claiming they were fighting to keep communism out of Africa. As the late Dr. Walter Rodney from Guyana who taught at the University of Dar es Salaam in Tanzania stated in his work *The Groundings with My Brothers*:

"The white world in their own way were saying that all these blacks amounted to nothing, for power was white....By being made into colonials, black people lost the power which we previously had of governing our own affairs, and the aim of the white imperialist world is to see that we never regain this power.

The Congo provides an example of this situation....After regaining political independence the Congolese people settled down to reorganise their lives, but white power intervened, set up the black stooge Tshombe, and murdered both Lumumba and the aspirations of the Congolese people. Since then, paid white mercenaries have harassed the Congo.

Late last year, 130 of these hired white killers were chased out of the Congo and cornered in the neighbouring African state of Burundi. The white world intervened and they all have been set free. These are men who for months were murdering, raping, pillaging, disrupting economic production, and making a mockery of black life and black society. Yet white power said not a hair on their heads was to be touched. They did not even have to stand trial or reveal their names."[22]

More than 100,000 Congolese were massacred during those turbulent years. By a strange coincidence, when Congo was still a colony, it also had about 100,000 Belgians living in the country. But most of them left when the country was plunged into chaos soon after independence.

There were a number of other African countries which also had substantial numbers of Europeans especially in East and Southern Africa. For example, in 1962 there were 66,000 white settlers in Kenya, mostly British; 27,000 in Tanganyika, mostly British; 75,000 in Northern Rhodesia, mostly British; 215,000 in Southern Rhodesia, also mostly British; 75,000 in Mozambique, mostly Portuguese; 250,000 in Angola, also mostly Portuguese; 70,000 in South West Africa, mostly from South Africa; and 3 million in South Africa, the bastion of white rule on the continent.

Except for Tanganyika which won independence in December 1961, Kenya which won hers in December 1963, and Northern Rhodesia in October 1964 when it was renamed Zambia, it would be decades before the rest of the countries with significant numbers of whites would win their freedom.

Unfortunately, the first country in the region with a substantial number of Europeans to win independence, Congo, also became the most traumatised; her agony compounded by the refusal of Western powers to leave the country when UN troops pulled out. Instead, they continued to wreak havoc in the bleeding heart of Africa.

The other players on the scene were, of course, on the nationalist side of the Congolese people. One of them was Che Guevara, an Argentine-Cuban doctor-turned-guerrilla fighter and one of the most influential revolutionaries in the twentieth century.

When Guevara arrived in Congo, nationalist forces were in disarray, to the consternation of the few African countries which were helping them. How and when Che Guevara got into Congo is an interesting part of this unfolding drama that had very much to do with the nationalist struggle itself which needed much support against the far superior forces mobilised by Western powers.

In the middle of 1964, Pierre Mulele who was minister of education under Lumumba and his heir apparent renewed fighting in Kwilu Province, his guerrilla base and stronghold in the central-western party of the country.

Another rebellion was going on at the same time in the northeast near Stanleyville, now Kisangani, the country's third largest city after Leopoldville (renamed Kinshasa) the capital, and Elisabethville (now Lubumbashi) the capital of Katanga Province.

It was led by the National Liberation Committee, an umbrella organisation of which Mulele was a leading member. The most prominent leaders in the Stanleyville uprising were Lumumba's former vice premier Antoine Gizenga and Christopher Gbenye. They all had one common enemy: the Western-backed government in Leopoldville installed three years earlier by the United Nations, the United States, and Belgium.

The Congolese government was about to collapse because of intensified fighting by the nationalist forces, prompting immediate intervention by the United States and Belgium. The two countries, especially the United States, were responsible for the creation of that government more than anybody else.

Compounding the problem was the fact that the United Nations was under strong Western influence exercised through the Security Council by the United States, Britain and France, all permanent members of the Council.

The other permanent member was, of course, the Soviet Union, providing a counterweight with its veto power wielded by all the permanent members.

Yet, because of their wealth and historical ties with the Third World during the colonial era, Western countries had a disproportionate impact on the formulation and adoption of UN resolutions including those on the former Belgian Congo, supported by their client states in the General Assembly. But that was not enough to stop the fighting in Congo.

In August 1964, the nationalist forces captured Stanleyville. The United States and Belgium responded militarily, justifying the invasion on their own terms regardless of what African countries said in protest to the invasion. Two months later, the two Western countries flew in several battalions of elite paratroops to rout the Congolese nationalist forces and succeeded in recapturing the city. They also seized control of the eastern part of Congo bordering Tanganyika, now Tanzania.

The border between the two countries runs through the middle of Lake Tanganyika from north to south; as does – or should – the one between Tanzania and Malawi, in the middle of Lake Nyasa (Malawi), a demarcation line recognised under customary international law, especially in disputes like this one, contrary to Malawi's dubious claims based on some old maps and agreements which do not even clearly show or define the boundary between the two countries as agreed upon by the British who then ruled Nyasaland, now Malawi; the Germans who ruled German East Africa, renamed Tanganyika, and Tanzania today; and the Portuguese who ruled Mozambique.

When the United States and Belgium took control of eastern Congo following their capture of Stanleyville, they also launched speedboat patrols on the entire Lake Tanganyika including the territorial waters belonging to Tanzania in clear violation of her territorial integrity ostensibly to intercept any help from this country going to the nationalist guerrillas in Congo.

The United States and Belgium also tried to justify their invasion on other grounds. As Jorge Castaneda states in his book *Companero: The Life and Death of Che Guevara*:

"Another ostensible goal was to prevent a repeat of the bloodbath that had occurred when the rebels entered Stanleyville, taking hostage the U.S. Consul, dozens of U.S. missionaries, and three hundred Belgian citizens and, according to some reports, executing 20,000 Congolese from the urban middle class."[23]

But the main reason for the invasion was to secure domination of the heart of Africa by the West. The United States and Belgium considered Congo to be their country, totally disregarding the interests of the Congolese people and the rest of Africa, because it was once a Western colony, ruled by Belgium, and therefore belonged to the Western sphere of influence.

Western countries had intervened in African affairs more than anybody else, beginning with the slave trade in the 1400s started by the Portuguese and the Spanish invaders on the West African coast, and going all the way through to the Berlin Conference of 1885 until the sixties and beyond. They also inflicted the greatest damage on Africa.

Therefore their intervention in Congo was also justified as a continuation of their "divine mandate" to rule members of the "lesser breed." As President Julius Nyerere said about the magnitude of such Western intervention in Africa, invoking the memories of what happened in Congo:

"It is incontrovertible that, both before and after independence, Western countries have interfered more actively – for both good and evil – in Africa than have the Eastern powers. Not only has Africa had more economic and technical assistance from the West; it has also had Stanleyville, Tshombe, and practical support for Verwoerd. If we talk about the first – and we should and do – then we must also talk about the second....

It is not possible for African states to compromise on the basic principles of African freedom and equality. A leader like Tshombe, who was willing to employ South African racialists in order to maintain his own power, and who was willing to dismember an African state if he could not control it – such a man could obviously not bring his nation into a coherent African entity...(because of) his deliberate betrayal of the basic principles of African freedom and African equality....

Treachery we cannot accept....Africa must never compromise with treachery to our cause....An African traitor was in charge of one of the largest, and potentially most powerful, of its states (the Congo)."[24]

President Kwame Nkrumah also expressed the same sentiment. As he stated in his letter to Tshombe, dated 12 August 1960:

"You have assembled in your support the foremost advocates of imperialism and colonialism in Africa and the most determined opponents of African freedom. How can you, as an African, do this?"[25]

It was Tshombe's treachery which alienated the African countries – Tanganyika (later Tanzania), Ghana, Algeria, Egypt, Guinea, and Mali – which supported the Congolese nationalists. It was also Tshombe's treachery which galvanised the nationalists, already enraged by Lumumba's assassination, into a potent force against the Western invaders who supported Tshombe and later Joseph Mobutu.

And it was the nationalist uprising by the Congolese guerrilla forces which influenced Che Guevara when he made his decision to go to Congo and join them in their fight against Tshombe, Mobutu and their Western supporters.

The uprising convinced Guevara that Lumumba's anti-imperialist struggle which had been neutralised by Western intervention soon after independence had now resumed. And the intervention by the United States and the former colonial power, Belgium, only confirmed what the Congolese nationalists and their supporters had been saying all along: They were fighting against imperialism and attempts by Belgium and other colonial powers to reconquer and continue to dominate Africa. Congo became the first battleground for such reconquest.

All that convinced Che Guevara to support the Congolese nationalist uprising which he saw as a just and noble cause in the struggle against imperialism.

When he led the Cuban delegation to the nineteenth session of the United Nations General Assembly in December 1964, he took the opportunity to talk at length with African and Arab delegates at the UN about the situation in Africa. In his speech to the UN General

Assembly, Guevara's strongest remarks focused on the Congo crisis, especially the invasion of Stanleyville by the United States and Belgium only a few months earlier in August. As he stated:

"Perhaps the children of Belgian patriots who died defending their country's freedom are the same ones who freely murdered millions of Congolese on behalf of the white race, just as they suffered under the German boot because their Aryan blood count was not high enough....

Our free eyes now look toward new horizons, and are able to see what our condition as colonial slaves kept us from seeing only yesterday: that 'Western civilization' conceals under its lovely facade a gang of hyenas and jackals.

That is the only possible name for those who have gone on a 'humanitarian' mission to the Congo.

Carnivorous animals, feeding on defenceless peoples: that is what imperialism does to man, that is what distinguishes the imperial 'white'....All the free men in the world must stand ready to avenge the crime of the Congo."[26]

A few months earlier in March, Guevara had taken the same position at the first United Nations Conference on Trade and Development (UNCTAD) in Geneva which he addressed as head of the Cuban delegation.

He had already become a legend by then. His mere presence even before he gave the speech electrified the international gathering:

"The hall at the Palais des Nations erupted into applause as Guevara made his way to the podium; he was already a legendary figure."[27]

He began his speech by severely criticising the conference for excluding China, North Vietnam and North

Korea and for inviting countries such as apartheid South Africa. Several times in his speech, he mentioned Lumumba and called attention to the plight of the poor, the people "struggling for their liberation...the needy of the world," rhetorically adding that "the imperialists will always insist that underdevelopment is caused by underdeveloped countries." And then he clearly defined his ideological position:

"We understand clearly – and express frankly – that the only correct solution to the problems of humanity at this time is the complete elimination of the exploitation of dependent countries by developed, capitalist countries, with all the consequences implicit in that fact."[28]

Articulating his position in those ideological terms at both conferences in New York before the UN General Assembly and at the UN Conference on Trade and Development (UNCTAD) in Geneva and in other international forums and interviews, it is clear that Guevara embarked on his mission to Congo as a champion of the oppressed and exploited masses of the world suffering at the hands of the metropolitan powers and their stooges in the underdeveloped countries. He had nothing but contempt for the imperialist powers whom he called "a gang of hyenas and jackals."

From Geneva he went to Algeria where he discussed with Ben Bella the African situation and what could be done to advance the nationalist struggle in Congo. Renewed fighting in Congo and the vulnerability of the Congolese central government which did not have the support of the general population were some of the main topics discussed in nationalist circles not only in Algeria but in other African countries such as Tanganyika where many of Lumumba's followers found sanctuary soon after his assassination in January 1961.

In Algeria's capital Algiers, Che also met with some of

the Congolese nationalists living in exile and discussed the situation in Congo. He became convinced that the 1961 nationalist uprising was about to start again. It was an assessment shared by the CIA. In one of its documents, now declassified, dated 5 August 1964 and drafted in March that year, the American intelligence agency stated:

"In recent months, regional dissidence and violence have assumed serious proportions, even by Congolese standards, and produced the threat of a total breakdown in governmental authority. The difficulties confronting Prime Minister Tshombe are enormous."[29]

Had it not been for American and Belgian as well as South African intervention, Tshombe would have been defeated by Lumumba's followers waging guerrilla warfare. And the history of Congo would have been entirely different. Che Guevara would probably not even have gone to Congo, and the Congolese people would not have suffered under Mobutu and his Western masters for more than 30 years. There would have been no Mobutu in power, another traitor the Congolese nationalists and Guevara fought just like they fought Tshombe.

Guevara's interest in Africa went beyond theoretical discussion about the nature of revolution and the struggle against imperialism. In January 1964 he had Pablo Ribalta, a black Cuban of African ancestry, appointed ambassador to Tanganyika. Ribalta was his close assistant going back to the late fifties when they fought together in the mountains – Sierra Maestra – against Batista's forces during the Cuban revolution led by Fidel Castro and Che Guevara himself. It was also in the same month and year, January 1964, that a revolution took place in Zanzibar, overthrowing the oppressive Arab regime.

Only about three months later, Tanganyika united with Zanzibar on 26 April 26 form the United Republic of Tanganyika and Zanzibar, renamed Tanzania on October

29th the same year.

Because of her commitment to African liberation and her proximity to Congo, Tanzania was to play a critical role in Guevara's mission in the former Belgian colony; so did his trusted aide, Cuban ambassador Pablo Ribalta whom he had strategically placed in Tanzania. He provided a critical link between Guevara – operating on the shores of Lake Tanganyika in eastern Congo – and Castro in Cuba.

Guevara was now ready to embark on his mission. But it was also a disappointing one, although he did not give up. As Peter Canby states:

"Che, the internationalist, left for Congo, where he and several hundred black Cuban volunteers joined forces with Laurent Kabila in a fight against Joseph Mobutu and a group of mercenaries led by the white South African Mike Hoare. It was a fiasco. While Mr. Kabila sped around the Tanzanian capital of Dar es Salaam in a green Mercedes, his troops, along with the Cubans, festered at the front."[30]

The use of Cubans of African origin was a critical factor in Guevara's calculations when the combat theatre was Africa itself.

First, he had Ribalto, a black Cuban, appointed ambassador to Tanzania as an advance man in preparation for his Congo mission; the Cuban embassy in Tanzania became the largest Cuban diplomatic mission on the African continent.

Next, as a tactical necessity and for political reasons as well, he led hundreds of black Cuban soldiers to Congo where they could easily blend in with the local black population and remove any suspicion among the Congolese that this was just another mission by whites, however well-intentioned, again taking charge in a black African country as if black people were not capable of doing things for themselves and on their own without white leadership.

The Cubans who went to Congo were said to be volunteers; probably not all of them were.

The element of colour as a tactical necessity and political consideration had also figured prominently in Guevara's calculations when earlier in September 1963 he tried to launch a revolution in his native Argentina.

He did not include any blacks in that expedition. Alberto Castellanos, one of his aides who took part in the Argentine mission, said in an interview in Havana, Cuba, on 23 January 1996, that the head of Guevara's escort, Harry "Pombo" Villegas, was not included in the Argentine expedition because he was of African origin. He quoted Che Guevara as saying, "There are no blacks where we are going."[31] In Congo, he and other black Cubans would fit right in.

Six African leaders, more than any others on the African continent, made the most determined attempt to help the Congolese nationalist forces in their war against the puppet government in Leopoldville and its Western sponsors. They were Julius Nyerere of Tanzania, Kwame Nkrumah of Ghana, Gamal Abdel Nasser of Egypt, Ben Bella of Algeria, Sekou Toure of Guinea, and Modibo Keita of Mali.

They even had a group of their own within the Organisation of African Unity (OAU) known as "the Group of Six" and secretly worked together as Ben Bella said in an interview years later in the 1990s. They were determined to liberate Congo. But as Ben Bella said in an interview in Geneva, Switzerland, on 4 November 1995:

"We arrived in the Congo too late."[32]

When Che Guevara arrived in Congo, the country was already torn apart by Western intervention and by internal conflicts – ethnic and regional, personal and ideological. He also led Cuban soldiers in combat against fellow

Cubans as well, pilots recruited by the CIA to fly bombing missions against nationalist strongholds in Congo.

Unfortunately, Ben Bella's poignant words could also be applied to Che Guevara and his Cuban troops: "We arrived in the Congo too late." By the time Guevara arrived in Congo, the nationalist insurgency had virtually been neutralised by Belgian paratroops and South African and Rhodesian – as well as French, German, and British – mercenaries backed up by American transport planes and other logistical support including "advisers" led by the CIA.

In what was code-named Operation Dragon Rouge, the United States, Belgium and other colonial powers including apartheid South Africa and Rhodesia captured Stanleyville in August 1964. It was their most successful military offensive in Congo and the most stunning defeat for the nationalist forces.

Only a month earlier, at the end of June, UN peacekeeping forces pulled out of Congo due to inadequate funding and lack of a large number of troops and logistical support necessary to bring about lasting peace in the country.

A much larger force, staying in Congo for a number of years probably five to seven while a new Congolese army was being trained, would have been needed to achieve that. But Western countries opposed additional funding which could have extended the UN peacekeeping mission in the embattled country. And that created a vacuum in a country already torn by strife the United States, Belgium and other Western countries – including South Africa and Rhodesia – were glad to fill.

The withdrawal of the UN forces also created a volatile situation with potential for catastrophe, leading to escalation of the conflict and greater international involvement.

UN Secretary-General Dag Hammarskjold was among those who warned about this dangerous prospect. As Fred

Greene stated in his book, *Dynamics of International Relations: Power, Security, and Order*:

"Hammarskjold warned that if the UN withdrew or became too weak, the Congo would become a center of civil and international war, much like Spain in 1936 – 1939. Any deep cut in the 19,000-man force would have destroyed the UN's capacity to maintain order or guard the vast state's borders with eight (sic) other lands."[33]

Congo is actually bordered by nine countries: Tanzania, Burundi, Rwanda, Uganda, Sudan, Central African Republic, Congo-Brazzaville, Angola, and Zambia.

It has the largest number of borders in Africa, together with its neighbour Tanzania which also has nine borders – eight countries and the Indian Ocean: Kenya, Uganda, Rwanda, Burundi, Democratic Republic of Congo (DRC), Zambia, Malawi, Mozambique, and the Indian Ocean.

And they are mostly porous borders, making it very difficult to guard them, especially for such poor and underdeveloped countries. The UN peacekeeping forces had already been spread too thin in Congo.

The UN peacekeeping mission also had already been weakened by "bitter opposition from the French and others....(And) to the very end Britain and Belgium decried the use of force to end the secession (of Katanga)."[34]

The United States and Belgium, of course, fully supported Moise Tshombe; so did apartheid South Africa, Rhodesia, and Portugal which was the oldest colonial power in Africa. The withdrawal of UN troops left the Congolese people entirely at the mercy of the mercenaries provided and funded by these very same countries.

One of the most frustrating experiences for the so-called Group of Six within the OAU – Nyerere, Nkrumah, Nasser, Ben Bella, Modibo Keita, and Sekou Toure – was that after the secession of Katanga was ended by UN forces, the rest of the OAU members were no longer interested in what was going on in Congo. And the OAU itself as a collective entity lost all interest in maintaining a UN peacekeeping mission in Congo despite the fact that the withdrawal of the peacekeeping troops would mean chaos.

Even leaders like Nkrumah and his colleagues in the Group of Six were not very enthusiastic about the UN operation for nationalistic reasons, although they conceded its necessity because of the inability of the Africans themselves to impose peace on Congo:

"15,000 to 20,000 UN troops entered the country. At first these were mainly from African states, for the Secretary-General felt that the Congo's neighbours should bear the burden of the operation....

The leftist states of Ghana, Guinea, and the United Arab Republic (Egypt), along with Morocco, envisaged their military contributions as support of Patrice Lumumba. At the start of 1961 they denounced the UN effort, and all but Ghana withdrew their small forces....

At this juncture India rallied to the UN's side with 4,000 combat troops. Equally significant politically was Ghana's decision to keep its token forces in the Congo. For President Nkrumah realized that all African efforts to put the Congo together had failed, though he could not publicly acknowledge that Africans could not manage their own affairs.

He hesitated also to support the Lumumba group in Stanleyville because he could not foresee what faction would triumph in a civil war after a UN withdrawal. Realizing that otherwise the Cold War would come to the heart of Africa with a vengeance, he, too, reluctantly supported the UN effort."[35]

As an ardent Pan-Africanist, Dr. Nkrumah's reluctance was understandable. He wanted Africans to take charge.

As he stated in his book, *Ghana: The Autobiography of Kwame Nkrumah*:

"It is far better to be free to govern or misgovern yourself than to be governed by anybody else."[36]

He also saw that the racial sovereignty of black Africans was at stake, as much as he did during the independence struggle when he said:

"It is only when people are politically free that other races can give them the respect that is due them. It is impossible to talk of equality of races in any other terms."[37]

With a stooge like Tshombe and later Mobutu, Congo was politically independent in name only; so were most countries in Francophone Africa – except Guinea under Sekou Toure and Mali under Modibo Keita – which remained satellites securely anchored in the French orbit. And when the situation in Congo degenerated into anarchy soon after independence, African countries wanted to play an active role in the resolution of the crisis for the same reason Western countries and others would like to resolve theirs without external intervention unless invited.

Therefore in supporting Tshombe, Western countries led by the United States did so in defiance of African continental sovereignty. As Uganda's Minister of State Mr. Grace Ibingira stated in January 1965 – before the bombing of two Ugandan villages by Congolese government forces using American-made-and-controlled planes – in asserting Africa's sovereignty and continental jurisdiction:

"The late President Kennedy demanded the Soviet withdrawal from Cuba on the grounds that Cuba was in the American sphere of influence....What is wrong when

African states demand to be responsible for the solution of the Congolese problem, since the Congo both geographically and even politically is naturally tied to them?"[38]

While the West was supporting Tshombe, the Congolese nationalists were also mobilising forces inside and outside the country.

The latest major fighting started in 1964. Revolts inspired and fuelled by the memory of Lumumba erupted in western Congo and threatened to spread or spark similar uprisings in other parts of the country.

The uprising was led by Pierre Mulele, guerrilla leader in Kwilu Province from 1963 to 1964. The 1964 revolt he led started in January and had an impact beyond the Congo. It was described by some observers as "the first great peasant uprising in an independent African country."[39]

Another writer, Ludo Martens, articulated the same position stating that the January 1964 insurgency led by Lumumba's education minister and spiritual and political heir, Pierre Mulele, was "the first great people's revolution against neocolonialism in post-independence Africa."[40] As the revolt spread, there was uncertainty in the government as to whether or not Lumumba's followers were about to win the war. Prime Minister Cyrille Adoula resigned.

His government was weak. He did not even have enough support in parliament; nor did he have a large national following or a powerful regional base which could have sustained him in office.

In July 1964, President Joseph Kasavubu appointed the notorious secessionist and Western puppet Moise Tshombe as prime minister. And that triggered even more violence from Lumumba's followers.

This was the second time that President Kasavubu had appointed a fervent tribalist as prime minister. Earlier in 1961 after Lumumba's assassination, he appointed Joseph

Ileo to that post. As Ileo bluntly stated in February 1961 within a month after Lumumba was murdered:

"The Congo is not a people. It is a collection of large ethnic groups and each of them is a people."[41]

Kasavubu himself was, of course, a tribalist with his strongest support coming from members of his ethnic group, the Bakongo, which was also his mother's. He was also partly Chinese and had clearly visible Oriental features; his maternal grandfather was Chinese.

Even the political party he led during the struggle for independence was solidly Bakongo, unlike Lumumba's which was national in scope, a feat that was never accomplished again.

Most Congolese leaders were, in fact, tribalist, including the nationalist guerrillas. That was one of the biggest problems which contributed to the defeat of the nationalist forces. And that was the kind of fiasco Che Guevara stepped into when he arrived in Congo about a year later in 1965.

But in spite of those difficulties, the uprising which started in Kwilu Province in western Congo spread eastwards throughout the first half of 1964.

The eastern front was led by Antoine Gizenga and Christopher Gbenye and other followers of Lumumba. Their operational base was Stanleyville, renamed Kisangani in 1971.

Lumumba's former aides in northern and eastern Congo had earlier formed the Committee for National Liberation (CNL) – also known as National Liberation Committee – which was supported by the Organisation of African Unity (OAU), the Soviet Union, and Cuba. Since it was supported by the OAU, it had the kind of legitimacy other insurgents did not have. And while the 1964 uprising was gaining momentum in the northeast, another leader arrived on the scene to help spearhead it in that region. He was "the dubious revolutionary, Gaston Sumialot."[42]

Since the early part of 1964, the Committee for National Liberation had established an operational base in Rwanda-Burundi close to the western shores of Lake Tanganyika and worked effectively within Congo itself.

By July 1964, not long after all UN troops had pulled out of the country at the end of June, the important mining town of Albertville, now called Kalemie, fell to the insurgents. Shortly thereafter in August, they captured Stanleyville, capital of eastern Congo and Lumumba's home region.

The establishment of an operational base in the Rwanda-Burundi area by the nationalist forces proved to be of great strategic importance. It was the only guerrilla base which survived when the insurgents were routed in late 1964. And that is where Che Guevara arrived in April 1965.

But his mission turned out to be not what he had expected. It was also one of the last two of his missions in the last two years of his life; the last was in Bolivia where he was killed in July 1967 in an operation masterminded by the CIA.

There were actually two guerrilla wars going on in Congo at the same time under two kinds of leadership. And both claimed to be the embodiment of Lumumba's ideals. As we noted earlier, there was the Committee for National Liberation operating in the northeast but which also served as an umbrella organisation; and the campaign in Kwilu Province in the west led by Pierre Mulele.

While the Committee for National liberation had more African and international backing, Mulele's insurgency was better organised. It was also more indigenous in inspiration, deeply rooted in Congolese society, and articulated a clearer ideological line, populist in content. Mulele was also acknowledged as a born-leader and the only one who could legitimately claim Lumumba's mantle of leadership. Antoine Gizenga also claimed the same honour since he had served as Lumumba's vice premier, while Mulele did as minister of education, yet did not have the charisma and populist appeal Mulele had.

But in spite of his legitimacy as Lumumba's successor, Mulele did not have a national following. His movement was confined to his regional and tribal base. It was supported by two tribes: the Bapende and the Bambunda in Kwilu Province in the west.

On the other hand, his rivals in the east captured more territory and therefore had a larger base. But the leaders of the eastern uprising were marred by corruption and personal rivalry and also had a reputation as cowards, at least a large number of them.

Neither of the two movements was extremist. In fact, the leaders of the Committee for National Liberation (CNL) in the east "maintained relations with both Belgian Foreign Minister Paul-Henri Spaak and the CIA station chief in the Congo, Laurence Devlin."[43]

However, that does not mean that the two Western countries most involved in Congo, the United States and Belgium, accepted the legitimacy of the CNL campaign, and for good reasons from the Western standpoint.

The insurgency in the east posed a serious threat to Belgium's economic interests in Congo represented by Union Miniere du Haut Katanga which owned Congo's vast mineral wealth and had earlier financed Tshombe's secessionist movement in Katanga Province and continued to support him in his new office as Congo's prime minister.

The CNL uprising was also seen as a threat to American geopolitical interests in Africa vis-a-vis the Soviet Union which was one of its main supporters, especially in such a strategically located and immensely rich country endowed with an abundance of natural resources.

The CNL was also a real danger to the South African and Rhodesian white mercenaries and Tshombe's Katangese secessionists who had wreaked so much havoc across the country, leading to the massacre of more than 100,000 Congolese. They all feared retaliation should the CNL shoot its way to victory. So the CIA decided to step in and destroy it.

The South African apartheid regime also came in with several hundred mercenaries led by the notorious bloodthirsty "Mad Mike" Hoare; so did the Belgians who had never really left Congo.

They all had one primary objective: wipe out the insurgents.

After they launched a full-scale offensive, they succeeded in isolating the CNL insurgents in Stanleyville, their nationalist stronghold. By November 1964, the nationalist forces were routed, but after putting up stiff resistance.

The final blow was delivered by Operation Dragon Rouge. That was when Belgian paratroops, South African and Rhodesian mercenaries and American "advisers" in American planes descended on Stanleyville with a vengeance and recaptured the eastern provincial capital. What followed was:

"A bloodbath, including the massacre of thousands of Congolese (including women and children) by South African mercenaries and the cold-blooded murder of about eighty Western hostages. The international outcry was deafening, but the mission succeeded. Though the rebels, called 'simbas' (meaning lions in Kiswahili), would survive in the area for years by November 1964 they were dispersed; and when, in March 1965, the white mercenaries captured the town of Watsa on the far eastern frontier...the rebellion was declared defeated....After the Dragon Rouge parachute operation in November 1964, the rebellion was not a serious threat."[44]

The massacre of thousands of Congolese in Stanleyville, including women, children and the elderly, was vehemently denounced by Che Guevara in his passionate speech to the UN General Assembly in December 1964 as head of the Cuban delegation.[45]

Many people, including Che, saw the rout of the nationalist forces in Stanleyville as a temporary setback and just another phase in the liberation struggle. They were years off target.

The Simba rebellion proved to be the last mass uprising in eastern Congo for more than 30 years until 1996 when Laurent Kabila emerged on the international scene as the leader of "the Alliance of Democratic Forces of Zaire and Congo"[46] which swept Mobutu out of power after a seven-month rebellion.

In Kwilu Province the insurgency, although weak and sporadic, went on until 1968 when its leader Pierre Mulele was tricked into accepting a "peace settlement" by General Joseph Mobutu, the military head of state who seized power three years earlier. Mobutu's rise to power was meteoric, from sergeant to general and president within a few years.

When fighting intensified after President Joseph Kasavubu appointed Tshombe prime minister in July 1964, Mobutu seized the opportunity as head of the army to position himself for the presidency. In October 1965, Kasavubu appointed Evariste Kimba to succeed Tshombe as prime minister. But neither – Kasavubu nor Kimba – lasted long in power.

Mobutu, now a general, proclaimed himself president and assumed full control on 25 November 1965. Kimba and other opponents, real and imagined, were hanged in a ruthless move by Mobutu to consolidate his position. He brooked no opposition and saw Mulele who was the embodiment of Lumumba's ideals as his biggest enemy; although Mulele no longer posed a serious military threat to the central government, and in fact never had, despite his lofty ideals.

And because Mobutu had played a critical role in the

assassination of Lumumba – he is the one who arrested him and had him flown to Elisabethville, Katanga, to be executed – he could not tolerate anyone who tried to resurrect the martyred independence hero as Mulele was trying to do by furthering Lumumba's ideals.

So, Mobutu set out to capture Mulele who was then living in exile in Brazzaville, the capital of the Congo Republic, just across the River Congo River from Kinshasa, then still known as Leopoldville, the capital of the former Belgian Congo. He used an amnesty offer to entice him.

The amnesty offer was extended even to some of the most brutal and notorious characters who served under Tshombe when he tried to dismember the country by declaring Katanga an independent state. When Mobutu offered the amnesty, he was secure in power and therefore had nothing to fear from his opponents. According to *Africa Contemporary Record 1968 - 1969*:

"The effectiveness of the President's administration was reflected in August (1968) by the release of all 19 political prisoners, including Godefroid Munongo, right-hand man of former President (Prime Minister) Tshombe. The officially-stated purpose of the amnesty was to facilitate national reconciliation."[47]

However, the unofficial and real purpose of the "amnesty" was to lure Mulele back to Kinshasa. And what happened to him when he returned to his home country contradicts the official version of what the amnesty was all about:

"One of the serious consequences of this amnesty, whether deliberately designed or not, was the subsequent execution of Pierre Mulele, the 39-year-old guerrilla leader of Kwilu Province from 1963 – 4, who was in exile in the neighbouring Congo Republic at the time.

Justin Bomboko (Mobutu's Foreign Minister who had also served under Lumumba in the same capacity) crossed the Congo River four times to urge Mulele to leave Brazzaville and to take advantage of the amnesty.

In an interview with Bomboko on 28 September – the day Mulele had agreed to return to Kinshasa on General Mobutu's Presidential yacht – Radio Brazzaville quoted the Foreign Minister as saying that Mulele believed the present Congolese regime was following Lumumba's ideal, so he now wished to take part in the country's current fight for economic independence.

The Kinshasa radio announced on the same day that Mulele's safety was assured by the government which was working towards national reconciliation.

Signed assurances had been given to the Brazzaville authorities, who were thus convinced that the amnesty would apply to Mulele.

On his arrival in Kinshasa, Mulele was received with all the honours due to his former office as Lumumba's Minister of Education. A reception was arranged in his honour at the residence of the Army Commander, General Louis de Gonzague Bobozo.

There was no hint of a reprisal until President Mobutu's return from an official visit to Morocco when he announced that 'the amnesty Decree was not intended to rehabilitate the rebel leaders who killed, burned and plunged whole regions into misery,' adding that Mulele would be tried as a 'war criminal.' Before a military tribunal *in camera*, and without legal representation, Mulele was condemned to death on 8 October and executed on the following day."[48]

In addition to the treachery of Mobutu's government for not honouring its promise of a blanket amnesty it claimed covered everybody including Mulele, Mobutu himself compounded the felony by saying that the amnesty decree did not apply to those who had killed, burned, and

166

wreaked havoc across the country.

JUSTIN BOMBOKO

Yet he could not explain why he went on to pardon Tshombe's top aides, including Tshombe's highly notorious right-hand man Godefroid Munongo, who plunged not regions but the whole country into anarchy, resulting in the death of tens of thousands of people when they led Katanga into secession, and even when Tshombe himself became prime minister of the Congo. If they deserved amnesty, why not Mulele? Mulele may also have believed the offer of amnesty was genuine because it was presented to him by Justin Bomboko whom he had known before when they were ministers in the same cabinet under Lumumba.

Mulele's uprising was not even as widespread as Tshombe's anarchy. It was confined mainly to his home region, Kwilu Province. And he was not a traitor like Tshombe. He was fighting to implement the ideals of Lumumba, the nation's independence leader who still had a large number of supporters in all parts of the country unlike Mobutu.

In fact, as late as the seventies, Lumumba was still the most popular leader Congo, far more popular than Mobutu, in spite of Mobutu's stature as president of a country he had supposedly rescued from anarchy, only to ruin it. As Crawford Young, professor of political science at the University of Wisconsin-Madison who once served as dean of the social science faculty at the National

167

University of Zaire, Lubumbashi, from 1973 to 1975, stated in his article "Zaire: The Unending Crisis" in *Foreign Affairs*:

"A 1975 survey of university students in the Kisangani heartland of Lumumbism provides fascinating evidence....The five African countries most esteemed, aside from Zaire, were Senegal, Congo-Brazzaville, Tanzania, Zambia, and Ivory Coast in that order. The three most admired African leaders were Kwame Nkrumah, Leopold Senghor, and Felix Houphouet-Boigny....Some 61 percent of the Kisangani students named Lumumba as the most important Zairian leader, with Mobutu coming in (a distant) second with (only) 11 percent."[49]

Unfortunately, because of tribalism, Mulele never commanded a large national following like his spiritual and ideological mentor Lumumba in spite of his stature and status as Lumumba's successor. But his end was as tragic as Lumumba's.

Both were betrayed, brutally murdered, and their bodies disposed of in the most gruesome way. Lumumba's body is said to have been dissolved in sulfuric acid. He was also severely beaten and tortured before being executed. Mulele fared no better; nor did his movement which was torn by tribal dissension and mostly supported by only two tribes, the Bapende and the Bambunda:

"The uprising in Kwilu dragged on until late 1968, when Pierre Mulele finally surrendered, theoretically in the context of a negotiated peace, to Mobutu Sese Seko. He was promptly dismembered, and his remains readily fed to the crocodiles of the Congo River.

In reality, however, his movement had been condemned by internal divisions since March 14, 1965. On that day, 'a grave defeat shattered Mulele's prestige and any faith in the future of the movement. The unity of Mulelism was broken; many youth abandoned the guerrilla movement. It was Mulele's only decision based on tribal considerations, but it had disastrous repercussions for him'."[50]

Thus, with the Committee for National Liberation (CNL) forces almost neutralised after the fall of Stanleyville in August 1964, and the virtual collapse of Mulele's nationalist movement in March 1965; the intervention of the six African countries – Tanzania, Ghana, Algeria, Egypt, Guinea, and Mali – after that to help Lumumba's followers came too late, as Ben Bella put it.

Che Guevara also came after the guerrilla movement had collapsed. Therefore his mission was a failure from the beginning even before he set foot on African soil on his way to Congo.

He arrived in Algiers, Algeria, on 14 December 1964 after leading the Cuban delegation to the UN General Assembly. By the time he arrived in the Algerian capital, the first stop among a number of African capitals he was to visit, the insurgency in eastern Congo led by the Committee for National Liberation (CNL) had fizzled out. The nationalist campaign led by the CNL, and by Mulele in Kwilu Province in the west, failed because of the geostrategic significance of Congo, located in the heart of Africa with immense mineral wealth. Every major world power was after this prized possession.

While in Algiers, Guevara – in addition to reviewing the situation in Africa with Ben Bella – talked not only with the Congolese nationalists but also with guerrilla leaders from the Portuguese colonies of Angola, Mozambique, and Portuguese Guinea (Guinea-Bissau).

He soon realised that the nationalist campaign in Congo was handicapped by two major problems. The first one was lack of united leadership and coordinated military campaigns – Mulele's and CNL's – under central command. In the next three months, he visited eight

African countries, promoting the idea (the imperative need for unity), but without success.

From left: Lumumba, Kasavubu, and Bomboko

The second problem involved securing continued assistance from the Soviet Union and the People's Republic of China for both groups on harmonious basis. The Soviet Union supported the Committee for National Liberation, while the Chinese backed Mulele.

Guevara sought to coordinate the flow of aid from the two powers but was frustrated in his effort by the Sino-Soviet rivalry in Africa.

Compounding the problem was the fact that assistance was not always obtained when it was needed, although the guerrillas ended up obtaining a lot of weapons. "Thus Che's emphasis on a third task during those months: persuading Ben Bella and other African leaders to fill in for tardy or inadequate Soviet and Chinese assistance as much as possible."[51]

Guevara continued with his African journey. On 26

December 1964, he left Algiers and flew to Bamako, the capital of Mali. The decision for him to go to Mali first before going anywhere else was attributed to Ben Bella who, according to an interview with him on 4 November 1995, "considered Modibo Keita the senior and most respected member of the group of Six,"[52] comprising Ben Bella, Modibo Keita, Nkrumah, Nyerere, Nasser, and Sekou Toure, the most uncompromising Pan-Africanists within the Organisation of African Unity (OAU).

And according to Jorge Castaneda who interviewed Ben Bella, Guevara's visit to Bamako "did not receive much attention: the joint communique was not signed by any member of the Politburo or senior minister. President Keita usually took holidays at Christmas, and there was no public welcome for Che in the streets of Bamako. Even press coverage was scant. The visit was in all likelihood scheduled at the last moment."[53]

That is probably because those who planned Che's African trip, including Che himself, did not want his activities publicized. In fact, according to an American intelligence cable, now declassified, none of the embassies or other representatives in Cuba of the countries Guevara visited were notified of his movements:

"According to a cable from the US Embassy in the Hague, Dutch sources in Havana reported this information."[54]

According to the same sources, Guevara's African trip was arranged from New York by the Cuban ambassador to Algiers, Jorge Serguera. That probably explains why Algiers was his first stop in his tour of a number of African capitals, Bamako, Mali, being his second.

In his talks with the leaders of Mali, Che emphatically stated that Cuba had made a mistake in aligning herself too closely with the Soviet Union and the People's Republic of China, according to the Mali cabinet minister who received him.[55]

On 1 January 1965, Che Guevara flew from Bamako to Brazzaville where he established some of the closest ties between Cuba and an African country. He also announced that 20 young men from the young African republic would undergo military training in Cuba. A few months later, a number of Cuban troops led by Jorge Risquet were sent to Brazzaville to provide security for President Alphonse Massemba-Debat.

Some of the black Cuban soldiers who went with Che Guevara to the former Belgian Congo in April 1965 later joined the presidential guard for Massemba-Debat in Brazzaville. When soldiers executed a coup three years later which ousted Massemba-Debat, the Cubans were still there. As Colin Legum and John Drysdale state:

"In July (1966), Massemba-Debat was nearly deposed when a military coup d'etat was thwarted by the loyalty of the Civic Guard (which included Cubans), a body exceeding the strength of the army. Yet, paradoxically, the Civic Guard was affiliated to the (ruling) party's left-wing youth movement (JMNR) which had been trained by Cuban instructors....

Although both factions of the army (one led by those who rose traditionally through the ranks and the other by younger officers some of them trained abroad) and the government appeared to have reached a compromise, the crisis was not in fact resolved.

The Civic Guard and JMNR were dissatisfied with the state of affairs, and fighting broke out at the end of August (1968). The headquarters of the dissident faction of the Civic Guard was the meteorology camp, where some Cuban instructors still remained."[56]

In December 1963, a year before Che Guevara went to Africa, Massemba-Debat had been elected to a five-year term as president and forged links with Cuba, the Soviet

Union, and China. On 3 August 1968, he was stripped of most of his powers by the army. He remained in office only as a figurehead. About a month later on 5 September, he was forced to resign.

The man behind the coup, Captain Marien Ngouabi in his twenties, did not become the new head of state but was the real power behind the new government, like Nasser was after the 1952 military coup in Egypt when General Mohammed Naguib became president in June 1953, only to be ousted by Nasser in November 1954.

Ngouabi was even more militant – Massemba-Debat had mellowed by the time he was ousted – and strengthened his ties with Cuba which Guevara had established in January 1965. On 1 January 1969, Ngouabi, promoted to major, became president, three years after Guevara left Africa.

While in Brazzaville in January 1965, Guevara also met with Dr. Agostinho Neto, the leader and founder of the Popular Movement for the Liberation of Angola (MPLA) waging guerrilla warfare against the Portuguese colonialists in Angola. It was the beginning of a long relationship between Cuba and Angola. The Cubans went on to support the MPLA in its liberation struggle which ended in victory in 1975. It was only in 1992 that Cuban troops finally left Angola.

They went to Angola during the seventies and played a critical role in pushing back South African soldiers who invaded that country – with American support – in an attempt to install a pro-Western regime; also to neutralise guerrilla fighters of the South West African People's Organisation (SWAPO) who used Angola as an operational base in their independence struggle against the illegal occupation of their country by apartheid South Africa.

Guevara stayed in Brazzaville for six days. From there he flew to Conakry, capital of Guinea, where he stayed from January 7th to January 14th. He met with President

Sekou Toure, an old friend, who also – like Ben Bella and a few others – was one of the biggest African supporters of the Cuban revolution. Guevara was warmly received in Guinea. But it was a different story when he travelled to neighbouring Senegal. Yet he never failed to say what he wanted to say, which was both a plea and a warning:

"(In Guinea), he was received more effusively than in Mali, except when he travelled with the President's (Sekou Toure's) entourage to meet with Leopold Senghor, the President of Senegal. The poet of *negritude* and his aides were 'indignant' at Guevara's inclusion in talks among African leaders.

Che renewed his call for support to liberation movements in Africa, emphasizing the need for unity in the 'struggle against imperialism.' The Congolese and other movements had to be united within and among themselves, and should draw closer to the Socialist countries, especially the two great powers (the Soviet Union and China). But not too close."[57]

As expected, the CIA was on his trail wherever he went. In a secret cable dated 15 January 1965, now declassified, the CIA reported that one of Guevara's concerns during his African trip "was to warn 'their friends' not to get too deep with the Soviet or Chinese communists. According to Guevara, while Cuba was as dedicated as ever to socialism, Cuban officials were very unhappy about the depth of interference in their internal affairs by the USSR and Communist China. Guevara said that it was too late for Cuba to do anything about it but that the Cubans felt it was not too late for the Africans to redress the situation. Guevara added that the Cubans were especially concerned about their friends the Algerians, and that he was proceeding directly to Algiers to deliver the same message to Ben Bella."[58]

Although the CIA cable was dated 15 January 1965, it

quoted information dated late December 1964. Guevara arrived in Algiers on 18 December 1964 on a flight from New York.

And that explains why the CIA in its cable stated that Che Guevara "was proceeding directly to Algiers to deliver the same message to Ben Bella" about not getting too close to the two communist powers; for, it was in Algiers that Guevara publicly expressed his anger at the Soviet Union, although he did that in February 1965.

But he undoubtedly warned Ben Bella right away when they met privately in December 1964. The warning must also have resonated well with the leaders in Conakry, Guinea, and in the Senegalese capital Dakar where the Francophile leadership, being pro-Western, was already not very friendly with the two communist giants.

Sekou Toure himself, a socialist, had already taken that step, suggested by Che Guevara, long before the Cuban leader went to Guinea. Back in December 1961, Toure expelled the Soviet ambassador for interfering in Guinea's domestic affairs, a move which surprised those who thought Guinea was a Soviet satellite.[59]

From Senegal, Che Guevara went to Ghana where he held extensive talks with President Kwame Nkrumah about the African situation. While still in Accra, Ghana's capital, Che also met with Laurent Kabila, the Congolese guerrilla leader based in eastern Congo on the western shores of Lake Tanganyika where Guevara would establish his guerrilla base:

"At least this is the account provided by Oscar Fernandez Mell (in an interview in Havana, Cuba, on 24 August 1996) who met Kabila in Dar es Salaam and spent four months with Che in the Congo."[60]

Che Guevara first arrived in Congo in April 1965. He went through Tanzania which also served as his operational base, especially Kigoma in western Tanzania;

Che and the other Cubans on the Congo mission also had a safe house in an area near the Dar es Salaam international airport.

More than 30 years after Che Guevara first went to Congo to support the nationalist forces, Laurent Kabila finally succeeded in ousting Mobutu from power in May 1997 after a life-long struggle – punctuated by years of absence from the combat zone – he had waged since he was in his early twenties as one of Lumumba's followers.

He spent most of those years in Tanzania which also served as a springboard for his operations against Mobutu, including the successful insurgency in 1996 –1997 that culminated in the ouster of one of Africa's most notorious and longest-ruling despots and which was supported by a number of African countries besides Tanzania.

Others were Rwanda and Uganda, the frontline states during the 1996 – 1997 rebellion; Burundi, Angola, Ethiopia, Eritrea, and even Zambia during the early stages of the offensive against Mobutu's regime.

Little did Che Guevara or anybody else back then in the sixties know that it would be another 30 years or so before the Western puppet regime in Congo would finally be defeated and ousted from power.

At the end of January 1965, Che Guevara returned to Algiers to talk to Ben Bella about his African tour during which he discussed the subject of the African liberation struggle with a number of African leaders including guerrilla fighters.

According to Ben Bella, Che believed that Africa was the best place to wage revolution and bring about fundamental change which would have global impact. As Ben Bella stated in an interview in Geneva, Switzerland, in November 1995:

"(Guevara had reached the conclusion that) Africa was the continent in the world most favourable for great changes; Africa set the course for the renewal of the anti-imperialist struggle."[61]

Guevara also felt that Congo was the best country in which to wage a revolution because it had two guerrilla movements already going on: one in the west led by Pierre Mulele, and the other one in the east led by the Committee for National Liberation (CNL). He also thought that because the United States was tied down in Vietnam, she would not be able to directly intervene in Congo on a large scale and turn back the tide.

Congo also reminded him of Bolivia, the country he felt was best suited for revolution in the entire Latin America. Bolivia was landlocked and bordered by many countries; so was Congo – bordered by nine – whose borders, at least some of them, were porous enough to serve as an outlet and compensate for the country's lack of direct access to the sea besides the Congo River.

There was yet another reason for Guevara's attraction to Congo as the ideal territory for revolution:

"Another decisive element in Che's approach to Africa, in Serguera's view, was its geostrategic situation. According to the Cuban ambassador to Algiers, who would later be accused of having 'dragged' Che into Africa by painting a rosy picture for him, Guevara gambled that the Soviet Union would tolerate Cuban support for the struggle in Africa, even if this was not quite the case in Latin America. Moreover, a success in Africa might induce Moscow to view more favorably Cuba's support for the revolution in Latin America."[62]

In an interview on 23 January 1996 in Havana, Jorge Serguera, the Cuban ambassador to Algeria during that time went on to say that Che Guevara also felt that Africa was somewhat of a no-man's land where the big powers had not yet established their spheres of influence.[63]

Guevara was probably, by analogy, thinking in terms of

177

the United States' influence in Latin America and domination by the Soviet Union of her satellites in Eastern Europe – where both super powers respected each other's hegemony – vis-a-vis Africa. He was wrong on both counts.

Neither super power, not even China, would hesitate to intervene in Africa at any cost if it felt that its interests were at stake. That was clearly demonstrated by American intervention in Congo where the United States even installed a puppet regime as much as she did in South Vietnam.

It was also demonstrated by Soviet and Chinese intervention as well, in Congo, although neither of the latter was as big and as effective as American intervention during the sixties and all the way through the years to the 1990s and beyond. Soviet intervention (although smaller than Cuba's) in Angola during the seventies where American clients – UNITA and the FNLA – lost the war also refuted Guevara's thesis. American surrogate forces in Angola included the South African army and air force.

Guevara's African journey also took him to Cairo, Egypt, during those early months in 1965. He went to Cairo twice; first, on February 11th when he returned from China, and in March when he spent three weeks in the Egyptian capital on his way back to Cuba from Tanzania. In his conversations with Nasser, he told him, only in general terms, what he intended to do next:

"First of all, Nasser detected in Che a 'deep personal anguish' and great sadness. Che did not discuss his inner concerns; he told Nasser only that he was going to Tanzania to study the prospects of the liberation movements in the Congo....

When he returned from Tanzania along with Pablo Ribalta, Che's ambassador in Dar es Salaam, Guevara recounted to Nasser his visit to the guerrilla camps in the vortex of the Congo-Tanzania-Burundi.

He had made up his mind to personally direct Cuban assistance to the Congolese rebels: 'I think I will go to the Congo because it is the hottest place in the world today. With the help of the Africans through the Committee in Tanzania, and with two battalions of Cubans, I believe we can strike at the heart of the imperialists' interests in Katanga.'"[64]

According to Mohammed Heikal, the influential editor of the Egyptian newspaper *Al-Ahram* whose editorials reflected official thinking and who also took notes of the conversations between President Nasser and Guevara, the Egyptian leader was greatly surprised when he heard what Che said and tried to convince him otherwise.

Nasser told him that because he was a white man and a foreigner, any attempt by him to lead blacks in Congo would be misinterpreted as a replay of Tarzan in real life. Guevara knew, of course, how offensive such a caricature of the African personality was to black people in general including those in the United States and elsewhere who felt offended as much as those in Africa.

He himself, according to Serguera in an interview in 1996, was greatly moved by racial oppression Africans – those at home and those in the diaspora – had suffered for centuries. As Prime Minister Jawaharlal Nehru of India stated in 1961:

"Reading through history I think the agony of the African continent...has not been equalled anywhere."[65]

But in spite of the danger that his attempt to help, however well-intentioned, could be misconstrued by Africans as a form of racial arrogance by a white person who thought he knew what was best for black people and was the only one best qualified to lead them, Guevara remained adamant in his position and even asked Nasser to commit troops to the cause. But Nasser denied his request, stating:

"If you go to the Congo with two Cuban battalions and I send an Egyptian battalion, it will be seen as a foreign intervention and do more harm than good."[66]

At that late date in the Congo crisis – "We arrived in the Congo too late," as Ben Bella put it – Nasser was obviously resigned to doing what he felt he could do best: train the Congolese guerrillas to fight the war themselves; not because he had turned a blind eye to the plight of the Congolese. After all, it was Nasser who undertook the responsibility of taking care of Lumumba's wife and children and had them taken to Egypt after the Congolese leader was assassinated.

He also allowed Cairo, Egypt's capital, to become the first major centre of refuge for African freedom fighters; used Cairo Radio to propagate worldwide on its external service information about the liberation struggle on the continent; and actively participated in the "struggle against the forces of neo-colonialism in the Congo"[67] more than most African leaders did except Nyerere, Nkrumah, Ben Bella, Milton Obote, Kenneth Kaunda, Sekou Toure, and Modibo Keita. As Nasser himself stated back in 1954 about the liberation struggle in Africa in his book, *The Philosophy of the Revolution*:

"We cannot, under any condition, even if we want to, stand aloof from the terrible and terrifying battle now raging in the heart of that continent between 5 million whites and 200 million Africans. We cannot stand aloof for one important and obvious reason – we ourselves are in Africa....

There is no denying the fact that Africa is now the scene of a strange and stirring commotion. The white man...is again trying to change the map of the continent. We surely cannot, under any condition, stand as mere onlookers, deluding ourselves into the belief that we are in no way concerned with these machinations."[68]

Therefore, Nasser's opposition to Guevara's mission to Congo was based on harsh realities, military and political, including the sensitive issue of race: black guerrillas in the heart of Africa being led by a white man from thousands of miles away.

Ben Bella also tried to dissuade Guevara from pursuing his Congo mission for the same reasons and warned him against playing saviour of black Africans. The racial issue was too delicate to be dismissed lightly. As he stated in an interview in November 1995:

"The situation in black Africa was not comparable to that prevailing in our countries; Nasser and I, we warned Che of what might happen."[69]

But Che Guevara was determined to go on with his mission despite the odds against it, especially in view of the recent defeat of the nationalist forces in Stanleyville in August 1964.

While in Cairo, Che held meetings with the Congolese nationalist leaders who fled their country after they were routed in Stanleyville by a combined invasion force of Belgian paratroops, South African mercenaries, and the Americans who provided planes, weapons and other material and logistical support.

Gaston Soumialot who lived on Zamalek island in Egypt met with Guevara several times on that island to discuss the armed struggle in Congo. Che also met again with Laurent Kabila who was one of the two vice-presidents of the National Liberation Committee (CNL). The other vice-president was Pierre Mulele.

Kabila was supposed to be leading the guerrilla campaign in eastern Congo from his operational base on the western shores of Lake Tanganyika; which he hardly was. Compounding the problem was the fact that the nationalist forces had been defeated in Stanleyville, and Mulele's campaign in the west had virtually collapsed, wracked by tribal divisions, although it did not completely die out until 1968.

Also, Mulele was not in Cairo, Egypt, or in Dar es Salaam, Tanzania, both serving as sanctuaries for the Congolese nationalists and others; he was living in exile in Brazzaville and it was not easy for him to travel freely in and out of the country, given the nature of his operations as a guerrilla leader.

All those factors complicated efforts by the nationalist guerrillas to mobilise funds and secure greater political support.

They therefore had to come up with a rescue plan in order to legitimise their campaign and obtain enough assistance to sustain the insurgency. That meant inflating figures as well as military preparedness and capability of the nationalist forces.

But it proved to be a formidable task. In eastern Congo, not only did Kabila's army lack capable fighters; it also lacked morale. The only credible element Kabila's "army" had was its potential capacity to establish a place of refuge in Kigoma, a Tanzanian port on Lake Tanganyika, for its guerrillas.

In mid-February 1965, Che Guevara, then in Dar es Salaam, left the Tanzanian capital and went to Congo via Kigoma to look at the guerrilla bases on the western shores of Lake Tanganyika.

What he found was pathetic. The guerrilla fighters he met were hardly soldiers by definition. Kabila's "army" needed all the help it could get in order to become a credible fighting force. That explains why Guevara insisted on sending Cuban soldiers to train the guerrillas and even provide a back-up force, although not to go into combat with them, let alone fight on their behalf. But that is exactly what happened.

The Cubans ended up on the battlefield, literally fighting a Congolese war for the Congolese. However, their military involvement was short and took place towards the end of their stay in Congo when they fought back in order to escape safely to Tanzania. As Jorge Castaneda states:

"Later, Che would spend long and frustrating months in the Congo waiting, in vain, for Laurent Kabila to lead his own troops into combat....Indeed, Guevara's adventure in the Congo would consist largely of the successive traps he fell into.

The expedition never recovered from the procrastination and corruption of Congolese leaders like Gaston Sumialot, Laurent Kabila, and Christopher Gbenye, who were supposedly struggling for their country's liberation. In the end, Che did realize how mistaken he was, but by then it was too late."[70]

Even more telling was Guevara's frustration with the Congolese nationalist leaders. They preached revolution but hardly practised it. They claimed they were fighting for the masses; yet, by comparison, they were living in magnificent splendour. They said they were on the battlefield, while they were in hotels, socialising.

It is true, they faced a big enemy, formidable forces marshalled by Western powers. But they also defeated themselves from within because of personal rivalry, tribalism, and their desire for comfort, hardly the life of a revolutionary. All that had a devastating impact on the guerrilla forces.

Jon Lee Anderson in his biography, *Che Guevara: A Revolutionary Life*, which, like Castaneda's, was also published in 1997, shows how little regard Guevara had for the Congolese nationalists in pursuit of power and personal glory. It is an assessment shared by Castaneda who, in his work, draws striking parallels between the

Congolese nationalist leaders and other Third World politicians.

Most of the Congolese leaders were "like many leaders of Afro-Asian decolonization – with the major exceptions of Ho Chi Minh, Nehru, Nyerere, and Nasser – essentially devious and corrupt reactionar(ies)."[71]

But Guevara's own searing indictment of the Congolese "revolutionaries" is probably the most powerful.

In an unpublished letter he wrote Fidel Castro from the shores of Lake Tanganyika in October 1965 just before he moved to Tanzania's capital Dar es Salaam where he stayed for many months, Guevara severely criticised the Congolese guerrilla leaders who had just been treated like royalty in Havana, soldiers he thought he could count on when he went to Congo to join the struggle against imperialism. He found them to be a despicable lot. As he told Castro in the letter:

"Sumialot and his companions have sold you an enormous bridge. It would take me forever to enumerate the huge number of lies they told you....I know Kabila well enough to have no illusions in his regard....

I have some background on Sumialot, like for example the lies he told you, the fact that he has not set foot on this godforsaken land, his frequent drinking bouts in Dar es Salaam, where he stays in the best hotels....

They are given huge amounts of money, all at once, to live splendidly in every African capital, not to mention that they are housed by the main progressive countries who often finance their travel expenses....The scotch and the women are also covered by friendly governments and if one likes good scotch and beautiful women, that costs a lot of money."[72]

Jon Lee Anderson in his autobiography on Che also notes how Guevara was disgusted with the Congolese nationalist leaders, including Kabila who was just riding around in Tanzania's capital Dar es Salaam in a green Mercedes Benz instead of being on the war front leading his troops. It was Che Guevara, instead, who was with those soldiers in Congo, fighting.[73]

Because of such bad leadership, the guerrillas fighting the CIA-installed regime in Kinshasa were very demoralized. Even the best weapons would not have helped rectify the situation.

Tribalism within the nationalist groups was also, like poor leadership, not a foreign-inspired but a home-grown problem, although Tshombe, Mobutu and their Western supporters also exploited it, making the situation worse. But that does not, in any way, make Kabila – or any other leader – any less responsible for ignoring his troops. In fact, he himself tried to build a guerrilla army based on tribal loyalties. As Christopher Hitchens states:

"At this time, Che Guevara formed a rather low opinion of Kabila, whose base and whose tactics were too tribal, who demonstrated a tendency toward megalomania, and who maltreated deserters and prisoners."[74]

But in spite of Guevara's disappointment, his biggest enemy in Congo, the CIA, did not win laurels, either, for what it did. It is true that Che Guevara failed in his mission. "Still, Mobutu had been the jewel in the CIA's African crown. So perhaps not all the historical ironies turn out to be at Guevara's expense."[75]

Guevara's analysis of the situation on the ground was still somewhat optimistic – he never gave up hoping for the best until he was killed less than two years later in Bolivia in July 1967 – as can be noted from his field journals in Congo, although he knew by then that everything was hopeless:

"There are two zones in which one might say there is

185

an organized attempt at revolution: the area where we are, and part of the province held by Mulele, who remains a big mystery. In the rest of the country there are only isolated bands surviving in the jungle; they lost everything without even fighting, just as they lost Stanleyville without a fight."[76]

The situation was worse than that. The Congolese nationalist guerrillas were hardly fighting, if at all. In eastern Congo where Che Guevara was, along the western shores of Lake Tanganyika, it was the Cubans, not the Congolese, who did the actual fighting, although the fiery encounter with the enemy was brief.

Mulele's insurgency in Kwilu Province in the west was dying slowly. And in Stanleyville, the nationalist forces had been routed by November 1964 – after losing the city in August the same year – by a combined force of Belgian paratroops, South African mercenaries, and American guns and planes as well as 'advisers," who massacred thousands of innocent Congolese including women and children.

In other words, the revolution Che Guevara went to join in Congo was over even before Che himself arrived.

It was when he was on his African tour in the early part of 1965 that Guevara decided to join the Congolese guerrillas without even going back to Cuba. Cubans closest to him confirmed that. They include Pablo Ribalta whom he had appointed as ambassador to Tanzania in preparation for his Congo mission. As Castaneda, who talked to several of Guevara's aides in Cuba and elsewhere in 1995 and 1996, states:

"Cuban sources have confirmed that Che decided to join the Congo rebellion before he returned to Havana.

The first is Cuba's former ambassador to Tanzania, Pablo Ribalta, dispatched to Africa by Che as his advance man in February 1964....In an interview with the author, in Havana, on January 23, 1996, Ribalta (said he) believes without a doubt that Che had determined to take the revolution beyond Cuba ever since his trip to the United Nations (in December 1964 as head of the Cuban delegation to the General Assembly where he gave a fiery speech condemning the American-backed Belgian invasion of Stanleyville in August the same year)....

By mid-January 1965 Che was obviously inclined to head for Africa permanently....(During) his week in Tanzania, he visited guerrilla camps in the Congo and verified the ideal rearguard position tacitly provided by the republic founded by Julius Nyerere,...the rebels' foremost supporter."[77]

While still in Africa, Guevara travelled from Algiers to China at the end of January 1965 to try to improve relations between Cuba and China which had deteriorated because Castro – unlike Guevara – had taken sides with the Soviet Union in the Sino-Soviet conflict.

By contrast, Guevara had publicly denounced the Soviet Union on February 24th when he was in Algiers, officially breaking with the communist giant; yet, he was still a Cuban leader, the closest to Castro besides Castro's younger brother Raul who was defence minister and who years later became president of Cuba, replacing his ailing brother. He became Cuba's acting president in 2006 in place of Fidel who was temporarily out of office because of an illness although the older brother remained in full control even form his hospital bed. Raul assumed full control in 2008 when he officially became president of Cuba.

Guevara knew that without Chinese approval, Cuban support for the Congolese guerrillas would not succeed for obvious reasons: the Chinese besides the Soviets provided weapons and were the biggest supporters of Pierre Mulele, although Mullele's guerrilla operation was by then a spent force.

Still, the other guerrilla group Che was working with in

eastern Congo needed weapons from China; also from the Soviet Union. But they came mostly from China. And they had to go through Tanzania which had very good relations with China; so did the weapons from the Soviet Union. They all came in through Tanzania.

Therefore antagonizing the Chinese would have meant no weapons for the Congolese nationalists and may be even no access through Tanzania.

But Guevara's mission to China, which besides being an attempt to improve Cuba's relations with the communist giant was also an attempt to improve Sino-Soviet relations, failed. So, he returned to Africa and went straight to Tanzania, the country which provided a safe haven for the Congolese guerrillas and for Che Guevara himself during his mission to the Congo:

"After his ten days in Beijing, Che arrived in Dar es Salaam on February 13 (1965). He was welcomed at the airport by a second-level minister, and the visit was relegated to inner pages by the local press. Perhaps Julius Nyerere had an inkling of what was afoot.

Che soon perceived the effects of his failed mission to China. The official dinner, hosted by the foreign minister (Oscar Kambona), was attended by all the African ambassadors and the Soviet representative, but there was nobody from the Chinese Embassy."[78]

In spite of the failure of his rapprochment mission to China, Guevara immediately began explaining to the Congolese guerrilla leaders in Tanzania how Cuban help would be provided to them to carry on their military campaign. He told Kabila that the fate of Congo was inextricably linked with that of the rest of the world. As Che himself stated, he offered Kabila "on behalf of the government (of Cuba) to send about thirty instructors and whatever arms we could. He accepted them gladly, recommending that we hurry, as did Sumialot; the latter also suggested that the instructors be black."[79]

Guevara then had lengthy discussions with the guerrilla fighters in the Tanzanian capital Dar es Salaam to determine for himself their readiness for waging guerrilla warfare. It was a large meeting attended by more than 50 guerrilla leaders from about 10 countries. They asked for Cuban assistance to carry on their military campaign, but drew a firm and cautious response from Che Guevara:

"I analyzed the requests they had expressed, almost unanimously, for financial help and training. I explained the cost of sending people to Cuba, the amount of money and time required, and the little certainty that they would return as combatants useful to the movement....

So I proposed that training take place not in our faraway Cuba, but in the nearby Congo, where the struggle was not against a puppet like Tshombe, but against United States imperialism....I spoke to them of the fundamental importance...of the liberation struggle in the Congo....

Their reaction was more than cold; though most refrained from making any comments, some asked for the floor to reproach me violently for my advice. They argued that their people, mistreated and debased by imperialism, would claim if there were victims that they would have died not for their own country, but to liberate another State. I tried to make them see that this was not a struggle bounded by any border, but a war against a common enemy, present everywhere...but nobody saw it in this light.

It became clear to us that there was a long way to go in Africa before achieving a truly revolutionary leadership, but we were glad to have met people who were ready to fight to the end. From that time, our task was to select a group of black Cubans, volunteers of course, and send them to reinforce the struggle in the Congo."[80]

Guevara also noted in his Congo journals that Laurent Kabila asked him to lead Cuban operations in Africa. Che said he did not share that view. In mid-March 1965, he went back to Cuba, having laid the groundwork for his return to Africa to pursue his mission in Congo. Castro sent a plane of the Cuban airline to Tanzania to fly Che Guevara back to Cuba.

Although he would return to Africa, he knew the difficulties he would encounter when he embarked on his mission to the continent. He noted that "the people in Africa had no sense of nationality; each tribe had its own chief, territory, and nation even though they all lived within a single territory."[81]

And that is fair characterisation. More than a generation later, Africa is still riven with ethnic tensions and rivalries some of which have exploded into full-scale war with unconstrained fury in a number of countries through the years. Guevara would not be surprised if he was still alive today to see what is going on in African countries. When he returned to Cuba:

"It was almost certainly at that time that a unit of about a hundred men, commanded by Che, was formed to train and support the Congo freedom fighters and, if necessary, to fight at their side – though never in their stead.

Perhaps some of the combatants were selected before the hasty decision to send them was actually made; others, like the subordinates of Rafael del Pino in the air force, were called up a few days before Che's return to Cuba.

Del Pino was instructed to pick out the 'blackest' troops from the Holguin base, especially those with anti-aircraft combat experience, since a large number of anti-Castro Cuban pilots (working for the CIA) were already in action against the Congo rebels.

Del Pino selected fifteen pilots, including Lieutenant Barcelay, who, under the name of Chango or Lawton, would save Che's life eight months later on the banks of

Lake of Tanganyika."[82]

As we noted earlier, Cuba also sent troops to Congo-Brazzaville where they played a critical role in the middle of 1966: they foiled an attempted coup against President Massemba-Debat. The Cubans, also almost all of them black, had been sent to Brazzaville to serve as presidential guards. The coup was French-inspired.

Unfortunately, the Cuban mission in the other Congo next-door (Congo-Leopoldville) was not successful, despite heroic attempts by the Cubans to help the Congolese guerrillas.

In addition to revolutionary commitment to the struggle against imperialism, the Cuban Congo mission served another purpose especially for Fidel Castro even if Che Guevara, ready to die anywhere for what he believed in, did not see it that way. That purpose, in Castro's mind, was to save Guevara's life.

Che wanted to go back Argentina to launch a revolution in his homeland, but Castro believed that his comrade would be killed by the Argentine army if he tried to do that. That is, at least, the interpretation of Emilio Aragones, a close friend and aide of Che Guevara who was also with him in Congo. As he stated in an interview in Havana on 23 January 1996:

"I knew that his dream was to go to Argentina: that was his ultimate goal. I believe Fidel encouraged or facilitated Che's trip to Africa in order to save him from a trip to Argentina. Fidel knew that the Argentine army was not the same as Tshombe's soldiers...

Che came back enamored of Africa because he spoke with all the African leaders and came out of there very enthusiastic....Fidel wound him up because there was less risk, rather than sending him off to Argentina he delayed him in Africa....What Fidel wanted was to gain time...he was trying to make sure by any means that Che would not

191

be killed."[83]

And as Castaneda, who interviewed Aragones, points out:

"During the course of three interviews and almost ten hours of recorded conversation, Aragones repeated this interpretation, almost obsessively, several times."[84]

Che Guevara would have been in great danger had he gone back to Argentina and tried to launch a revolution against the Argentine army and security forces, some of the best trained, and best equipped, in the entire Latin America. His compatriots who had tried to do so earlier, were wiped out.

It is also true that Tshombe's army was not by itself a formidable military machine; it was not even a credible fighting force. But it was backed up by well-trained and battle-hardened mercenaries from South Africa supported by Belgium and the United States. In fact, it was the CIA which was behind the rise of Tshombe. It was also the CIA which put Tshombe in power.

Therefore, the danger to Che Guevara came not from the Congolese government and its army and security forces but from the CIA as was tragically demonstrated only about a year-and-a-half later when he was finally killed in Bolivia in a plot masterminded by the CIA; in one of the first pictures taken soon after he was shot was a CIA agent.

So, when he went to Congo, he was still in great danger from enemies bigger than Tshombe and Mobutu. In fact, he almost got killed by the mercenaries when they closed in on his guerrilla base and virtually surrounded it, until he and his aides and others miraculously escaped across Lake Tanganyika to safety in Tanzania.

Among the aides he selected to accompany him to the Congo were Victor Dreke, and "Pombo" Harry Villegas whom Guevara excluded from the Argentine expedition in September 1963 because he was black – "There are no blacks where we are going," Che Guevara said – but chose him for the Congo mission precisely because he was. Guevara and his fellow Cubans arrived on the shores of Lake Tanganyika in April 1965; although he himself had been there earlier to check on the guerrilla camps. He was in Tanzania for one week in February and went to Congo to check on the guerrilla camps.

Almost all of the 130 Cubans who accompanied Che Guevara were black. Many of them were volunteers, but not all. A number of them had not even been told where they were going, for security reasons. However, their lack of knowledge about the mission proved to be costly; so did their ignorance about the country where they were headed and about Africa in general.

They knew nothing about the culture and history – including colonial history – of the people they were going to help. Military defeat also took its toll, as did dysentery which struck Guevara himself as well, after they had been in Congo for several months. As Che Guevara conceded towards the end of 1965 when he was staying in Dar es Salaam, Tanzania:

"In Cuba very few of our principal military or mid-level cadres with good training were black. When we tried to send primarily black Cubans, we sought them out among the best elements of the army, with some combat experience. The result is that our group has...a very good combat morale and precise tactical knowledge in the field, but little academic training....

The fact is that our comrades had a very scant cultural background, and also a relatively low political development."[85]

Compounding the problem was the fact that the Cuban force was assembled in a hurry, according to the people themselves who went on the Congo mission and who were still alive in the 1990s, talking about their expedition. Aragones said he told Guevara after they had been in Congo for some months:

"Che, nobody knows what the hell we're doing here."[86]

The result was frustration, low morale, anger, and indiscipline among the Cuban troops, although there was no mutiny. In fact, preparation for the Congo mission took barely two months. Then it was time to leave Cuba:

"At daybreak of April 2, 1965, Che's head shaved and with a dental prosthesis in place, he, Dreke, and Papi (Jose Maria Martinez Tamayo) departed from Havana's Jose Marti airport for Dar es Salaam, Tanzania. As Castro would reveal twenty years later: 'I myself suggested to Che that he should gain some time and wait; but he wanted to train cadres, develop through experience'....
The departure of the other combatants – who would arrive in Tanzania little by little – was also arranged in haste, as were the arms shipment....A first unit, commanded by Che, landed at the Tanzanian capital on April 19. Four days later they embarked upon their trek across the savannah to Kigoma on the lakeshore (of Lake Tanganyika) facing the Congo."[87]

At the end of April, Guevara and his team arrived at the guerrilla base in Kibamba on the western shore of Lake Tanganyika in eastern Congo. They were received with military honours. Then they introduced themselves: Dreke, also named Moja, which means One in Kiswahili; Martinez Tamayo, or Mbili, meaning Two; and Che, or Tatu, meaning Three, in Kiswahili. Che was also registered at the camp as an interpreter and as a physician.
The Swahili designations denoted "rank"; hence Che Guevara ranked number three, for obvious reasons. It was

not an obsession with security but simply a fact of life. The danger was real, and the enemy was not faraway. And their mission floundered. For about seven months, they just waited, languishing in the camp. They had come to fight. But where was the war?

Right from the beginning, the Cubans faced a problem: Should they tell the Congolese guerrillas who Tatu, the "lowest-ranking" member, really was? Laurent Kabila, the leader of the guerrilla soldiers in that region, knew who Tatu was, of course. And he wanted Tatu's presence and identity to remain a secret. But Kabila was not even on the scene. He was still in Cairo with his aides where the Congolese nationalists had formed the Supreme Council of the Revolution headed by Gaston Soumialot.

But the main reason, shared by the Cuban ambassador to Tanzania, Pablo Rabalta, for refusing to divulge Tatu's identity was simple. If it became publicly known that more than one hundred Cuban troops had arrived in Congo, the conflict would be internationalized.

The reaction would be even worse if the news spread that it was none other than Che Guevara himself who was leading the troops. That would draw in untold numbers of South African mercenaries and others, and trigger a violent reaction by the United States, Belgium and other Western countries.

To avoid all that, Che simply sneaked in, although it is hard to believe that the CIA did not know his whereabouts until July 1965, despite earlier reports during the same year by CIA operatives in the field that Che was already in Congo. The CIA is said to have discounted those reports, until a few months later when it accepted their validity. Che, nevertheless, had good reason to keep his identity secret. As he stated in his Congo diaries:

"To be frank, I was afraid that my offer of support might cause extreme reactions, and that some of the Congolese or the friendly government (of Tanzania) might ask me to stay away."[88]

Yet the United States, Belgium and other Western powers including apartheid South Africa had already internationalized the struggle by effectively intervening on Tshombe's and Mobutu's side. In fact, it was the CIA which brought in the Cubans first – the ones who served under Cuban leader Batista who was overthrown by Castro in January 1959 – to fight against the Congolese nationalists.

Therefore the invitation of Che Guevara and other Cubans under Castro by the Congolese nationalists was merely a response to Western intervention in Congo dating back to 1960 when the United States, Belgium and their allies ousted Lumumba and assassinated him the following January; so was the involvement of African countries – Tanzania, Algeria, Egypt, Ghana, Guinea, Mali, and later Uganda – in support of the Congolese nationalist guerrillas; it was also in response to Western intervention in Congo.

Unfortunately for the people of Congo who were forced to live under Western puppets, Tshombe and Mobutu and their treasonous coterie, Cuban intervention on behalf of the nationalists was not as effective as it could have been – even if it had meant prolonged guerrilla warfare to tie down the mercenaries – partly because of the guerrilla leaders themselves. Laurent Kabila and his colleagues did not provide effective leadership critical to a successful guerrilla campaign.

Che Guevara spent most of his time just waiting for Kabila and his deputies to come back to Congo and start fighting. They never did, wasting seven months. The guerrilla base was also deserted. And Guevara and his Cuban aides could not even move about – to another hill or terrain – without permission from Kabila. Yet, he wasn't even there in the combat zone. So they had no other choice but to wait, and wait.

The waiting period included waiting for visitors and supplies from Cuba whose arrival punctuated the monotony Che and his troops had to endure in Congo. Guevara worked as a doctor and helped train the Congolese guerrillas but he and his compatriots could have done much more, a point Che himself made when he wrote in his Congo journals, complaining:

"We had to do something in order to avoid complete idleness....Our morale was still high, but some comrades began to grumble as they saw the days pass in vain."[89]

In the first week of May, the rest of the Cuban troops and advisers, all combat-ready, arrived at the guerrilla camp on the western shores of Lake Tanganyika. Kabila's deputy also arrived from Cairo and repeated Kabila's order not to reveal Che Guevara's identity. Che, an international figure, had to obey orders from an obscure guerrilla leader who had sought his help, and had to learn the hard way to live as a subordinate, at least temporarily, until he was out of Congo.

A voracious reader, Guevara had also been known in the past to read Immanuel Kant for mental relaxation, including Kant's magnum opus and difficult philosophical work *Critique of Pure Reason*. But nothing could help him with his boredom in Congo.

Che Guevara was also handicapped in another way by a deadly tropical fever which weakened him so much that he suffered from "extraordinary fatigue, so I didn't even want to eat."[90] His health had always been poor since his childhood in Argentina – he suffered from asthma – and got worse in Congo where he faced a different environment and diseases he had never encountered before.

Around the same time Guevara was debilitated by illness, Kabila's deputy made a momentous decision, and an irrational one. He decided to capture Albertville, now known as Kalemie, a large mining town about 125 miles south of the main guerrilla base. Albertville also had a Belgian military station. The timing was bad, and the guerrillas were not ready for the attack; nor was there anyone to rescind the order.

Kabila was still out of the country and there was no one to lead the invasion of Albertville even if the guerrillas had been prepared for it. All of Kabila's deputies lacked the military skills and leadership qualities to spearhead the attack on Albertville. Like Kabila himself, they were not even in the combat zone except the deputy who decided to invade this important mining town.

There were more problems. The fact that Albertville was not some kind of obscure village or minor settlement but a major mining town made things worse. It had a lot of people and foreign-owned businesses, especially Belgian. No military commander or guerrilla leader in his right mind, and with no combat troops and enough weapons, would have contemplated such a move at that time. It was a foolish gamble.

The odds were totally against the guerrillas. And there was nothing Che Guevara could do to reverse the decision or delay the invasion.

He was not the guerrilla commander; Kabila's incompetent deputy was. And being in poor health added to his anguish. He was debilitated by constant asthma attacks and lost one-quarter of his weight.

Oscar Fernandez Mell, Guevara's close colleague in the Sierra Maestra (Maestra Mountains) in the late 1950s during the Cuban revolution and the war against Cuban dictator and American stooge General Batista, was sent to Congo by Castro to watch over him and make sure everything was all right.

But things were not going well for Che. As Fernandez Mell wrote:

"He was not there as a leader, or anything; his role was

one that he especially hated: to send people (into combat), without going himself."[91]

In what probably is one of Guevara's most realistic assessments of the Congo situation, the legendary guerrilla leader wrote the following in his journal in 1965:

"The main defect in the Congolese is that they don't know how to shoot....Discipline here is very poor, but it seems that things are changing on the front....Today we can say that the apparently greater discipline on the fronts was false....

The main feature of the People's Liberation Army is that it was a parasite army which didn't work, didn't train, didn't fight, and demanded supplies and labour from the population, sometimes by force.

It is clear that an army of this sort can be justified only if it occasionally fights, like its enemy counterpart....But it didn't even do that....The Congolese revolution was irreparably doomed to failure owing to its internal weaknesses."[92]

Guevara made it clear that he was not talking about just one place, the guerrilla camp at Kibamba, but all the other operational bases throughout eastern Congo where Kabila's forces were operating. Other guerrilla camps included those in Baraka, Lulimba, and Katenga.

He sent investigators to all those sites, and what they found was bad, very bad, to say the least. The "guerrilla soldiers" were always drunk, lazy, without discipline, and had absolutely no interest in fighting, not even in self-defence. They just ran. They were soldiers in name only.

What made the whole situation so frustrating was that all the guerrilla bases were fully stocked with weapons from the Soviet Union and China, shipped to the nationalist forces through Tanzania. Yet they did nothing with all those weapons.

In June 1965, Chinese Prime Minister Chou En-Lai made an official visit to Tanzania and promised even more weapons and other help for the Congolese nationalist guerrillas. It was also during this visit that Chou En-Lai boldly stated in the Tanzanian capital Dar es Salaam that Africa was ripe for revolution, a statement which was received with apprehension in neighbouring Kenya.[93]

It became one of the most famous statements the Chinese leader ever made and was widely quoted in the international media. Besides Kenya, a number of other African countries were not pleased with what Chou En-Lai said in Tanzania.[94] They included the former Belgian Congo, and Malawi under Dr. Hastings Kamuzu Banda, an Anglophile.

They felt that they were among those targeted for revolution; a fear publicly expressed by President Banda and Congolese Foreign Minister Justin Bomboko. Several others were just as concerned, although not all of them issued public statements on the subject. As W.A.C. Adie stated in "China's Revived Interest in Africa" in *Africa Contemporary Record*:

"According to the *Far Eastern Economic Review* leading OAU Governments are concerned at the new evidence of Chinese subversive activity, particularly in the training and arming of rebel groups, in both Congos and Zanzibar, Cameroun, Guinea and Mali. According to the Foreign Minister of Congo Kinshasa (Justin Bomboko), the first targets are to be his own Government and those of the Central African Republic, Chad, Cameroun and Gabon."[95]

In 1965, Burundi, Dahomey, the Central African Republic, Ghana and Tunisia broke off diplomatic relations with the People's Republic of China. In the same year, Kenya expelled Chinese diplomats. And in May 1968, President Leopold Sedar Senghor of Senegal spoke of foreign interference in student demonstrations and a general strike, referring to a "secret opposition" inspired by Maoism. Shortly afterwards, the New China News correspondent and some of his assistants were expelled from Senegal.

According to the Peking *People's Daily*, it was an excellent thing that there was a "smell of gunpowder" all over the world, a statement that was not well-received in many African capitals anymore than Chou En-Lai's was when he said Africa was ripe for revolution. And as *Afrique Nouvelle*, Dakar, Senegal, commented in its 6 – 12 June 1968 edition:

"The Chinese have chosen to penetrate from the Atlantic and the Indian Ocean into the heart of Africa."[96]

Congo's Foreign Minister Justin Bomboko was therefore right when he said his government was targeted for revolution. But he was only partly right.

The Kinshasa government was already targeted by its own people, fellow Congolese, and would have been targeted by the nationalist guerrillas, anyway, even if the People's Republic of China or the Soviet Union – which supplied them with weapons – did not exist. The uprising in Congo was an indigenous phenomenon, not a foreign-inspired insurgency like the secession of Katanga or the assassination of Lumumba.

But as time went on without any military action being taken by the Congolese guerrillas, their prospects for success grew dimmer and dimmer.

Albertville was still their target. Yet it was not within striking range; nor was its capture a realistic goal, which became even more unrealistic when mercenaries closed in on the guerrillas.

After the South African mercenaries led by "Mad Mike" Hoare and his small air force neutralised other guerrilla bases along the Congolese border with Sudan and

Uganda in the northern part of the country, they headed south, with dire consequences for Kabila's soldiers and the Cubans led by Che Guevara, and for the entire guerrilla operation in eastern Congo.

"Mad Mike" Hoare in Congo in 1964 injured by shrapnel

Out of boredom and as a preemptive strike against the enemy in anticipation of the major attack on Albertville by the guerrillas, Che Guevara and Kabila agreed through correspondence quoted in Che's journals to attack Front de Force, also known as Bendera (which means flag in Kiswahili), a small town about 25 miles south of the guerrilla base at Kibamba. Bendera was also near a dam, only a few miles from the main target, Albertville.

However, Guevara was not too enthusiastic about the attack on Bendera for strategic reasons. He wanted them to try and capture Katenga which was a much smaller town than Bendera; it was also more accessible from their main guerrilla base in Kibamba. But Kabila refused to change the plan.

He was determined to seize Bendera, although such an attack carried a very high risk of alerting Tshombe's troops and mercenaries to the presence of the Cubans in Kabila's guerrilla army. Guevara wanted to go to the battle front and directly take part in the attack on Bendera but had to hold back since Kabila had not authorised him to do so. Instead, Dreke, known as Moja, was assigned to lead fewer than 40 Cubans and 160 Rwandans to try and capture Bendera.

The offensive was launched towards the end of June 1965. It was a tragedy. But even worse was the fact that the unsuccessful invasion exposed the presence of Cuban troops among the Congolese guerrillas. Four of the Cubans were killed and their bodies were taken away by Tshombe's mercenaries.

The Cuban soldiers also made one big mistake. They did not follow Che Guevara's strict orders not to carry any personal items and documents when going into combat. When the South African mercenaries examined the bodies and the items they had on them, they found out that they were Cubans and immediately notified the American "advisers" operating in Congo.

In his memoirs, "Mad Mike" Hoare, leader of the mercenaries, tells how his troops discovered the passport and diary of one of the Cubans killed in combat. The passport showed which African countries he – and the other Cubans – had visited. And the diary lamented how "the Congolese were too lazy even to carry a 76mm howitzer and its shells."[97]

The CIA station chief in Congo, Laurence (Larry) Devlin, had always suspected the presence of Cubans. His suspicions were now confirmed: the guerrillas near Albertville were being supported by the Cubans sent by Castro. According to a CIA report about Congo declassified in the 1990s, the American embassy in Congo-Kinshasa did not disclose the recovery of the four dead Cubans until 6 July 1965. Coincidentally or not, it was also in the same month that President Joseph Kasavubu appointed Moise Tshombe to be prime minister of Congo.

It was not until September 21st that the embassy confirmed there were 160 Cubans in Congo helping the guerrillas, although as far back as February, the American embassy in Dar es Salaam, Tanzania, had sent sent a report to Washington about Che Guevara's activities in Tanzania. However, the estimate provided by the CIA of the number of Cubans in Congo was off by 40.[98]

The military disaster the Cuban soldiers and the African guerrillas suffered at Bendera greatly affected the morale of the Cubans. They became very bitter when they realised that the Congolese guerrillas would not, and could not, fight.

They either dropped their weapons and ran, or simply fired into the air, wasting ammunition and obviously trying to provide cover for their flight from the battlefield. Several of the Cubans said they wanted to go back home. And Kabila was still not on the scene.

Finally on July 11th, Che Guevara met with Kabila in Kigoma, the town on the eastern shore of Lake Tanganyika in Tanzania. But Kabila stayed in Kigoma only for a few days and told Guevara that he had to go back to Dar es salaam and talk to Soumialot.[99]

The decision by Kabila to return to the Tanzanian capital was the last straw for the Cubans. Their morale was totally undermined.

They couldn't see how Kabila and other guerrilla leaders could keep on staying away from the combat zone when they were supposed to be leading their troops – and the Cubans – into war but instead chose to live in comfort in Dar es Salaam and other African capitals, totally against the rules of revolutionary warfare.

Two Cuban doctors and several other Cubans at the guerrilla base in Kibamba threatened to leave, prompting a violent reaction from their true – though "undercover" – leader, Che Guevara. He decided to go directly into combat himself, only to be overruled by the African guerrilla leaders who, in Guevara's view and which probably was the real reason, feared such a move would make them look bad; especially if their troops saw that a foreigner was willing to risk his life and lead them into combat while they weren't.[100]

However, the morale improved somewhat at the end of July when 25 Cubans and 25 Rwandan guerrillas launched a successful ambush against enemy troops. But several Cubans were still not impressed. They insisted on going back to Cuba.

By August 16th, Guevara himself had also run out of patience. He didn't care what Kabila said about not going into combat without permission. He simply went.

That same night, of August 16th, he arrived in Bendera, weak and tired. While in Bendera, he uncovered vast quantities of weapons and ammunition stocked up by Tshombe's forces, but the guerrillas were spread out along the Albertville highway. The month of August was the best so far, at least for him, in terms of anticipated military action. As he wrote in his August journal:

"In general this month has been very positive; besides the Front de Force (Bendera) operation (which was a total disaster), there has been a qualitative change in the people. My next step will be to visit Lambo in Lulimba and visit Kabambare, then convince them of the need to take Lulimba, and keep going along that path. But for all this it is necessary that this ambush and subsequent operations be successful."[101]

However, the improvement of the situation during the month of August – although not much – invited a retaliatory response from the Congolese government and the South African mercenaries and their Belgian and

American supporters. According to Major Bem Hardenne, the Belgian chief of staff of Belgium's military mission in Albertville, intelligence extracted from guerrilla prisoners showed that the guerrillas were in fact stronger than expected. As he put it:

"The certainty that there are numerous Cubans on Congolese soil aggravates the rebel threat against the cities of Albertville and Kongolo."[102]

The CIA reached the same conclusion,[103] and worked with the Belgians and the South African mercenaries to neutralise the Cubans. The Belgians decided to attack the rebels and the Cubans without delay, preferably before the end of September 1965. The offensive also involved the South African mercenaries and the CIA.

Within two months, the Fifth Battalion of South African commandos totalling 350, led by "Mad Mike" Hoare, surrounded the guerrillas and their Cuban supporters at their camp in Kibamba. But this also proved to be the most severe test for the mercenaries in their Congo campaign.

The guerrilla soldiers, especially the Rwandans fighting together with the Congolese nationalists, put up stiff resistance far more than the mercenaries had expected.

The South African mercenaries also faced another problem. As Major Hardenne stated, the Congolese government soldiers were no better than their fellow countrymen on the other side they were supposed to be fighting. As soon as the first shots were fired, they dropped their weapons and ran. That was bad enough.

They went even further and spread the myth that the guerrilla soldiers were invincible; any attempt to go against them, suicidal. Thus, they helped to defeat themselves, although the performance of the guerrilla fighters on the battlefield should have been enough to disabuse them of that notion.

Far from being invincible, many of the guerrilla soldiers were plain cowards just like their brethren in the Congolese national army supported by the CIA, Belgium, and the South African mercenaries.

Yet, in spite of the stiff defence put up by the Rwandans and the weakness of the Congolese national army, the South African mercenaries and the Congolese government soldiers led by Belgian officers pushed on relentlessly towards the western shore of Lake Tanganyika where the Cubans and the nationalist guerrillas were based. Altogether, they comprised two battalions specifically assigned to eliminate the guerrillas and the Cubans.

Unable to destroy or capture them, they sent them fleeing across Lake Tanganyika to Tanzania where they found sanctuary. But it was not easy to dislodge them because of the presence of well-trained Cuban troops at the guerrilla camps, a concession also made by the South Africans as noted by Belgian Major Hardenne:

"The South Africans report that the rebel units display discipline and aggressiveness, and that they move in the field like well-trained troops. They have not detected any Cubans, but are certain of their presence because several messages in Spanish were intercepted by the Fifth Commandos' portable radios."[104]

In late October 1965, several hundred guerrilla soldiers were killed when they fought the mercenaries in Baraka where one of the guerrilla bases was located. The South African mercenaries saw a number of white Cubans leading the guerrilla fighters into pitched battles, but failed to capture any.

The CIA station in Congo was now absolutely sure that Tatu (Number Three in Kiswahili) was none other than the legendary Che Guevara. In an interview in Princeton, New

Jersey, in November 1995, Laurence Devlin, the CIA station chief in Congo who played a major role in planning the elimination of Patrice Lumumba in January 1961, although he died that, said he had long suspected the presence of Cuban troops among the guerrillas:

"He (Devlin) showed photos of Che to twelve prisoners, who stated that they had talked with Tatu in Kibamba and later in Bendera; in the pictures he alternately wore a moustache or a beard, or was clean-shaven. Eleven of the twelve soldiers recognized Tatu, making his identity virtually certain. Shortly afterward, Devlin confirmed Che's presence thanks to war diaries seized from fallen rebels."[105]

And according to a CIA report, now declassified, dated 26 August 1965:

"Several thousand rebels do hold a considerable redoubt in the Fizi area on the northwestern shore of Lake Tanganyika. The insurgents there are well-armed, probably accompanied by at least a few Cuban and Chinese advisors, and seem better trained and more resolute than were their counterparts in the northeast."[106]

Also Gustavo Villoldo, an anti-Castro Cuban who fought at the Bay of Pigs and who was sent to Congo by the CIA to help Tshombe's government, said in an interview in Miami in the United States on 21 November 1995 that he knew Che Guevara was in Congo, and became enraged when he learned that Che and the other Cubans were not captured or killed.

He confronted his CIA recruiter stating that he had not come all the way to Congo to fight the Castro regime, only to see the Cubans Castro sent to help the nationalist guerrillas return home alive and well.[107]

What the anti-Castro Cubans – who were all white,

according to Devlin – wanted the most when they went to Congo was just to wipe out the Castroists – who were all black except Che Guevara, Papi, Benigno, Fernandez Mell, and Aragones.

On the other hand, what the other Cubans led by Che wanted the most was just to get out of Congo and return home.

But the two groups never confronted each other directly, apart from sporadic but intense machine-gun-fire exchanges involving aircraft piloted by anti-Castro Cubans and Cuban-Congolese guerrillas forces spread out along the highway to Albertville. The guerrillas and their Cuban supporters fought back ferociously when they were attacked from the air.

But the Lake Tanganyika area of eastern Congo where the guerrilla fighters and the Cubans were based was becoming increasingly vulnerable to attack by the South African mercenaries and the Congolese government soldiers commanded by Belgian officers.

Che Guevara spent the months of September and October travelling through the area to assess its vulnerability and potential for counterattack. He went to Fizi, Baraka, Lilamba, and other towns and settlements, travelling on foot from town to town. In all those places, all the guerrilla leaders he talked to, as well as their troops, asked him to send Cuban troops and financial assistance. During his exploratory journey, he came under fire from the mercenary and anti-Castro air force several times. But his life was never in serious danger.

As he travelled through the region, he constantly worked on military strategy and tactics, debating whether to disperse his small force in order to rebuild the Congolese guerrilla army, or concentrate his troops so that he could organise a formidable combat unit. This dilemma was frustrating. As he himself explained, because of illness, low morale and indiscipline among his troops, he never deployed more than 40 soldiers who were in the best shape for combat.

However, by the end of September 1965, all that became irrelevant: the Congolese guerrilla army was falling apart and there was nothing the Cubans could do about it. Guevara himself bitterly admitted that he had been blind to reality and unduly optimistic:

"Our situation was getting more and more difficult and the notion of building an army was slipping through our fingers, with all its arsenal of weapons, men, and munitions. Still imbued with a sort of blind optimism, I was incapable of seeing it."[108]

One of the main reasons he was so misguided and unduly confident is that no one had the courage to confront him and tell him the truth. As Dariel Alarcon Ramirez (Benigno), who was with Che Guevara in Congo, stated in an interview in Paris on 3 November 1995: "Nobody ever confronted him."[109]

Even senior Cuban military advisers who were with him in Congo feared to ask any questions about his plans or raise any doubts about his judgment, lest they be denounced as cowards.

Guevara looked at Congo from his perspective in the Sierra Maestra during the late fifties when he and Castro led a successful revolution against Batista from those mountains. He expected the Congolese guerrillas to react in a similar way and perform well in combat. But the Congolese never did.

Emilio Aragones, who also was with Che in Congo, still wondered 30 years later how an intelligent man like Guevara could have been so naive. As he stated in an interview in Havana on 23 January 1996:

"I don't know if he really believed it, or if he said so in part because he didn't want to leave, he didn't want it to fall apart, I don't know. But a man as intelligent as he can hardly have believed it would work."[110]

At the beginning of October 1965, the Cuban minister of health, Machado Ventura, went to Congo via Tanzania with a message to Che Guevara from Castro, and with the news that Congolese guerrilla leader Gaston Soumialot was in Havana in September on a much-trumpeted visit; although, like Laurent Kabila, Soumialot was not on the battlefield or anywhere in the combat zone like Che and the other Cubans were, together with the Congolese guerrillas, dodging bullets from battle-hardened South African mercenaries.

According to Che Guevara, Castro in his message advised him "not to despair, he asked me to remember the first period of the struggle and recalled that these problems happen."[111]

But he never told Castro the great difficulties he was having in Congo, although he could have given that message to the different envoys who travelled from Cuba to Congo to see him. On October 5th, he wrote a long letter to Castro, stating, among several other things, the following:

"I will say only that here, according to those close to me, I have lost any reputation for objectivity because I am unduly optimistic in the face of the existing, real situation....

In my previous letters I had asked you not to send lots of people, but cadres. I said we are not short of weapons, aside from a few special ones; on the contrary we have too many and not enough soldiers. I especially warned you not to give out funds except in very small amounts and only after many requests. None of these things have been taken into account....

Forget about sending more men to ghost units; prepare me up to one hundred cadres, who should not all be black....Treat the issue of boats very tactfully; do not forget that Tanzania is an independent country and we have to play it clean here. Send, as soon as possible, some mechanics and a man who can navigate to get us across the lake at night in relative safety."[112]

His Congo mission was finally coming to an end as he was now contemplating seeking safety, across Lake Tanganyika, in Tanzania.

Guevara's first, and last, direct participation in combat was also a disaster. It took place on 24 October 1965 when his guerrilla camp was attacked by the mercenaries. Che had to decide whether to withdraw or fight back. He decided to fight.

His camp had stocks of gunpowder, mortars, communications gear and other military equipment enough to launch a formidable counterattack. But it did not have the soldiers to do that.

As expected, the Congolese guerrillas fled for their lives. Guevara himself, after holding out on a hill for several hours with other Cubans, ordered a retreat.

All the gunpowder and military equipment at the guerrilla base was destroyed or seized.

The Congolese guerrilla soldiers had again proved that they could not fight. As Che Guevara himself conceded in a grim assessment probably of his entire Congo mission:

"Personally, I felt terribly depressed, I felt responsible for the disaster due to my lack of foresight and weakness."[113]

Finally, realism prevailed over blind optimism. It was during the same month of October that Guevara probably concluded that his mission was doomed.

Robert W. Kormer, the African specialist at the United States National Security Council (NSC), reached the same conclusion. As he reported to national security adviser McGeorge Bundy in a secret memo, 29 October 1965, now declassified: "The war in the Congo is probably over."[114]

And it was indeed, for all practical purposes.

Then one day, as his mission was coming to an end, inexorably propelled in that direction by forces beyond his control, Che Guevara said something which amounted to a farewell to Congo.

He was reading one of his many books at a guerrilla camp not far from the Kibamba operational base when the sound of an approaching bombardment led him to instruct Fernandez Mell:

"Make sure they put a Cuban at the door of each hut so that the Congolese won't escape."[115]

Just a few minutes after he started reading his book again, the South African mercenaries launched a vicious attack on the camp. The Cubans couldn't even tell which route the South Africans had taken as they advanced towards the camp or which one the Congolese guerrillas had taken fleeing for their lives. And that created a serious problem for Che Guevara which required immediate attention.

He did not know which way to go to save his troops. They were virtually surrounded. When the intensified attack made the whole area extremely dangerous, Guevara immediately ordered:

"Let's leave by that path down there, and hope they'll come the other way."[116]

Throughout October, the mercenaries and the Congolese government soldiers led by Belgian army officers had been making a steady advance towards the western shore of Lake Tanganyika where they knew the guerrillas were based, recapturing villages and other areas which had once been occupied by the insurgents. In his

October diary, which was also the last of his Congo journals, Che Guevara admitted:

"A month of disasters without any extenuating circumstances. To the disgraceful fall of Baraka, Fizi, and Lubonja...we must add...total discouragement among the Congolese....The Cubans are not much better, from Tembo and Siki (Aragones and Fernandez Mell) to the soldiers."[117]

So, he didn't have much choice left, except three options: escape, be captured, or get killed on the shores of Lake Tanganyika.

He and his followers were not only surrounded but their chances of getting out of there alive grew slimmer and slimmer every minute.

From the north and south, the mercenaries were advancing towards the Cubans and the Congolese guerrillas; to the west was a mountain; and to the east was Lake Tanganyika of course, 420 miles long, 45 miles wide, and patrolled by the CIA on speed boats; incidentally, it is also the world's second deepest lake after Lake Baikal in the former Soviet Union and is infested with crocodiles.

Castro also, from reading Guevara's letters and other reports brought back to him by his envoys he sent to Congo, reached the inevitable conclusion that the mission had failed:

"He promptly sent communications equipment to Tanzania and sailors with suitable boats to prepare for an eventual retreat. He also sent Osmany Cienfuegos to persuade Che to recognize defeat, abandon the expedition, and save himself."[118]

Castro also wrote Che Guevara a letter which Che received on November 4th while still in eastern Congo on the western shore of Lake Tanganyika. It was Castro's fervent hope that Che would abandon the mission instead of courting disaster. As he stated in the letter:

"We must do everything, except for the absurd....If in Tatu's view our presence becomes unjustifiable and futile, we must think of retreating. We must act in accordance with the objective situation and our men's frame of mind. If they believe we should stay, we will try to send whatever human and material resources they consider necessary. We are worried that you will make the mistake of fearing that your attitude will be considered defeatist or pessimistic....Avoid annihilation."[119]

Although Guevara had renounced his Cuban citizenship when he left Cuba for Africa to go to Congo, Castro left a way open for him to return to the island; if not, he said he would support him in whatever new mission he was going to undertake after leaving Africa.

But he did not want him to go back to Argentina, at least not right away. Castro felt that it would be too dangerous for Che Guevara to return to his native land during that time. He feared Che would be killed by the Argentine army against which he had very little hope of succeeding if he started a revolution, as he was in fact determined to do; not only in Argentina but throughout Latin America. As for Congo, that was the end of the mission.

But even if Che Guevara still wanted to pursue his Congo mission in spite of the odds against him, several other factors militated against such an undertaking because of what had taken place on the African continent.

On 13 October 1965, just before the OAU annual conference of African heads of state and government opened in Accra, Ghana, Congolese President Joseph Kasavubu dismissed Prime Minister Moise Tshombe and replaced him with Evariste Kimba. Less than a month later on November 24th, Joseph Mobutu overthrew Kasavubu and executed Kimba and several other leading politicians.

Different analysts strongly suspect that the CIA and its station chief Laurence Devlin were involved in the ouster of Kasavubu, but not in Tshombe's dismissal. And there are those who believe that the two events were an integral part of a single operation, still masterminded by the CIA and Laurence Devlin.

There seems to be good reason for such suspicion, including the role Devlin played in the arrest and subsequent assassination of Lumumba in collaboration with Tshombe and Mobutu.

Mobutu could not have arrested Lumumba and had him flown to Katanga, which amounted to a death sentence at the hands of his arch enemy Tshombe, without Devlin's knowledge and approval as the CIA station chief in Congo. He was on the CIA payroll and had been working for the CIA for a long time.

Devlin had a very close relationship with Mobutu. And it is, of course, an open secret that the CIA was behind Mobut's rise to power; he had been on the CIA payroll as an army officer even before Congo won independence, and when he was Lumumba's secretary.

The close relationship between Devlin and Mobutu was also corroborated by the American ambassador to Congo during that time, Mr. Goodley, when he made the following remark:

"Devlin is closer to Mobutu than any non-Congolese I know."[120]

The removal of Tshombe from office as Congolese prime minister led to an improvement of relations between the government in Leopoldville and other African countries almost all of which considered him to be a traitor. And the Congolese government adopted a more friendly attitude towards neighbouring countries especially Tanzania, Congo-Brazzaville, and Uganda which did not want to have anything to do with it as long as Tshombe was in power.

Such an improvement in relations made Che Guevara's mission to Congo no longer relevant, now that Tshombe was out of power; although not Mobutu who was just as treacherous especially in the view of the so-called Group of Six in the OAU – Tanzania, Ghana, Algeria, Egypt, Guinea, and Mali – as well as Uganda which became increasingly militant under the leadership of Dr. Milton Obote who also strongly supported the Congolese nationalists.

The support of these countries for the Congolese nationalists – hence for Che Guevara and other Cubans supporting the nationalist insurgency in Congo – was critical. But it was no longer available for a number of reasons. As Jorge Castaneda states:

"For its part, the group of radical states had lost any reason to continue supporting the rebels; indeed several leaders had already ceased to do so. Ben Bella was deposed by Houari Boumedienne in June (1965); Obote of Uganda had already suspended his assistance; and Nkrumah of Ghana would fall a few months later (on 24 February 1966 in a CIA-engineered coup).

Julius Nyerere, the rebels' foremost supporter, found himself practically alone, without any real rationale for continuing to support a struggle which was disintegrating anyway."[121]

The October 1965 OAU conference held in Accra, the capital of one of the radical states supporting the Congolese nationalist guerrillas, focused on the Congo crisis. Another major African crisis developed only a month later when the white minority regime in Rhodesia led by Prime Minister Ian Smith illegally declared independence on November 11th.

217

Nyerere and Nkrumah

In fact, the host of the conference, Dr. Nkrumah, was the first African leader to propose formation of an African High Command – to address the continent's defence needs and security problems – when the Congo crisis first erupted in 1960. He was strongly supported by all the leaders of the Casablanca Group and by Nyerere and Obote whose countries were not members of the group. As Nyerere stated:

"During the difficulties in the Congo, when the idea of an African High Command was first proposed, I was very taken with it....

I have often thought we must try and find a method which will enable us, in Africa, to avoid the weaknesses of the 'national' state....

The African national state is an instrument for the

unification of Africa, and not for dividing Africa. African nationalism is meaningless, is dangerous, is anachronistic, if it is not at the same time Pan-Africanism."[122]

But the support given to the Congolese nationalists by the staunchly Pan-Africanist leaders had reached its limit. Now that the guerrilla struggle in Congo had failed, a new arrangement had to be made to accommodate that reality, however harsh and painful for the radical states:

"Nyerere even proposed to Kasavubu (just a month before he was overthrown by Mobutu) that he meet with the rebel leadership immediately after the Accra summit.

The Congolese president opened talks with Congo-Brazzaville as well, aimed at reducing its aid to Pierre Mulele's rebellion in Kwilu (Congo-Leopoldville's western province bordering Congo-Brazzaville).

By the end of October the situation in the region had changed radically: the front of progressive countries was crumbling in tandem with the (guerrilla) front by the lake (Tanganyika).

The missing link was for Nyerere to ask the Cubans to depart, along with the South African mercenaries, in accordance with the Accra resolutions on nonintervention. He did so at the beginning of November (1965).

Mike Hoare left the Congo that month, though his men lingered on through the following year.

On November 1, the Cubans received a message from Dar es Salaam: Nyerere formally requested that Cuban assistance be discontinued. This effectively cut off all aid to the Congo rebellion – or what was left of it. As Che noted, 'it was a death blow to a dying revolution.'"[123]

Che Guevara was not blaming Nyerere for stopping Cuban assistance to the Congolese guerrillas but was simply acknowledging that the nationalist insurgency had failed. Even if President Nyerere had asked the Cubans to continue giving assistance to the Congolese guerrillas, the situation would not have improved.

He asked Castro to withdraw Cuban troops from Congo because there was very little chance that the guerrilla movement would have been revived. That was partly because of the weakness of the Congolese themselves. And Nyerere knew that.

Nyerere greeting Castro

If he thought the guerrilla nationalist forces had the chance to succeed, he would not have asked the Cubans to leave Congo. He was, after all, the strongest supporter of the Congolese guerrillas and the only one left. But he was also realistic enough to know that the nationalist insurgency had collapsed.

Now, contrast that with his position on Angola when that country was invaded by South African troops during the seventies in an attempt to overthrow the MPLA government with the help of the CIA; they came within striking distance of the Angolan capital Luanda before Cuban troops were rushed in at the request of the Angolan government to help stop and repel the invaders. As Nyerere stated in an interview on ABC American television, "Issues and Answers" programme, at the State House in Dar es Salaam in June 1976 when he was asked about the situation in Angola, the Cubans were not the cause of what was going on in Angola. He said that in response to the question:

"Can you use your influence, which is tremendous influence, and ask Castro to withdraw his troops from Angola?"

Nyerere responded by saying: "Even if I had that kind of influence, it would be unnecessary. First, you remove the cause...."[124]

Therefore, in the case of Congo, he was not opposed to continued assistance to the guerrillas but to the provision of aid which would not have achieved anything, although the cause of the crisis – Western intervention in Congo – which led to Cuban involvement was still there.

In the case of Angola, the cause – "First, you remove the cause," as Nyerere put it – was South African and American intervention in that country, especially the massive infusion of aid to anti-MPLA forces and the invasion of Angola by South African troops with American support.

That is what triggered the Cuban response as much as Western intervention did in the Congo.

But, unfortunately, the insurgency in Congo was virtually dead, a fact also conceded by Che Guevara when he commented on Nyerere's request to Castro asking him to withdraw Cuban troops from the Congo: "It was a death blow to a dying revolution."

Yet, in spite of all that, Che Guevara refused to give up, weak and undernourished as he was. He said as long as the South African mercenaries were still in Congo hunting down the guerrillas and wreaking havoc in the country, it would be unfair for him to leave the Congolese nationalist soldiers to fight alone unless they themselves asked him to do so.

They did not even have their leaders around. The only leader who was there then, on the western shore of Lake Tanganyika in eastern Congo, was Masengo, Kabila's deputy.

Che Guevara met Masengo in the middle of November 1965 as the South African mercenaries tightened the noose around the nationalist forces; the guerrillas had, in fact, been surrounded since October.

The two leaders discussed strategy as the campaign was coming to an end and Guevara offered this: "Resistance and death, or retreat." He was talking about Cubans fighting to the end.

But Masengo disagreed: "No, I don't agree. If we are not capable of contributing a Congolese fighter, a single one, beside each Cuban in order to die together, we cannot ask the Cubans to do so."

Guevara responded by saying:

"Fine, but the decision has to come from you and has to be perfectly unambiguous. Whatever you decide we should do, we will do it, but the decision is clearly yours."[125]

The military situation did not look good at all for the Cubans and for the Congolese guerrillas led by Masengo during those final hours.

The nearest hill – vital for observation, tactical retreat, and for launching a counterattack – had already been seized by the South African mercenaries, putting the Cubans and the Congolese nationalist guerrillas in extreme danger.

The Cubans told Masengo and other Congolese guerrilla soldiers that they should be given formal authorisation to leave:

"You must give us a document saying that you believe the Cuban advisers should withdraw, as their presence here has exacerbated the repression."

Che Guevara stated his position once again to Masengo:

"Look, they (the mercenaries) are already here, the issue for us is to be ready for a final confrontation. The situation is clear: resistance and death, or retreat."[126]

Masengo and his fellow Congolese guerrillas finally agreed, and the Cubans prepared to catch the boats which would take them across Lake Tanganyika to safety in Tanzania.

Yet at the very last minute, Guevara tried one more time to keep on pursuing his mission. Just as they were getting ready to leave, he told Aragones and Fernandez Mell that he would like to stay in Congo with a few Cubans and march west across the country – about 940 miles – to Kwilu Province and join Pierre Mulele to re-ignite the guerrilla uprising.

His friends were stunned. Fernandez Mell, Guevara's comrade-in-arms during the Cuban revolution when they fought side by side in the Sierra Maestra against Batista, and who had been sent to Congo by Castro to watch over Guevara, lost all patience with Che. He threw his hat on the ground when he heard what Guevara said.

Aragones, older and wiser, was more self-controlled but took a firm stand, and told Guevara:

"Listen, Che, I have obeyed everything you have said here without discussion, to the letter, as your subordinate. But Che, let me tell you this: don't even think that you can dare to tell me to leave while you stay here."[127]

Guevara agreed with him, but he really didn't mean it.

He still had something else in mind to try and maneuver his way out and stay in Congo. This is what he came up with:

"I'll stay here with five strong men to recover our dead or missing in action....The idea of leaving completely and departing as we had arrived, leaving behind defenceless peasants and armed but defenceless men, given their little capacity to fight, defeated and feeling that they had been betrayed, hurt me deeply."[128]

It was time to leave Congo.

Entire families started fleeing as the South African mercenaries approached their villages which also provided cover for the rebels, and got into boats to escape to Tanzania.

Lawton, the Cuban who was sent by Castro to direct the emergency evacuation, was horrified to see boats filled with the villagers who begged him not to leave them behind; while his leader Che Guevara refused to go aboard, still determined to stay in Congo and march out west to join Mulele in Kwilu Province. His excuse for not getting on any of the boats?: Children and women must go first.

Lawton vehemently disagreed, telling Guevara: "Look, those blacks belong here in the jungle, they are willing to live here. These blacks are not whom the mercenaries are after. They after you and the black Cubans." But Che insisted: "When they get here, they are going to massacre these people." To which Lawton responded: "Yes, but my orders are that those who must not be massacred are yourselves, and I have to get you out. I respect you, but I am here under orders from Fidel; if I have to tie you up to take you out of here, I will."[129]

Finally, but reluctantly, he went along. Their escape across Lake Tanganyika to safety in Tanzania also enlarges the legendary character of Che Guevara as someone who defied and constantly went against overwhelming odds to achieve whatever objective he had in mind, although he is not the one who masterminded the rescue operation. But how was it possible for one hundred Cubans and dozens of Rwandan and Congolese guerrillas to cross Lake Tanganyika to safety in Tanzania?

The entire lake – including the Tanzanian side in clear violation of Tanzania's territorial integrity – was constantly patrolled, twenty-four hours a day, by speedboats operated by the South African mercenaries and by the CIA as well as by the Congolese government troops. They also crossed the lake, not under cover of darkness but at dawn illuminated by daylight, with the South African mercenaries right behind them in hot pursuit. So how was Che Guevara and the Cubans – who were the prime target – able to escape to Tanzania?:

"Benigno raised the issue with greater precision. The Cubans were ready to fight to the last man, as they traversed the lake in their leaking and overcrowded vessels, surrounded by enemies who were fully aware of their schedule and itinerary. But they did not have to. Either nobody saw them, or those who did decided not to attack. The outcome was hardly believable: the Cubans, though surrounded, were able to escape safely."[130]

Benigno (Dariel Alarcon Ramirez) himself, in an interview on 3 November 1995, had an even more chilling story to tell about what happened on that day. He was there:

"I was very surprised by a place we passed at dawn. I thought it was impossible for us to get by without being seen, because we passed between two sloops, we had to turn off the motors and all of us dove into the water, those who knew how to swim dove in and pushed the raft to pass between the two sloops that were there. I at least

225

expected them to start shooting at us any second. It was humanly impossible for them not to see us."[131]

By all accounts the escape was a miracle, but a great disappointment to those who would have loved to capture the Cubans, especially Che Guevara, and bring them in dead or alive.

The Belgian military officers in Congo were enraged; they had a permanent mission in the country and troops in every major city, and in the fields fighting the insurgents. In fact, they did not even believe that the Cubans had left Congo.

The CIA station chief in the capital Kinshasa, Laurence Devlin, offered one explanation how Che Guevara and the Cubans as well as a number of Congolese guerrillas and their Rwandan compatriots were able to escape to Tanzania:

"I assigned a boat to prevent the Cubans from crossing the lake; but it broke down, and the Cubans got away. I will never forgive myself."[132]

Still that does not fully explain, if at all, how the Cubans got away.

There was more than one patrol boat on Lake Tanganyika; not only did the CIA have more than one boat, the South African mercenaries and the Congolese army also had patrol boats on Lake Tanganyika. And they were high-speed boats, much faster than what the Cubans and the guerrillas escaped in.

And they all – the CIA, the South African mercenaries, and the Congolese army under Belgian officers – worked together and knew the Cubans had embarked on boats to flee to Tanzania; that is why they were in hot pursuit of them.

So why were they not able to intercept them, knowing full well that they were trying to escape? Major Bem

Hardenne, the Belgian chief of staff of OPS/SUD (Belgium's military station in Albertville), explained what happened on that day:

"Weather conditions had improved, so the command post and CPS/SUD were directing operations from a plane. They realized that the Cubans were fleeing on several boats, crossing the lake or navigating southward along the coast.
For reasons that will never be explained, the ANC planes and boats piloted by mercenaries were not only not there despite orders, but did not respond to calls from the plane....This bad execution of orders allowed the Cubans to escape."[133]

But there are those who dispute these explanations. Jules Gerard-Libois, who had been studying wars in Congo for more than 30 years at the *Centre de Recharche et d'Information Socio-politique* (CRISP) in Brussels, Belgium, found it hard to believe how the Belgians, the South African mercenaries, the CIA, and anti-Castro Cubans in Congo working for the CIA and for the Congolese government, could have failed to prevent Che Guevara – whom they knew was there – and the Cubans from escaping.
According to his findings, the Belgian military mission in Albertville ordered the Congolese battalions under its command to let the Cubans go. The two Belgian CIA pilots who were supposed to have been directing operations against the fleeing Cubans, and who could have rained destruction on them, were confined to their rooms on orders from their superiors.
The CIA station chief in Albertville admitted to two Belgian officers that he had received instructions to avoid any confrontation with the Cubans before December 1st (1965). The CIA ordered its planes and high-speed boats to launch an "operational destruction of the enemy," but

the order was not obeyed.[134]

Gerard-Libois said the CIA spared the lives of Che Guevara and the other Cubans – much as the Americans wanted them destroyed, which is what they did to Che and his compatriots in Bolivia in July 1967 in a plot masterminded by the CIA – because Castro had reached an immigration agreement with the American government. Under that accord, Castro agreed to allow more than 45,000 Cubans to leave the island and go to Florida during the first year of the agreement's implementation.

On 27 October 1965, the Cuban leader announced that anybody who wanted to leave would be allowed to do so.

Had the Cubans including Che Guevara been attacked, let alone killed, in Congo when they were escaping to Tanzania, Castro would not have honoured the agreement. And he probably would have contemplated other moves in retaliation, although Gerard-Libois does not mention that.

But there was another dimension to the problem. The United States government did not intentionally spare Guevara's life or that of his colleagues. As Jorge Castaneda states:

"Gerard-Libois believes that the accord (allowing tens of thousands of Cubans to emigrate to the Unites)...led the United States to avoid any conflict which might have blocked its implementation. In this perspective, it seems logical that Washington should have instructed its mission abroad to avert any friction or confrontation with the Cubans during those weeks, until the Comarioca immigration agreement had been fulfilled.

Obviously, the US Government had not foreseen that its general guidelines would allow Che Guevara to escape. Officers in Congo may well have misinterpreted the instructions, and allowed the encircled Cuban fighters to flee from Kibamba (to Tanzania)."[135]

But none of the American officials who were directly

involved in the matter recalled anything like that or accepted this interpretation.

The CIA station chief in Congo, Laurence Devlin, said he never received any such order; nor did his former agents in Albertville, especially Richard Johnson, head of the CIA base in that city, say they did.

Gustavo Villoldo, a Cuban exile who fought at the Bay of Pigs and who was assigned to Congo by the CIA to work for Tshombe, swears that even if he had received such an order not to attack Che Guevara and the Cubans when they were fleeing across Lake Tanganyika to safety in Tanzania, there is no way he would have obeyed it; that was totally out of the question.

But he never received such an order, he said, in an interview in Miami, Florida, in the United States on 21 November 1995.

William Bowdler, the American diplomat who negotiated the Camarioca immigration accord, said in an interview on 8 November 1996 that he did not remember any such deal with Castro or a unilateral decision by the American government to avoid confrontation with the Cubans in Congo.[136]

Therefore, it is still a mystery why Che Guevara and all the Cubans were allowed to escape from Congo to Tanzania; or why the CIA failed to intercept them, if it failed at all to do that.

The question is open to interpretation. And there have been several such interpretations as we just saw.

Maybe the CIA, for whatever reason, did not really want to kill Che Guevara in the heart of Africa, in the very same country where only five years earlier the American intelligence agency helped capture and assassinate Patrice Lumumba.

Maybe it did not want to create two martyrs in the same country; not because it wanted to spare Guevara's life – otherwise it would not have helped to get him captured and killed in Bolivia less than two years later.

After the failure of his mission in Congo, Che Guevara had only another year-and-a-half to live. And a legend was born. But he still would have been one, had he died in Congo, no matter how.

Guevara fled to safety weighing less than 110 pounds, having lost 40, mainly due to dysentery. His congenital condition, asthma, had also taken its toll. According to his secretary in Tanzania, Colman Ferrer, in an interview in Havana on 25 August 1995:

"He was skinny, pallid, and underfed."[137]

Also, spending several weeks in a bedroom and in an office set up form him on the first floor of the Cuban Embassy in Dar es Salaam did not help his condition. He began to recover only when plans for his next mission became clearer.

His secretary during the months he spent in Tanzania recalled in the same interview:

"I don't think he left in a spirit of defeat, but rather with a critical attitude toward the organization's political leadership, with a spirit of love and compassion toward the Congolese brigades."[138]

The months he spent in Dar es Salaam also gave him ample opportunity to talk to his old friend, Pablo Ribalta, Cuba's ambassador to Tanzania; it was Che Guevara himself, as you may recall, who had him appointed to that strategic post in anticipation of his Congo mission.

He wanted someone very close to him to have the ambassadorial post in a country which played a critical role in supporting the nationalist guerrillas in Congo as well as in southern Africa through the years; in May 1963, Tanzania was chosen by the Organisation of African Unity (OAU) to be the headquarters of the OAU Liberation Committee responsible for all the liberation movements in

Africa.

While in the Tanzanian capital, Guevara also got the chance to see his wife, Aleida, who travelled from Cuba to see him. Ribalta later recalled Aleida's trip to Tanzania:

"His wife arrived in Dar es Salaam. They were staying at the Embassy. Che was very friendly, very happy, they talked about the children, they hugged....She stayed until later."[139]

It was also when he was in Dar es Salaam that Che Guevara wrote his book, the famous Congo diaries: *Pasajes de la guerra revolucionaria (el Congo)*. Although it remained unpublished for a long time, it was quoted extensively before being published. In writing the book, Guevara used his notes taken in Congo. The English version of the book is *The African Dream: The Diaries of the Revolutionary War in the Congo*.

Colman Ferrer, a young secretary at the Cuban embassy in Dar es Salaam, served as his assistant. She took dictation and transcribed the text; then Che Guevara revised and corrected the final manuscript. The project kept him busy. As Ferrer stated:

"He was careful in the things he was going to write, avoiding any mistakes. He took great care, he analyzed and reread the transcription repeatedly."[140]

And in the words of Ambassador Ribalta:

"He wrote day and night. His only distraction was an occasional game of chess with me. One day when I was about to checkmate him, he looked at me is if he had not realized what was happening; it was obvious that he wasn't really in the game."[141]

The months he spent in Tanzania were his last on

African soil, a continent he first visited in June 1959 when he travelled to Egypt where President Nasser received him with full honours; then on to Sudan and Morocco.

He left Tanzania in early March 1966. As Ulises Estrada, a black Cuban who also was with Che Guevara in Tanzania and who was a specialist in African affairs, stated in an interview in Havana on 9 February 1995:

"Everybody (who was with Che Guevara in Congo) returned to Cuba and he stayed on alone in Tanzania. And then I decided to get him out of Tanzania and take him to a safe place until he decided what he was going to do."[142]

What he decided to do next cost him his life at the age of 39.

His Congo mission also had another tragic dimension. It was when he was in Congo that he received news of his mother's death back in his native Argentina. The news was sent to him by Castro.

He mourned his mother's death in the green hills of Africa, a continent he felt was the best battleground in the struggle against imperialism. But fighting the world's most powerful country, the United States, which was firmly entrenched in Congo, ended in tragic failure of the first nationalist revolt against a client state on the African continent.

Cuba's, hence Guevara's, involvement in Congo was used by the United States as a pretext to justify her intrusion in the heart of Africa and even accused the Cubans of internationalising the conflict; although the Americans had already intervened in Congo years before the Cubans went in. Not only did the United States go into Congo before the Cubans; she went in even before the Russians and the Chinese did.

Cuban involvement in Congo was a response, by invitation, to American intervention including the assassination of Lumumba in a CIA-masterminded plot; as much as Cuban involvement in Angola was also a response, again by invitation, to South Africa's invasion of that country, an invasion which was also backed up by the United States.

Had apartheid South Africa not invaded Angola, there would have been no need for Cuban intervention. Cuban involvement in Angola was also in response to American intervention – directed by the CIA – in support of UNITA in order to overthrow the MPLA government which had been recognised by the Organization of African Unity (OAU) and by most African countries including American allies on the continent.

Yet the United States defied the wishes of Africa as much as she did earlier in Congo when she supported Moise Tshombe, a leader most African leaders shunned because he was a traitor.

And America's direct role in the assassination of Lumumba did little to help the United States win friends in Africa – besides Tshombe and Mobutu – and keep other countries out of the Congo imbroglio; it accomplished exactly the opposite.

The CIA plot to assassinate Lumumba started with the Eisenhower Administration and remains, to this day, one of the saddest chapters in the history of relations between the United States and Africa. That the United States was largely responsible for his assassination is an open secret, as much as it has been for more than a generation.

It is as much a sad story about the weakness of African countries as it is one of total disregard for the interests and rights of Africans – for racist reasons as well – by the world's most powerful country whose white majority, according to national surveys, still refuse to accept African Americans as full human beings; hence the belief among millions of whites – if not the vast majority – that black people are genetically inferior to whites and members of others races, a racist doctrine given pseudoscientific validity by *The Bell Curve*[143] and other works.

233

Therefore by killing Lumumba, the United States was also just getting rid of "another nigger," although the main reasons for their intervention in Congo and subsequent assassination of Lumumba were geopolitical, ideological, and economic: control of Congo, the heart of Africa, by the United States and her Western allies for their benefit and keeping the Russians and the Chinese out of there.

But the racial factor in Lumumba's elimination can not be overlooked. In fact, when President Dwight Eisenhower and his subordinates discussed how they should get rid of Lumumba, they used derogatory language – in describing him – which amounted to racism, as Chrsitopher Andrew showed in his book, *For the President's Eyes Only: Secret Intelligence and the American Presidency from Washington to Bush.*

And evidence against the United States is overwhelming, although some people, while conceding American complicity in Lumumba's assassination, tend to minimise her role. One of them is Jon Lee Anderson who wrote an excellent biography of Che, *Che Guevara: A Revolutionary Life*, which also deals with the Congo crisis.

Yet he downplayed America's role in the assassination of Lumumba. He also failed or deliberately refused to see the United States as an imperial power capable of manipulating and controlling world events to the detriment of weak countries; not necessarily as a global tyrant although it is hard to refute that after America's invasion of Iraq and threats to invade other countries.

The United States controls their economies; intimidates, manipulates, and even overthrows their governments, and has even ordered and sponsored the assassination of leaders the American government does not like.

Yet some people fail to see or are unwilling to accept that, sometimes out of blind patriotism in the case of Americans, although Anderson is not cast in that mould as a blind patriot. His book is massive and rich in detail. But that does not compensate for lack of objective analysis. As Jane Franklin stated in *The Nation*:

"Anderson seems not to share Guevara's view of US imperialism, and downplays the US role in global events. Speaking at a 1961 rally to mobilize Cubans for the imminent US invasion, Guevara cited the recent murder of Patrice Lumumba as 'an example of what the empire is capable of'....

In the many pages devoted to events in the Congo, Anderson contests this claim. Though he reports a plan by Dr. Sidney Gottlieb of the CIA's 'medical division' to poison Lumumba, he states that 'before the CIA could get close to Lumumba, however, his own Congolese rivals did.'

But the CIA and the US Embassy had already connived with these Congolese rivals – Moise Tshombe and Joseph Mobutu – to murder Lumumba. Mobutu, who turned Lumumba over to Tshombe to kill, was actually on the CIA payroll.

Four years later, when Guevara left Cuba to fight against Tshombe and Mobutu on the side of Lumumba's followers, the CIA had already dispatched a band of Cuban exiles, trained for the Bay of Pigs, to fly bombing raids for Tshombe. This CIA operation, ignored by Anderson, suggests that Washington shared Guevara's view of the dimensions of the struggle."[144]

Some supporters of President Dwight Eisenhower refused – and even today probably still refuse – to accept the fact that the president did authorise the assassination Lumumba.

He is the same leader who didn't care how many people were killed in order to "fight communism" in Latin America; didn't have any qualms about overthrowing the populist government of Guzman Arbenz of Guatemala in 1954 and the government of Dr. Mohammad Mossadeq in

Iran a year earlier in 1953 because it nationalised the oil industry which belonged to the Iranians – not to the British or the Americans.

Then there was the plot to assassinate Castro, also conceived and hatched by the Eisenhower Administration; and next, the one against Lumumba.

Just as in the case of Castro when Eisenhower felt that the CIA was not doing enough, and fast enough, to eliminate him, the president also felt that the intelligence agency was not working fast enough to get rid of Lumumba. As Christopher Andrew stated in his book, *For the President's Eyes Only: Secret Intelligence and the American Presidency from Washington to Bush*:

"Just as Eisenhower had regarded the 5412 Committee's February (1960) proposals for dealing with Castro as too feeble, so he was equally critical of its initial plans for covert actions against Patrice Lumumba.

When the committee met to discuss action against Lumumba on August 25, Gordon Gray reported that the president 'had expressed extremely strong feelings on the necessity for very straightforward action in this situation, and he wondered whether the plans as outlined were sufficient to accomplish this.'

Thus admonished, the committee 'finally agreed that planning for the Congo would not necessarily rule out 'consideration' of any particular kind of activity that might contribute to getting rid of Lumumba.'"[145]

As part of the plot to eliminate Lumumba, the CIA also launched a smear campaign against the Congolese prime minister and prepared different kinds of poisons to accomplish the mission. All this and much more was revealed during US Senate investigations, conducted by a special committee chaired by Democratic Senator Frank Church of Idaho, into assassinations of foreign leaders by the CIA.

The hearings also covered CIA plots – some of them successful – to overthrow foreign governments including a number of them in Africa: for example Nkrumah's government in Ghana which the CIA succeeded in overthrowing in February 1966; Nyerere's in Tanzania which the CIA tried more than once, in 1964 and thereafter, to overthrow; and Lumumba's, of course, with Lumumba himself being targeted for assassination not just for removal from office. And the smear campaign against him by the CIA knew no bounds:

"Allen Dulles (the CIA director, also known as DCI – Director of the Central Intelligence) told Eisenhower that Lumumba was insane; later reports alleged that he was also 'a dope fiend.'

On September 21 the DCI reported to an NSC (National Security Council) meeting, chaired by the president, that 'Lumumba was not yet disposed of.'

Still fascinated by the use of poisons in covert action, Richard Bissell (head of CIA's covert operations) instructed a CIA scientist (Dr. Sidney Gottlieb) to prepare biological toxins designated to assassinate or incapacitate an unnamed 'African leader' (Patrice Lumumba)."[146]

More than a decade later, the CIA was still denying its involvement in the assassination of Lumumba in spite of overwhelming evidence implicating the American intelligence agency in the diabolical plot.

In a television interview on 27 February 1975 by Daniel Schorr of CBS News, CIA Director William Colby was asked about the agency's role in assassinations: "Has the CIA ever killed anyone in this country?" Schorr asked. "Not in this country," replied Colby. The CIA chief was then asked about assassinations abroad, but he refused to give any names.

Schorr suggested Dag Hammarskjold, the UN secretary-general killed in a mysterious plane crash in

Ndola, Northern Rhodesia (now Zambia) in 1961. "No, of course not!" said Colby. But when Schorr mentioned Patrice Lumumba, also killed in 1961, Colby refused to comment. As the Church Committee later revealed, there had indeed been a CIA plot to poison and assassinate Lumumba.[147]

The plot included infecting Lumumba's toothbrush with deadly bacteria. Finally, the CIA concluded that getting rid of Lumumba right away was the best solution. And that is exactly what it did, in collusion with Tshombe and Mobutu.

After the assassination of Lumumba in January 1961, who reportedly was shot by a Belgian CIA mercenary in the presence of Tshombe and his right-hand man, interior minister Godefroid Munongo and other Katangese cabinet members on the outskirts of Elisabethville, capital of Katanga Province, another tragedy befell the Congolese people: Lumumba's followers lost the war against the American-backed Congolese government of Moise Tshombe and Joseph Mobutu.

The year 1965 was probably their worst year when they lost against the combined forces of South African mercenaries mobilised by the CIA, anti-Castro Cubans also recruited by the CIA, the Congolese army led by Belgian officers, and against the CIA itself which ran the entire Congo operation with the help of Belgium, the former colonial power which once ruled Congo. But Lumumba's followers never gave up the fight despite their weakness.

However, even by the 1970s, opposition to Mobutu's regime was not as well-coordinated as it could have been; a problem which had plagued his nationalist opponents since November 1965 when he seized power, and which also divided the nationalist guerrillas against the CIA-backed Tshombe-Mobutu alliance from 1960 to 1965.

And there was no single ideology which united Mobutu's opponents except shared antipathy to his regime.

As Professor Crawford Young, who taught in Congo (later Zaire) for a number of years, stated in 1978 in his article, "Zaire: The Unending Crisis," in *Foreign Affairs*:

"Opposition groups...remain fragmented, riven by personal, ethnic and ideological divisions....The most potent threat is the FNLC – *Front National pour la Liberation du Congo* – lineal descendants of the old Katanga *gendarmes* (who invaded Shaba Province, former Katanga, from Angola in 1977 and 1978)....

It is fundamentally a military grouping that has taken on the name of a political party, has had access to sanctuary in Angola, and has been able to acquire arms.

However, as a political alternative it is severely hampered by its regional base and its chameleon past, having successively served Moise Tshombe and European capital, white mercenaries, the Portuguese, and most recently the MPLA.

Many secretly hoped it might be an anti-Mobutu detonator, triggering a chain reaction of events that would bring to power not (its leader) Nathaniel Mbumba, but some other national leader or perhaps a transitional regime, like that of 'Field Marshall' John Okello in Zanzibar in 1964."[148]

Even Lumumba's deputy, Antoine Gizenga, failed to mobilise national support for his agenda, although he repeatedly invoked Lumumba's name to justify his claim to the mantle of leadership that supposedly passed on to him after his mentor was assassinated:

"Antoine Gizenga, Lumumba's vice premier, has been at times backed by Luanda and Moscow as an ideological alternative to the present regime.

He has led a succession of paper organizations, and speaking in the political metaphors of 1960, continues to insist that he alone enjoys a claim to apostolic succession to Lumumba.

Mobutu's scornful characterization of him as 'a stinking corpse whom only the Russians refuse to bury' is not entirely unfounded."[149]

Others fared no better, and sometimes even worse, especially those who operated from overseas. They had little influence – let alone following – at home and were characterised by ideological confusion, putting Lumumba and Tshombe together as national heroes:

"The Brussels-based *Movement d'Action pour la Resurrection du Congo* (MARC), led by former Provincial President and Regional Commissioner Monguya Mbenge, has some following in Belgium but little in Zaire.

The eclecticism of its leader is suggested in the dedication of his recent anti-Mobutist book to Lumumba, Kasavubu, Tshombe and Mulele – a spectrum of 1960 political figures that spans the entire ideological range."[150]

The confusion in his mind was obvious, as he lumped all those leaders together, trying to make a national hero out of a traitor, Moise Tshombe.

Even for Laurent Kabila's movement, prospects were just as bleak in the 1970s – as well as during the 1980s and even in the early and mid-1990s – although he never gave up his dream to oust Mobutu. As Professor Young stated during the the late 1970s:

"One insurgent movement within the country lingers from the 1964 – 65 wave of rebellions.

Localized in the Fizi-Baraka area of Lake Tanganyika (where Che Guevara was based), this group – known in recent years as *Parti de la Revolution Pupulaire (PRP)* – achieved notoriety in 1975 by kidnapping four Stanford University students from a zoological research station in (western) Tanzania.

Its composition is ethnically restricted to the Bembe, though its leader, Laurent Kabila, is a Shaba Luba (from the former Katanga Province renamed Shaba, in Kiswahili, meaning copper). The movement now has only a few hundred followers, and has no possibility of enlarging its base of operations."[151]

But it did, against all odds, defying political pundits who said it had no national appeal and would not be able to mobilise support from other parts of the country. Besides its nationalist rhetoric, what inspired many people to support Kabila and his political organisation was the sentiment they shared against Mobutu. They all wanted him out of power.

Kabila's party, based in Kivu Province in eastern Congo since the sixties, joined forces with the Tutsi – known as Banyamurenge or Banyamulenge, named after the Mulenge mountains on which they live – in the same province and formed the Alliance of Democratic Forces for the Liberation of Congo-Zaire under the leadership of Laurent Kabila; and eventually ousted Mobutu Sese Seko in May 1997 after a seven-month triumphant march across the country to the capital Kinshasa on the banks of the Congo River more than a thousand miles away.

Mobutu's rag-tag army hardly fought back. The soldiers fled as soon as they heard Kabila's troops were within striking range. Some of them joined the nationalist insurgents.

After Kabila came to power, many questions were raised about the nature of his leadership until his assassination by one of his bodyguards on 16 January 2001 in a plot conceived and authorised by Rwandan leaders.

He may not have been a democrat; few are, on a continent notorious for dictatorship. But whatever his shortcomings, he played a critical role in kicking Mobutu out of power with the help of neighbouring countries,

241

especially Rwanda, Uganda, Angola, Tanzania, Burundi, and even Ethiopia and Eritrea as well as Zimbabwe. That was the most important task at that time.

Whatever it took to get Mobutu out of power was acceptable. And anybody who did it has to be thanked for that. Kabila did, and for that, he deserves credit despite his dubious credentials as a democrat.

His tenacity was legendary, which is not necessarily a bad quality for a leader and may be vital in handling the herculean task of national reconstruction of a country Mobutu left in tatters.

But Laurent Kabila's past also raised a number of important questions which should not be overlooked if the new Congo is to shed its past characterised by tyranny and corruption.

So, any leader who follows in the footsteps of Kabila – including his son Joseph Kabila who succeeded him after his father was assassinated – will not be able to redeem the country unless he introduces fundamental change under democractic rule. As Cindy Shiner stated in her report from Kigoma, Tanzania, "Despot or Democrat? Friends and Foes Illuminate the Faces of Kabila," in the *International Tribune*, 20 May1997:

"His revolutionary roots reach to the 1950s, yet questions are invariably raised about how pivotal a player he was in Zaire's many upheavals....

Born into the Luba tribe 56 years ago in the restive Katanga region...he was a youth leader in a party allied with Patrice Lumumba....Mr. Kabila participated in the Lumumbists' 1963 – 1964 uprising at Stanleyville – renamed Kisangani – where he was described as a second-echelon operative."[152]

When Che Guevara arrived in the Congo in April 1965, Kabila – although absent from the combat zone – was the acknowledged leader of the guerrilla fighters in the part of eastern Congo where the Argentine-born Cuban revolutionary took his Cuban troops to join the insurgency against the American-installed puppet government in Leopoldville (renamed Kinshasa by Mobutu in 1971). Kabila was no longer the "second-echelon operative" he was during the 1963 – 1964 uprising in Stanleyville:

"(After the defeat in Stanleyville) he eventually emerged as the head of a Marxist organization, the People's Revolutionary Party, and established an enclave in the far eastern Kivu Province that encompassed the area around the towns of Fizi and Baraka.
There, along the shores of Lake Tanganyika among the Bembe people, he lived and governed outside the rules of Marshal Mobutu's rigid state. A Zairian writer described him as 'a typical African warlord.'"[153]

Members of the Bembe tribe were among his harshest critics.
Many of them, living in Kigoma, Tanzania, told horror stories about their lives under Kabila and his guerrilla soldiers who wanted to overthrow Mobutu Sese Seko.
Yet even among those critics, there were some who said they understood why he did some of the things he did: Revolution requires discipline and maximum sacrifice. And that entails suffering. But such a perspective did nothing to diminish the bitter resentment many of the Bembe had against Kabila:

"While some Zairians hail him as their liberator, many Bembe interviewed here in this Tanzanian town resent the way he ruled them from 1964 until the early '80s through a system of power games and terror.
A group has been formed of Mr. Kabila's opponents among the Bembe, called the Council of Resistance and National Liberation, and many Bembe hope it will topple Kabila."[154]

What did he do to them that made many of them resent and hate him so much?

Hated as he was, how was he able to live among them for so long?

He was not even a member of their tribe or from the same region, Kivu Province. Kabila was a Luba from Shaba Province; he was also partly Lunda, Tshombe's tribe in the same province, the former Katanga. Yet somehow, he was able to dominate them:

"In Kigoma, across Lake Tanganyika but within sight of the hills of Mr. Kabila's former enclave, numerous Bembe recalled how Mr. Kabila lived off their land, exploiting their region's gold.

Several people cited allegations that he used extreme tactics to cling to power, including having enemies and rivals burned at the stake.

Their accounts, while consistent, could not be verified. 'It is the worst memory that the Bembe hold in their minds about Kabila – that he burned people alive,' said a former ally of Mr. Kabila's who asked not to be identified."[155]

Some of his biggest opponents had a broader interpretation of what went on in spite of the tyranny they say they lived under. In fact, many of the Bembe did not even ostracise or abandon him:

"Despite the allegations about Mr. Kabila's regime, people stayed with him.

'The Bembe respected him a lot,' said Lubunga Lwa Ngabo, spokesman for the Council of Resistance and National Liberation.

'He was the chief. You have to respect him. You have to do what he says. We understood that it was within the scope of the revolution, and to make order you have to rule like that,' Mr. Ngabo said."[156]

And he remained an elusive character – not atypical of revolutionaries – even in Tanzania, a country which had been his second home since the sixties, and more or less a permanent one since the eighties; even his son Joseph Kabila who succeeded him as president of the Democratic Republic of Congo was born and brought up in Tanzania:

"In the capital of Tanzania, Dar es Salaam, where Mr. Kabila spent most of the last decade, his former neighbours said they suspected him of being an agent for the Tanzanian government because of his wealth...including two large homes...and what they called duplicitous behaviour.

He has been known not only as Laurent Kabila, but as Raul Kabila, Mzee Mtwale, Collins Mtwale, and Christopher Mtwale, according to Tanzanian newspaper reports.

But Mr. Kabila's friends depict him as a private man who stuck with his vision to oust Mobutu."[157]

Some of his critics said he was worse than many people realised. As one of his implacable foes bluntly stated:

"'He's not a liberal. He's a dictator – worse than Mobutu,' said a Bembe intellectual who requested anonymity."[158]

But given a choice between Kabila and Mobutu, how many Congolese would have chosen to live under Mobutu? How many wanted to return to the status quo ante of the *ancien regime*?

It is in this context that Kabila's contribution to the liberation of Congo must be viewed.

He played a critical role in removing from power a despotic regime that had been imposed on the Congolese people by the United States and other Western powers in the 1960s to serve Western interests. And for more than 30 years, Mobutu served them well at the expense of his own people.

Yet the West was no less responsible than Mobutu for the misery and suffering the Congolese people had to endure for an entire generation. They are still suffering today. And they will continue to suffer for at least another generation because of the devastation wrought in this bleeding heart of Africa mainly because of Western intervention and support of one of the most rotten regimes in modern history.

When Mobutu was ousted from power, Zaire was no longer a country but an empty shell. It was totally ruined.

When Kabila renamed it Congo, a new one was born. It was a rebirth of a nation from the ashes of the sixties, and from the pillage and plunder, ruin and neglect of the seventies, eighties and nineties under Mobutu.

Thanks to Western powers for going into Congo. And they never left.

The Congo crisis, the first and most horrendous tragedy Africa suffered during the early days of independence, demonstrated in a very painful way the devastating impact the Cold War and Western greed had on the embattled continent.

Most African countries won independence when rivalry between the East and the West was most intense. They ended up being caught in the middle, unable to resist foreign intervention in their affairs.

Compounding the problem was the brutal fact that the young nations were already burdened with enormous problems which were the inevitable result of their transition from colonial tutelage to independent status.

They have, since the sixties, gone through a generation of triumph and tragedy in what has been the most severe test of the viability of the modern African state which itself was, towards the end of the twentieth century, in a state of decay in most parts of the continent because of self-inflicted wounds under rotten leadership.

It is only now, since the late nineties, that some countries on the continent have begun to make some progress in the political and economic arena to improve the lives of their people. But they still have a long way to go.

Tragically for Congo, little has improved through the years even after Mobutu was overthrown. It is as if this bleeding heart of Africa never left the sixties.

Notes

1. Dan Snow, "Too Rich for its Own Good: DRC: Cursed by Its Own Wealth," BBC News Magazine, 8 October 2013.

2. Kwame Nkrumah in his letter to Moise Tshombe, 12 August 1960, reproduced in Ghana Government's White Paper, No. 6/60, p. 8, Accra, Ghana, August 1960; quoted by Ali A. Mazrui, *Towards A Pax Africana: A Study of Ideology and Ambition*, London: Weidenfeld & Nicolson, 1967, p. 38.

3. Brian Urquhart, "The Tragedy of Lumumba" in *The New York Review of Books*, 4 October 2001.

4. Ibid.

5. D'Lynn Waldron, ""Patrice Lumumba, Stanleyville, Belgian Congo."

6. Ibid.

7. Frank Carlucci, interviewed in June 1997 by Charles Stuart Kennedy, *Ambassador Frank Charles Carlucci III, The Association fr Diplomatic Studies and Training Foreign Affairs Oral History Project*; continuation of interview; initial interview date, 1 April 1997, copyright 2000 ADST, pp. 5, 7 – 28.

8. Jane Franklin, "Che Guevara: Guerilla Heroica,"

The Nation, New York, May 19, 1997, p.28. See also Jon Lee Anderson, *Che Guevara: A Revolutionary Life*, Nnew York: Grove Press, 1997.

9. Christopher Andrew, *For the President's Eyes Only: Secret Intelligence and the American Presidency from Washington to Bush*, New York: Harper Perennial, 1997, pp. 293 – 301.

10. Ibid., p. 253.

11. Stephen Weissman, "Opening the Secret Files on Lumumba's Murder," *The Washington Post*, 21 July 2002.

12. Keith Kyle, "The UN in Congo: Initiative on Conflict Resolution and Ethnicity," 1995.

13. John Reader, *Africa: A Biography of the Continent*, New York: Vintage, 1999, pp. 659, 660, and 662.

14. Adam Hochschild, *King Leopold's Ghost: A Story of Greed, Terror, and Heroism in Colonial Africa*, New York: Houghton Mifflin, 1998, pp. 301 – 302.

15. Brian Urquhart, "The Tragedy of Lumumba," *The New York Review of Books*, 4 October 2001.

16. Patrice Lumumba, letter to his wife.

17. Julius Nyerere, "Tanzania Rejects Western Domination of Africa," to members of the diplomatic corps, at the State House, Dar es Salaam, Tanzania, 8 June 1978; issued by the Ministry of Information and Broadcasting, Dar es Salaam, Tanzania, 8 June 1978; reproduced in *Tanzanian Affairs*, London, Britain-Tanzania Society, Bulletin of Tanzanian Affairs No. 6, July 1978.

18. Herman Kinder and Werner Hilgemann, *The Anchor Atlas of World History, 2: From the French Revolution to the American Bicentennial*, New York: Anchor, 1978, p. 268.

19. Ibid.

20. Leonce Ndikumana and Kisangani, "The Economics of Civil War: The Case of the Democratic Republic of Congo," Peri Working Paper No.63, 1 July 2003.

21. Piero Gleijeses, *Conflicting Missions: Havana, Washington, and Africa, 1959 – 1976*, The University of North Carolina Press, 2002, pp. 84 and 85.

22. Walter Rodney, *The Groundings with My Brothers* (London: The Bogle-L' Ouverture Publications, 1969), pp. 18 - 19. See also Walter Rodney, *How Europe Underdeveloped Africa* (Dar es Salaam, Tanzania: Tanzania Publishing House, 1974).

23. Jorge G. Castaneda, *Companero: The Life and Death of Che Guevara* (New York: Alfred A. Knopf, 1997), p. 271. See also G. Michael Schatzberg, *Mobutu or Chaos?: The United States and Zaire 1960 - 1990* (New York and Philadelphia: University Press of America/Foreign Policy Research Institute, 1991), p. 28; and G. Madeleine Kalb, *The Congo Cables* (New York: Macmillan, 1982), pp. 378 - 379.

24. Julius Nyerere, *Freedom and Socialism: A Selection from Writings and Speeches 1965 - 1967* (Dar es Salaam, Tanzania: Oxford University Press, 1968), pp. 194, 295, 296, and 377.

25. Kwame Nkrumah, in his letter to Moise Tshombe, August 12, 1960; reproduced in Ghana Government's White Paper, No. 6/60, p. 8, Accra, Ghana, August 1960; and Ali A. Mazrui, *Towards A Pax Africana* (London: Weidenfeld & Nicolson, 1967), p. 38.

26. Che Guevara, in his speech to the UN General Assembly, December 1964, quoted by Jorge G. Castaneda, *Companero: The Life and Death of Che Guevara*, op. cit., pp. 272 - 273. See also Tad Szulc, *Fidel: A Critical Portrait* (New York: Avon, 1987), p. 66. As Szulc states: "Che's gradual withdrawal from economic policy-making, and his growing concentration on contacts with the Third World, (was) evidently in concurrence with Castro. Guevara seemed to enjoy this mission."

27. J.G. Castaneda, *Companero*, op. cit., p. 266.

28. Che Guevara, in his speech to the United Nations Conference on Trade and Development (UNCTAD),

Geneva, Switzerland, March 25, 1964; quoted in Ernesto Che Guevara, *Temas Economicos* (Havana, Cuba: Editorial de Ciencias Sociales, 1988), p. 416; and J.G. Castaneda, *Companero*, ibid.

29. Director of Central Intelligence Agency (CIA), "Special National Intelligence Estimate: Short-term Prospects for the Tshombe Government in the Congo," August 5, 1964 (Secret), in "Declassified Documents Catalog," Research Publication (Woodbridge, Connecticut), Vol. 16, #5, September - October 1990, file series No. 2439; quoted by Castaneda, ibid., p. 268.

30. Peter Canby, "Poster Boy for the Revolution," in *The New York Times Book Review*, May 18, 1997, p. 8.

31. Che Guevara, quoted by Alberto Castellanos who was interviewed by Jorge G. Castaneda, in Havana, Cuba, January 23, 1996. See Castaneda, ibid., pp. 248, and 432 - 433 footnotes nos. 17 and 18.

32. Ahmed Ben Bella, in an interview with J.G. Castaneda, in Geneva, Switzerland, November 4, 1995. See Castaneda, ibid., p. 276.

33. Fred Greene, *Dynamics of International Relations: Power, Security, and Order* (New York: Holt, Rinehart and Winston, 1964), p. 544.

34. Ibid., p. 546.

35. Ibid., p. 544.

36. Kwame Nkrumah, *Ghana: The Autobiography of Kwame Nkrumah* (New York: Thomas Nelson and Sons, 1957); reprinted, Kwame Nkrumah, "Background to Independence," in Paul E. Sigmund, Jr., editor, *The Ideologies of the Developing Nations* (New York: Frederick A. Praeger, 1963), pp. 184 - 185.

37. Ibid.

38. Grace Ibingira, quoted in *Uganda Argus*, Kampala, Uganda, January 15, 1965; cited by Ali A. Mazrui, *Towards A Pax Africana*, op. cit., p. 273.

39. Catherine Coquery-Vidrovitch, Alain Forest, and Herbert Weiss, *Rebellions-Revolution au Zaire, 1963 -*

1965 (Paris: Editions L'Harmattan, 1987), Vol. 1, p. 164; cited by Castaneda, ibid., p. 277.

40. Ludo Martens, *Pierre Mulele, ou la Seconde Vie de Patrice Lumumba* (Antwerp, Belgium: Editions, EPO, 1985), p. 12; and Castaneda, ibid.

41. Joseph Ileo, in *The New York Times*, February 12, 1961, p. E9; quoted by Ali Mazrui, *Towards A Pax Africana*, op.cit., p. 10.

42. Castaneda, *Companero*, ibid., p. 277.

43. Ibid., p. 278. On relations between the Commitee for National Liberation (CNL) leadership and the CIA as well as the Belgian Foreign Minister Paul-Henri Spaak, see also madeleine G. Kalb, *The Congo Cables: The Cold War in Africa - From Eisenhower to Kennedy* (New York: Macmillan, 1982), p. 378.

44. Castaneda, *Companero*, ibid. See also David Gibbs, *The Political Economy of Third World Intervention: Mines, Money and U.S. Policy in the Congo Crisis* (Chicago: University of Chicago Press, 1991), p. 157.

45. Che Guevara, cited by Castaneda, ibid., pp. 272 – 273.

46. "Zaire Rebels Aim to Oust Mobutu," *Africa Analysis*, No. 259, London, 1 November 1996, pp. 1 – 2.

47. Colin Legum and John Drysdale, *Africa Contemporary Record: Annual Surveys and Documents 1968 - 1969* (London: Africa Research Ltd., 1969), pp. 441 - 442.

48. Ibid., p. 442.

49. Crawford Young, "Zaire: The Unending Crisis," in *Foreign Affairs*, Fall 1978, pp. 182 - 183. See also Crawford Young, *Politics in the Congo* (Madison, Wisconsin: University of Wisconsin Press, 1965); Otto Klineberg and Merisa Zavalloni, *Nationalism and Tribalism Among African Students* (Paris: Mouton, 1969).

50. J. G. Castaneda, *Companero*, ibid., 279; and Coquery-Vidrovitch et al., *Rebellions-Revolutions au Zaire*, op. cit., pp. 158 - 159.

51. Castaneda, ibid., p. 280.

52. Ibid., pp. 280, and 436 footnote no. 9.

53. Ibid.

54.Ibid.

55. United States Department of State, "Airgram AmEmbassy The Hague to DOS, African Travels of Che Guevara," February 1, 1965 (Confidential), NSF, Country File, Box 17, Vol. 4, #71 airgram, LBJ Library; and Castaneda, ibid., p. 436.

INR/Thomas Hughes to the Secretary, "Che Guevara's African Venture," RAR-13, April 19, 1965 (Secret), NSF, Country File, Cuba, Activities of Leading Personalities, no. 18 memo, LBJ; cited by Castaneda, ibid.

56."Congo Democratic Republic (Congo-Brazzaville)," in *Africa Contemporary Record*, op. cit., pp. 454, and 456.

57. Castaneda, *Companero*, op. cit., p. 280.

58. Central Intelligence Agency (CIA), Intelligence Information Cable, "Statements of Ernesto Che Guevara on the Primary Purpose of His Mission to Africa" (Secret). The cable quotes information dated late December 1964, and is itself dated January 15, 1965, NSF, Country File, Cuba, Vol. 4, LBJ Library. As Castaneda states:

"Its main thrust is supported by the fact that Che publicly expressed his anger at the Soviet Union six weeks later, precisely in Algiers.

This account of Che's warning against close relations with the USSR and China was repeated in a report by the State Department's Intelligence and Research section, signed by Director Thomas Hughes, and addressed to the Secretary of State.

Knowing the professionalism of Hughes and Adrian Basora, who wrote the reports on Cuba during those years, it is difficult to imagine that they would have given credence to any dubious information."

See INR/Thomas Hughes, April 19, 1965, NSF,

Country File, Cuba, Activities of Leading personalities, no. 18 memo, LBJ Library; and Castaneda, p. 281.

59. Sekou Toure, in Paul E. Sigmund, Jr., *The Ideologies of the Developing Nations*, op. cit., p. 154.

60. Castaneda, ibid., p. 281.

61. Ben Bella, in an interview with J.G. Castaneda, Geneva, November 4, 1995, ibid., pp. 281, and 436.

62. Castaneda, ibid., p. 282; and Piero Gleijeses, "Cuba's First Venture in Africa: Algeria, 1961 - 1965," in the *Journal of Latin American Studies*, London University, no. 28, Spring 1996, p. 175.

63. J. G. Castaneda, *Companero*, ibid., p. 281.

64. Ibid., p. 283; and Mohammed Heikal, *The Cairo Documents* (Garden City, New York: Doubleday, 1973).

65. Jawaharlal Nehru, "Portuguese Colonialism: An Anachronism," in *Africa Quarterly*, Vol. 1, No. 3, October – December 1961, p. 9. See also Nehru, "Emergent Africa," in *Africa Quarterly*, Vol. 1, No. 1, April – June 1961, pp. 7 - 9.

66. Gamal Abdel Nasser, quoted by Mohammed Heikal, *The Cairo Ducuments*, op. cit., and J.G, Castaneda, *Companero*, ibid.

67. Boutros Boutros-Ghali, "The Foreign Policy of Egypt," in Joseph E. Black and Kenneth W. Thompson, *Foreign Policies in A World of Change* (New York: Harper and Row, 1963). See also Jacques Raulin, *Arab Role in Africa* (London: Penguin African Library, 1962); and Vernon McKay, "The Impact of Islam on Relations among the New African States," in J. Harris Proctor, editor, *Islam and International Relations* (New York: Frederick A. Praeger, 1964).

68. Gamal Abdel Nasser, *The Philosophy of the Revolution* (Cairo, Egypt: Information Department, 1954; Buffalo, New York: Economica English edition, 1959), pp. 74 – 75.

69. Ben Bella, in an interview, Geneva, November 4, 1995, in Castaneda, *Companero*, op. cit., p. 283.

70. J. Castaneda, Ibid., pp. 163 - 164.

71. Ibid., p. 163.

72. Che Guevara, in his letter to Fidel Castro, written in the Congo, October 1965; quoted by Castaneda, p. 164. The letter comes from Che's unpublished writings: Eernesto Che Guevara, *Pasajes de la guerra revolucionaria (el Congo)*, Havana, p. 86. As Castaneda, who obtained the letter and interviewed Guevara's compatriots who fought with in the Congo, states:

"This text, based on Che's Congo campaign journals, remains unpublished although it has been extensively quoted, particularly in Paco Ignacio Taibo II, Felix Guerra, and Froilan Rodriguez, *El ano que estuvimos en ninguna parte* (Mexico City: Planeta, 1994)....

The complete manuscript was made available to me in Havana (in 1996) by generous Guevaristas.

Its authenticity was corroborated on comparing the copy thus obtained to that held by several of Che's aides, including Jesus Parra, a former secretary of Che's, who allowed me to compare the manuscript with his own in Havana." See J. Castaneda, ibid., p. 5.

73. Jon Lee Anderson, *Che Guevara: A Revolutionary Life* (New York: Grove Press, 1997). See also Guevara's first book, *Guerrilla Warfare*; and Guevara, *The Motorcycle Diaries: A Journey Around South America* (New York: Verso, 1997).

74. Christopher Hitchens, "The Truth About Che Guevara," in *The New York Review of Books*, July 17, 1997, p. 20.

75. Ibid.

76. Ernesto Che Guevara, *Pasajes de la guerra revolucionaria (el Congo)*, Havana, p. 86; cited by J.G. Castaneda, *Companero: The Life and Death of Che Guevara*, op. cit., p. 284.

77. J. Castaneda, ibid., pp. 285, and 320.

78. American Embassy, Dar es Salaam, Tanzania, to Secretary of State, February 16, 1965 (Confidential), Country File, Cuba, Activities of Leading Personalities, Box 20, #32 Cable, LBJ Library, based on a report from the Nigerian Charge d' Affaires, Dar es Salaam; cited by Castaneda, ibid., pp. 289, and 437.

79. Ernesto Che Guevara, *Pasajes de la guerra revolucionaria (el Congo)*, written in Dar es Salaam, Tanzania, November 1965 - March 1966, and kept in Havana, Cuba, p. 4; quoted by Castaneda, ibid., p. 289.

80. Che Guevara, *Pasajes...(el Congo)*, pp. 3 - 4; and Castaneda, ibid., pp. 289 - 290.

81. Castaneda, ibid., pp. 292 - 293.

82. Ibid., pp. 297 - 298.

83. Emilio Aragones, in an interview with Castaneda, Havana, Cuba, January 23, 1996, ibid., pp. 298, and 299.

84. Castaneda, ibid. p. 299.

85. Che Guevara, *Pasajes...(el Congo)*, pp. 25, and 148; and Castaneda, ibid., p. 300.

86. Emilio Aragones, quoted by Castaneda, ibid.

87. Castaneda, ibid., pp. 300, and 301.

88. Guevara, *Pasajes...(el Congo)*, p. 7; and Castaneda, ibid., p. 307.

89. Ibid.

90. Ibid.

91. Oscar Fernandez Mell, in an interview with Castaneda, Havana, Cuba, August 24, 1995, ibid., pp. 308, and 438 footnote no. 61.

92. Guevara, *Pasajes...(el Congo)*, pp. 18, and 19; and Castaneda, ibid., p. 308.

93. Chou En-Lai's visit to Tanzania, in *The Standard*, and *The Nationalist*, Dar es Salaam, Tanzania, June 7, 1965. See also Chou En-Lai, in the *East African Standard*, and the *Daily Nation*, Nairobi, Kenya, June 1965; and Lawrence Fellows, "Chou's Visit Perils East Africa Unity," in *The New York Times*, June 8, 1965.

94. W.A.C. Adie, "China's Revived Interest in Africa,"

in Colin Legum and John Drysdale, *Africa Contemporary Record*, op. cit., p. 48; *Far Eastern Economic Review*, Hong Kong, November 7, 1968, p. 315; *Afrique Nouvelle*, Dakar, Senegal, June 6 - 12, 1968.

95. Ibid. See also Ali A. Mazrui, *Towards A Pax Africana* (London: Weidenfeld & Nicolson, 1967), pp. 154, and 190:

"By a curious coincidence, Chou En-Lai was expected to arrive in East Africa at just about the time when Britain was called upon to 'protect' the area (following the army mutinies in Kenya, Uganda, and Tanganyika in January 1964).

And Sir Alec Douglas-Home was soon to justify British military aid to East Africa partly by citing Chou En-Lai's remark that revolutionary prospects were excellent in Africa....

A Kenyan Minister expressed the concern of his Government about the activities of some foreign embassies in Nairobi.

There was reference to an occasion when a high-ranking Communist diplomat had shared a political platform with Mr. Oginga Odinga, then Kenya's Minister of Home Affairs.

Since then ideological disagreements between Oginga Odinga and his colleagues in the Kenya Government have become more open.

Bitter public arguments were carried on during the months of April and May 1965....

The formation of a new opposition party (Kenya People's Union - KPU) under Odinga confirmed the ideological split in Kenya."

However, neither Communist China nor the Soviet Union was behind the army mutinies in East Africa in 1964. As Mazrui states:

"Sir Alec was probably misreading the events on the East African mainland when he detected a communist design behind the mutinies."

See Mazrui, *Towards A Pax Africana*, ibid., p. 154. See also Sir Alex Douglas-Home, in the *East African Standard*, Nairobi, Kenya, February 7, 1964. On Oginga Odinga, see the *East African Standard*, October 23, 1964; *Reporter: East Africa's Fortnightly Magazine*, Nairobi, Kenya, September 11, 1964, p. 13; *Kenya Weekly News*, Nairobi, Kenya, June 21, 1968; and "Kenya," in *Africa Contemporary Record*, op. cit., pp. 155 - 157.

96. *Afrique Nouvelle*, Dakar, Senegal, June 6 - 12, 1968.

97. Cuban soldier killed in the Congo, in his diary, cited by Mike Hoare in Richard Gott, "The Year Che Went Missing," in the *Guardian Weekend*, London, 30 November 1996, p. 30.

98. American Embassy, Dar es Salaam, Tanzania, to Secretary of State, February 16, 1965 (Confidential), Country File, Cuba, Activities of Leading Personalities, Box 20, #32 Cable, LBJ Library; Goodley/American Embassy/Leopoldville to Secretary of State, September 21, 1965 (Secret), NSF, Country File, Congo, Vol. II, no. 7 cable, p. 49, LBJ Library; cited by J. G. Castaneda, *Companero: The Life and Death of Che Guevara*, op. cit., p. 309.

99. Castaneda, ibid., pp. 309 - 310.

100. Che Guevara, *Pasajes...(el Congo)*, pp. 41, and 44; in Castaneda, ibid., p. 310.

101. Guevara, *Pasajes...(le Congo)*, p. 63; Castaneda, ibid.

102. Bem Hardenne, *Les Operations Anti-Guerillas dans l'Est du Congo en 1965 - 1966*, February 1969, mimeograph, pp. 19 - 20; and Castaneda, ibid., p. 312.

103. CIA, cited by Castaneda, ibid.

104. B. Hardenne, *Les Operations Anti-Guerillas...du*

Congo..., p. 22; and Castaneda, ibid., p. 313.

105. CIA station chief in the Congo, Laurence Devlin, cited by J.G. Castaneda, *Companero: The Life and Death of Che Guevara*, ibid.

106. Central Intelligence Agency (CIA), Intelligence Memorandum, "Situation in the Congo," August 26, 1965 (Secret), NSF, Country File, Congo, Vol. II, no. 16 memo, LBJ Library; and Castaneda, ibid.

107. Gustavo Villoldo, in an interview with Castaneda, Miami, Florida, November 21, 1965, ibid.

108. Che Guevara, *Pasajes...(el Congo)*, p. 85; and Castaneda, ibid., p. 314.

109. Che Guevara, Darield Alarcon Ramirez (Benigno), in an interview with Castaneda, November 3, 1995, ibid., pp. 314, 437 footnote no. 41, and 439 footnote no. 80.

110. Emilio Aragones, ibid., pp. 314, and 437 footnote no. 25.

111. Fidel Castro, quoted by Che Guevara, *Pasajes... (el Congo)*, p. 85; and Castaneda, ibid., p. 314.

112. Che Guevara, letter to Fidel castro, October 5, 1965, written in the Congo, quoted in *Pasajes...(el Congo)*, pp. 86 - 87; and Castaneda, ibid., p. 315.

113. Guevara, *Pasajes...(el Congo)*, p. 99; and Castaneda, ibid., p. 318.

114. Robert W. Kormer to Bundy McGeorge, The White House, October 29, 1965 (Secret), NSF, Country File, Congo, Vol. 12, October 1965 - 66, memo, LBJ Library; and Castaneda, ibid.

115. Che Guevara, quoted by Emilio Aragones, in an interview with Castaneda, ibid., pp. 318 - 319. See also pp. 437 footnote no. 25, and 439 footnote no. 89.

116. Ibid.

117. Che Guevara, *Pasajes...(el Congo)*, p. 99; and Castaneda, ibid., p. 319.

118. Castaneda, ibid.

119. Fidel Castro, in his letter to Che Guevara, received

in the Congo on November 4, 1965, quoted in *Pasajes...* (*el Congo*), pp. 118 - 119; and Castaneda, ibid.

120. American Embassy, Leopoldville, to Secretary of State, November 25, 1965 (Secret), National Security File (NSF), Country File, Congo, Vol. 12, cable no. 47, LBJ Library; cited by Castaneda, ibid., p. 320. On CIA's involvement in the ouster of President Joseph Kasavubu, see for example, Ellen Ray, William Schapp, Karl Van Meter, and Louis Wolf, editors, *Dirty Work: The CIA in Africa*, Vol. 2 (Syracuse, New York: Lyle Stewart, 1979), p. 191.

121. Castaneda, ibid. See also Kwame Nkrumah on the Congo crisis; Crawford Young, "Zaire: The Unending Crisis," in *Foreign Affairs*, Fall 1978, pp. 169 - 185.

122. Julius Nyerere, "Nationalism and Pan-Africanism,' in Paul E. Sigmund, Jr., *The Ideologies of the Developing Nations*, op. cit., pp. 209, 210, and 211.

123. Castaneda, and Guevara, *Pasajes...*(*el Congo*), ibid. See also Thompson, *Ghana's Foreign Policy* (Princeton, New Jersey: Princeton University Press, 1967).

124. Julius Nyerere, on American television programme, ABC's "Issues and Answers," June 1976.

125. Che Guevara, quoted by Castaneda, *Companero: The Life and Death of Che Guevara*, op. cit., p. 321.

126. Ibid.

127. Emilio Aragones, in an interview with Castaneda, Havana, Cuba, January 23, 1996, ibid.

128. Guevara, *Pasajes...*(*el Congo*), p. 138; and Castaneda, ibid.

129. Quoted by Castaneda, ibid., pp. 321 - 322.

130. Ibid., p. 322.

131. Benigno (Dariel Alarcon Ramirez), in an interview with Castaneda, Havana, Cuba, November 3, 1995, ibid.

132. Laurence Devlin, CIA station chief in the Congo, based in Kinshasa, quoted ibid.

133. Bem Hardenne, quoted ibid., pp. 322 - 323.

134. Castaneda, ibid., p. 323.

135. Ibid.

136. Ibid., pp. 323 – 324, and 440 footnote no. 102.

137. Colman Ferrer, quoted by Castaneda, ibid., p. 326.

138. Ibid.

139. Pablo Ribalta, quoted in Froilan Escobar, Felix Guerra, and Paco Ignacio Taibo II, *El ano que estuvimos en ninguna parte* (Mexico City: Joaquin Mortiz/Planeta, 1994), pp. 242 - 243; cited by Castaneda, ibid., p. 327.

140. Colman Ferrer, quoted by Castaneda, ibid., p. 328.

141. Pablo Ribalta, quoted in Taibo et al., *El ano que estuvimos en ninguna parte*, op. cit., p. 239; and Castaneda, ibid., p. 328.

142. Ulises Estrada, in an interview with Castaneda, Havana, Cuba, February 9, 1995, ibid.

143. Richard Herrnstein and Charles Murray, *The Bell Curve: Intelligence and Class Structure in American Life* (New York: Free Press, 1994), pp. 269, and 311:

"The average white person tests higher than about 84 percent of the population of blacks and the average black person higher than about 16 percent of the population of whites.

The average black and white differ in IQ at every level of socioeconomic status. Attempts to explain the difference in terms of test bias have failed....

It seems highly likely to us that both genes and the environment have something to do with racial differences."

Lynne Duke, "Whites' Racial Stereotypes Persist: Most retain Negative Beliefs About Minorities," in *The Washington Post*, January 9, 1991, p. A1:

"A majority of whites...said (in national opinion polls) they believe blacks and Hispanics are likely to prefer welfare to hard work and tend to be lazier than whites, more prone to violence, less intelligent and less patriotic."

Richard Morin, "What Americans Think: Southern Discomfort: Racially Bigoted Attitudes Linger in Many parts of Dixie," in *The Washington Post*, National Weekly Edition, July 15 - 21, 1996, p. 35:

"It's surprising how many Americans do openly claim in public opinion polls that blacks are inferior to whites....

Polls show that millions of Americans support blatantly discriminatory laws as well as freely assert that blacks are inferior to whites,...which is almost certainly an underestimate because of people's reluctance to offer potentially inflammatory views to polltakers....

While Martin Luther King, Jr., a Southerner and a black, had a dream of an integrated society where African Americans and whites lived together in harmony, that dream is rejected by about half of all Americans in the South as well as in the country as a whole, according to surveys conducted by the Center for the Study of the American South at the University of North Carolina and co-sponsored by the *Atlanta Constitution*."

Nadine Strossen, president, American Civil Liberties Union (ACLU), in the conservative journal, *Policy Review*, Washington, D.C., September - October 1997:

"Many avenues of opportunity have remained narrow and constricted, available only to the relative few.

Today, the hopes and dreams of millions of Americans are still stifled, not because of their individual failings, but solely because of their skin color.

That is why I, along with other ACLU leaders, believe that the most pervasive, overarching civil-liberties problem in this country is race discrimination.

According to the National Opinion Research Center, a majority of white Americans still believe that blacks and Hispanics are less intelligent, less hardworking, and less patriotic than whites.

It would be naive to think these negative stereotypes do not influence the decisions made by employers and school administrators - the vast majority of whom are white - every hour of every day all over the country, translating into millions of lost opportunities.

We are still generations away from the-blind merit system that critics of affirmative action like to think we already have....

In this country, government spending on public education is clearly linked to race. Schools serving mostly minority, inner-city children receive half as much money per student as schools in the surrounding white suburbs. This unequal distribution of public resources based on skin color denies both equality of opportunity and equality of results."

And as Professor Nathan Glazer states in his book *We Are All Multiculturalists Now* (Cambridge, Massachusetts: Harvard University Press, 1996), the main problem in the United States even today is "the fundamental refusal of other Americans to accept blacks."

And they probably will never be accepted as equals by the vast majority of whites and others including Asians and Hispanics as well as other non-blacks.

All what we have cited here is highly relevant to the way the United States treated the Congo and the rest of black Africa when she intervened in the Congo to support the arch-traitors Moise Tshombe and Joseph Mobutu and assassinate Patrice Lumumba. It is also relevant to the way the United States treats black Africa even today.

All those national surveys conducted through the years – and much more including continuing racial discrimination against African Americans in education, employment, housing, health care – and the popularity of *The Bell Curve* which became an instant best seller for reasons which had nothing to do with sympathy for blacks when it was first published in March 1994, show clearly that the United States still is a racist society, in practice even if not in the legal sense, despite professions to the contrary. As Professor Cornel West, an African American, states in his best selling book *Race Matters*, the United States is "chronically racist."

It would therefore be extremely naive for anyone to

believe that such a society, which denies African Americans racial equality – for no other reason than that they are an African people – is going to respect the rights of black people in Africa.

This is the same country which deliberately supported apartheid South Africa to persecute and keep black people down. As President Julius Nyerere said with regard to South Africa:

"Despite the protestations of belief in human equality, the domination of a white minority over blacks is acceptable to the West....It is time for Britain and the United States of America to make clear whether they really believe in the principles they claim to espouse, or whether their policies are governed by considerations of the privileges of their 'kith and kin.'"

That is why the assassination of Patrice Lumumba with the help of the United States in January 1961 was, besides eliminating a leader the American government didn't like, also a matter of just getting rid of another nigger, whom the CIA also called "a dope fiend."

A racist government could not have felt any other way when killing a black person, regardless of his status. That is why even President Dwight Eisenhower himself who ordered Lumumba's assassination was opposed to racial integration.

Black people meant absolutely nothing to him. In fact, one of his black assistants, Frederick Morrow who once worked for CBS News but joined Eisenhower's presidential campaign staff, was not even allowed to work in the White House after Eisenhower won the 1955 presidential election.

See also Julius Nyerere, "Rhodesia in the Context of Southern Africa," in *Foreign Affairs*, New York, April 1966; and Nyerere, *Freedom and Socialism: A Selection from Writings and Speeches 1965 - 1967* (Dar es Salaam, Tanzania: Oxford University Press, 1968), pp. 155, and 156.

144. Jane Franklin, Guerrilla Heroica," in *The Nation,* May 19, 1997, p. 28.

145. Christopher Andrew, *For the President's Eyes Only: Secret Intelligence and the American Presidency from Washington to Bush* (New York: Harper Collins, 1995), p. 253. See also "(Senator Frank) Church Committee, Alleged Assassination Plots," Washington, D.C., April 26, 1976, pp. 13 – 18; and Stephen Ambrose, *Ike's Spies: Eisenhower and the Espionage Establishment* (Garden City, New York: Doubleday, 1981), pp. 293 - 301.

146. Christopher Andrew, *For the President's Eyes Only*, ibid., p. 253; Stephen Ambrose, *Ike's Spies,* op. cit., 301 - 303; and Church Committee, "Alleged Assassination Plots," ibid., p. 19 – 33.

147. Christopher Andrew, ibid., p. 406.

148. Crawford Young, "Zaire: The Unending Crisis," in *Foreign Affairs*, Fall 1978, pp. 169, 177, and 178.

149. Ibid., p. 178.

150. Ibid.

151. Ibid.

152. Cindy Shiner, "Despot of Democrat? Friends and Foes Illuminate the Faces of Kabila," in the *International Herald Tribune,* 20 May 1997, p. 6; and in *The Washington Post*, 20 May 1997.

153. Ibid.

154. Ibid.

155. Ibid.

156. Lubunga Lwa Ngabo, quoted ibid.

157. Ibid.

158. Ibid.

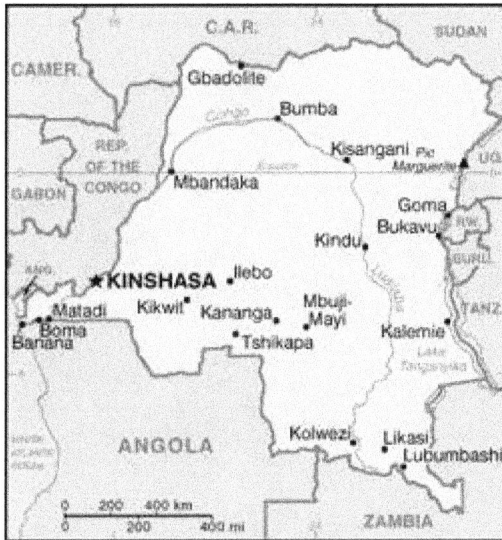

Democratic Republic of Congo (DRC)

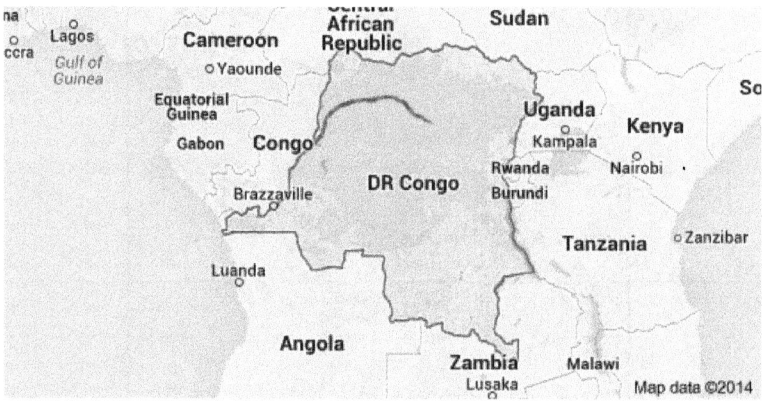

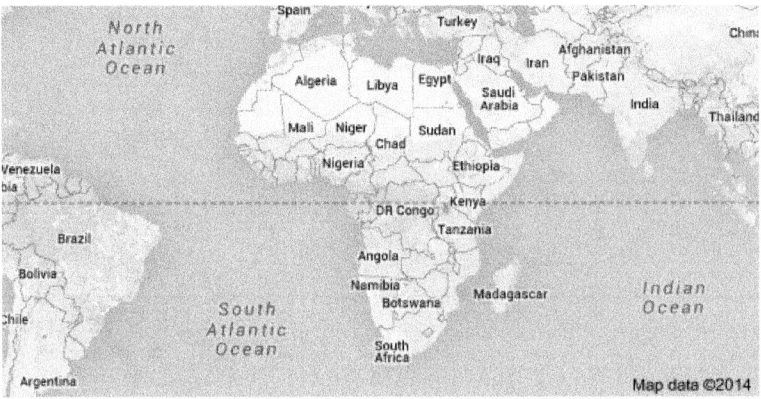

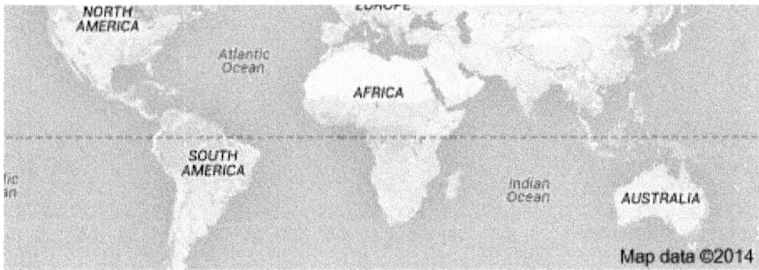